P9-DUT-541

ESSENTIALS OF EXPORTING AND IMPORTING
U.S. Trade Policies, Procedures, and Practices

ESSENTIALS OF EXPORTING AND IMPORTING
U.S. Trade Policies, Procedures, and Practices

Harvey R. Shoemack
Illinois Institute of Technology—Chicago
Oakton Community College

Patricia Mink Rath
Consultant, Marketing Education—Chicago

FAIRCHILD BOOKS
An imprint of Bloomsbury Publishing, Inc.

B L O O M S B U R Y
NEW YORK · LONDON · NEW DELHI · SYDNEY

FAIRCHILD BOOKS
An imprint of Bloomsbury Publishing Inc

1385 Broadway 50 Bedford Square
New York   London
NY 10018   WC1B 3DP
USA   UK

WWW.BLOOMSBURY.COM

FAIRCHILD BOOKS, BLOOMSBURY and the Diana logo are trademarks
of Bloomsbury Publishing Plc

First edition published 2010

© Bloomsbury Publishing Inc, 2014

All rights reserved. No part of this publication may be reproduced or transmitted in
any form or by any means, electronic or mechanical, including photocopying,
recording, or any information storage or retrieval system, without prior permission in
writing from the publishers.

No responsibility for loss caused to any individual or organization acting on or
refraining from action as a result of the material in this publication can be accepted
by Bloomsbury Publishing Inc or the authors.

Library of Congress Cataloging-in-Publication Data
Shoemack, Harvey R.
Essentials of exporting and importing : U.S. trade policies, procedures,
and practices / Harvey Shoemack, Patricia Mink Rath. — Second edition. pages cm
Includes bibliographical references and index.
ISBN 978-1-60901-889-4 (paperback)
1. Exports—United States. 2. Imports—United States. 3. United States—Commerce.
4. Foreign trade regulation—United States. I. Rath, Patricia Mink. II. Title.

HF1416.5.S56 2014
658.8'4—dc23
2014010909

ISBN: PB: 978-1-60901-889-4

Typeset by Precision Graphics / Lachina Publishing Services
Text Design Alisha Neumaier
Cover Design Untitled
Printed and bound in the United States of America

CONTENTS

EXTENDED CONTENTS

INTRODUCTION

GLOBALIZATION AND THE BENEFITS OF TRADE

Think of what modern global trade means: having access to goods and services from around the world that brings people choices never before known in history. Being part of the process of marketing your products to customers in Europe, Asia, and South America, or supplying people in the United States with goods from Australia, Africa, and other far places has the potential to offer your customers a wider range of goods at a profit to you.

Sometimes global trade occurs even without a business seeking it, as when out of the blue, a Chicago wholesaler of formal gowns receives an Internet order from a retailer in the Emirate of Abu Dhabi for an assortment of silk jacket dresses. More often, establishing agreements overseas with customers and suppliers is the result of months of planning and negotiating; however, when successful, such agreements can last for years, to the advantage of both parties.

The fields of exporting and importing that comprise global trade are areas with expanding opportunities. As this text points out, U.S. businesses conducted more than $2.2 trillion dollars in export trade 2013 and imported more than $2.7 trillion worth of goods that same year. And businesses are not alone in their efforts to connect with other countries.

The federal government traditionally supports the growth of global trade. Historically, at the end of World War II, the United States led the way in establishing and promoting international trade to rebuild devastated European and Asian countries in the hope of preventing future wars. One way to build trade alliances is to lower tariffs, or taxes, and other nontariff barriers (NTBs) to trade, such as foreign-language packaging requirements or product safety certification. The book describes various regional trade alliances such as the North American Free Trade Agreement (NAFTA) among the United States, Canada, and Mexico, plus emerging agreements with the European Union and Asia. It also explains the efforts of international organizations, such as the World Trade Organization (WTO), to encourage global *free trade*—the open exchange of goods, services, and information among nations with few or no government-imposed protectionist barriers—and *fair trade*—a system of international commerce that respects the rights of workers to have fair wages and a workplace that is not dangerous to them or to the global environment.

Fair trade practices focus on alleviating poverty, enhancing gender equality, improving working conditions, protecting the environment, and promoting equality and justice among all peoples of the world. Free trade proponents believe that free trade will create the environment for fair trade to flourish, as the markets will solve the issues of equilibrium, a goal that unfortunately has yet to eliminate the economic and social barriers between industrialized and emerging nations. The goal, whether through free trade and/or fair trade, is to combine business success with an improved standard of living for people everywhere.

This revision of *Essentials of Exporting and Importing: U.S. Trade Policies, Procedures, and Practices,* Second Edition, is not intended to be a thorough analysis of U.S. or global trade policy. Instead, the authors offer a basic, step-by-step approach for the novice student or trader whose career path includes potential ventures into the dynamic world of exporting American-designed goods and services, or of sourcing imports from countries all over the world in response to the needs and wants of American consumers. Exporting and importing goods are emerging occupational fields offering opportunities full of adventure, challenges, risks, and rewards. In writing and bringing this text up-to-date, the authors, through their years of international business management, teaching, writing, and marketing experience, hope to alert you to the opportunities and spare you the pitfalls so frequently encountered by the uninitiated. We wish you enjoyable reading and successful ventures!

ACKNOWLEDGMENTS

The authors are indebted to the following people at Fairchild Books, a division of Bloomsbury Publishing, for their contributions to this effort: Amanda Breccia, Acquisitions Editor—Fashion; Joe Miranda, Editorial Development Manager; Edie Weinberg, Art Development Editor; Charlotte Frost, Production Manager; Kirsten Dennison, project manager; and Nan Reinhardt, copyeditor.

The authors are also grateful to the following individuals and organizations from business, government, and academia:

- Paul S. Anderson, partner, Sonnenberg & Anderson, Attorneys at Law, Chicago, and Honorary Consul General, Honorary Royal Norwegian Consulate General, Chicago
- James Foley, Director of Operations, Turner Center for Entrepreneurship, Bradley University, Peoria, IL
- Foreign Policy Association, New York, *Great Decisions* 2014
- Ric Frantz, CEO, LR International, Wood Dale, IL
- Kathryn Kerrigan, owner, Kathryn Kerrigan, Inc., Libertyville, IL
- The Illinois District Export Council, Richard Paullin, Chairman, and the volunteer members dedicated to the promotion of U.S. exports
- Bob Rosenbaum, principal, Sales Source, Lincolnshire, IL
- Gerry Sky, CEO, Le Fleur Imports, Ltd., Northbrook, IL
- The U.S. Department of Commerce, Chicago office, and the U.S. Export Assistance Center, Chicago
- Gregory Arend, Nassau Community & Fashion Institute of Technology
- Kathryn Eason, West Virginia University
- Melinda Adams, University of the Incarnate Word

Harvey Shoemack is very thankful to Patricia Mink Rath for her unique ability to juggle writing and editing more than one publication at a time. He believes this second edition of *Essentials of Exporting and Importing* could not have happened without her patience and constant encouragement. He sincerely appreciates her fashion-focused inputs that make this text much more readable and enjoyable, while also teaching students the importance of U.S. global trade policies, procedures, and practices. He also acknowledges the encouragement and patience of his wife Frieda and his family, friends, and colleagues who have been so understanding of the time and effort devoted to this second edition. He has dedicated this book to the memory of his father, Theodore.

Patricia Mink Rath is grateful to Harvey Shoemack for again inviting her to participate, this time in the revision of this text. The humor, patience, and love of her husband Philip Balsamo provide continuing encouragement in the development of this work and others; and the enthusiasm of son Eric Rath, his wife Kiyomi, and daughter Dana, remains a constant inspiration.

In conclusion, both authors are indebted to Olga Kontzias, Executive Editor Emerita, Fairchild Books, for her initial endorsement of this text and subsequent revision. Her enthusiasm and support remain a memorable beacon in the preparation of this work.

I

Globalization and the U.S. Export-Import Business

Figure 1.1 The fabric and production of fashionable jeans draws from resources throughout the world.

CHAPTER 1
AN OVERVIEW OF GLOBAL BUSINESS TODAY

NAUTICA SAILS AHEAD LIKE ITS FOUNDER DAVID CHU. Nautica sportswear, a clothing marketer for men, women, and children, ranks with Ralph Lauren and Tommy Hilfiger brands in major stores throughout the world. The name alone—resembling the word *nautical*—reveals the company's seafaring emphasis. In addition to jackets, sweaters, and pants, all with a nautical flare, items such as sunglasses, fragrances, footwear, household goods, and outdoor furniture bear the brand name. Available in the United States and Canada, plus stores in Europe, China, Russia, Turkey, Brazil, and other countries, totaling 75 in all, Nautica's annual sales exceed $1.5 billion. Who is responsible for creating this brand?

Nautica's creator is David Chu. Born in Taiwan with a love for the sea, Chu originally wanted to become an architect. However, after taking a class in illustration at New York's Fashion Institute of Technology, he realized his future was in fashion design and marketing. After college he returned to Taiwan, where at age 23, along with some friends, he started a clothing business. Although this first business failed, Chu was not discouraged. Better to fail when you are young than later on in life, he thought.

Chu returned to the United States and worked for an apparel manufacturer for several years. One day, he decided to create a few men's jackets designed for sailing that were both colorful and practical. New York's Bloomingdale's and Barneys were among his first customers. He named his company Nautica, as its initial focus was nautical gear for sailing enthusiasts. In its first year, Nautica's sales amounted to $700,000, rising to $2.5 million the following year. As sales boomed, larger companies became interested in Nautica. In 2003, VF Corporation (owner of such brands as Lee, Wrangler, and the North Face) bought Nautica for $600 million. Chu stayed with the company through its transition and then moved on to create a new men's tailored clothing brand, Lincs under David Chu. He also started other business ventures, including a made-to-measure line of menswear. Both David Chu and Nautica have surged ahead.[1]

Just as entrepreneurs such as David Chu are exploring ways to grow their businesses, other companies are on the lookout for profitable opportunities in new locations. Influencing business expansion, however, is the worldwide rise of terrorism and political instability, which have permanently altered ways of conducting business. Recent changes in the world's economic, political, legal, technological, and sociocultural environments have made it both easier and more difficult for companies of any size, in any country, to conduct international trade. More efficient production results in better products, lower prices, and more choices for their customers—all key to more sales and larger profits. Why should American workers and business owners—as well as government administrators—promote and engage in global business?

BENEFITS OF TRADE

Global trade, the exporting and importing of goods and services, is critical to U.S. economic growth and stability. As the world's largest economy, the United States is also the world's largest exporter and importer of goods and services. Export and import trade supports one out of every five of the 38 million U.S. jobs. U.S. free trade agreements (FTAs) sustain more than five million of those jobs, according to the U.S. Chamber of Commerce. Every billion dollars of exported goods and services supported more than an estimated 4,900 jobs in 2012.[2]

U.S. exports of goods and services totaled $2.3 trillion in 2013, according to the Export-Import Bank of the United States.[3] The United States and developed economies in Europe and Asia have slowly recovered from one of history's worst recessions. U.S. factories have nearly doubled their output over the past 20 years and now account for 20 percent of world manufacturing value-added—a larger share than the combined economies of China, India, Brazil, and Russia.[4]

Trade fuels industrial growth, supports quality jobs at home, and raises living standards for Americans. U.S. industry in total—not just the multinational corporations—benefits by specializing in the production of goods that can be produced and marketed most efficiently. Of the 293,000 U.S. exporting companies, 97 percent are small and medium-sized enterprises. Of course, larger companies, such as Boeing Aircraft or Caterpillar Tractor, account for a majority of U.S. merchandise exports, but small and medium-sized firms account for more than 33 percent of U.S. international sales.[5]

Figure 1.2 **As one of the world's largest exporters and the largest importer, the United States depends on foreign trade to enhance its economy.**

From a national perspective, these goods and services can then be exchanged for imports from other countries that offer U.S. consumers lower prices or quality options not available from domestic manufacturers. The U.S. Chamber reports that access to imports increases the purchasing power of the average American household by about $10,000 annually.[6] All these benefits of two-way trade are possible because of globalization.

Globalization, the increasing interdependency and interaction of nations, economies, and businesses all over the world, has had a positive effect on American *marketers, producers,* and *consumers*. The foundation for globalization has been twofold: free trade and technological innovation.

Free Trade

Free trade is the absence of government-imposed trade barriers—laws or protectionist policies—that would prevent the free flow of goods or services between two or more countries. Free trade allows U.S. businesses or individuals to market, or sell, their products or services in virtually any country (with the exception of national or international boycotts, such as the current situation with Iran).

The United States has a history of using trade restrictions to protect domestic manufacturers or to raise revenue. In its early years, the U.S. government imposed revenue-raising tariffs to help pay off its Revolutionary War debts and built protectionist walls to keep out cheap imported products that would unfairly compete with new American manufacturers.[7]

Even though the country no longer needed the revenue-raising tariffs after the 16th Amendment authorized the personal income tax in 1913, the United States continued to impose a tax on imports. The U.S. Congress in 1930 tried to protect U.S. manufacturers, following the stock market crash and economic crisis, with the devastating Smoot-Hawley Tariff. Rather than protect U.S. manufacturers during the Great Depression, the tariff was so antitrade that more than 60 other trade partner nations countered with import tariffs, barring U.S. products. Smoot-Hawley is often credited with exporting the U.S. depression worldwide and possibly creating the perfect economic environment for World War II.[8]

Fortunately, the days of severe U.S. protectionism ended with the end of World War II and the start of the Cold War with Russia. The U.S. promoted trade and cultural exchanges among its allies throughout the Cold War. It offered an alternative to the Communist system. The lowering or elimination of barriers to export/import—free trade—got its real start in July 1944 at the Bretton Woods conference. The New Hampshire ski resort hosted delegates from 44 allied nations, including Russia, in an attempt to save, and rebuild, the postwar international economic system.[9]

Over the past four decades work that began at Bretton Woods has continued through the international organizations that were founded there. Chapter 2 of this text provides more details on these organizations—and their roles in promoting financial stability, economic assistance, and trade liberalization to this day.

On the production side, free trade means U.S. firms can turn to **outsourcing** production or locating factories or distribution centers in virtually any country to take advantage of raw materials sourcing, lower-cost labor, or distribution efficiencies gained when facilities are located closer to their customers.

Through free trade, American consumers can choose from a vast variety of goods at the most competitive prices. Many products would not be on store shelves today if only domestic producers supplied all the goods. A good example is the fashion industry, where in 2011, 98 percent of the apparel and 99 percent of the footwear sold in the United States was produced internationally. The majority of these imports come from Asia, a growing source for very low retail prices for goods of reasonable quality.[10]

Technological Innovation

The second major development that laid the groundwork for globalization was **technological innovation**. In recent years, the introduction of the personal computer and the Internet allowed businesses of any size, as well as individuals, to access market and manufacturing data necessary for entry into the global marketplace. Countries, companies, and personnel became linked via worldwide communications technology. Advanced transportation technologies, such as global positioning system (GPS) tracking, have led to faster, safer, and more efficient shipping worldwide.

Why are globalization and export-import trade so important to the United States? As a free and democratic nation, the United States is dedicated to world peace and security that come from increasing the integration of economies around the world. Trade is critical to the prosperity of the nation, fueling economic growth and supporting jobs at home.

Most nations try to exchange goods or services that they produce most efficiently. These actions help raise living standards and provide families with affordable goods and services. The U.S. economy continues to grow and is a model for the free world. But foreign governments often restrict U.S. exported goods, with domestic farm products and services facing numerous protectionist trade barriers. Reducing global trade barriers will give farmers, ranchers, manufacturers, and service providers better access to the 95 percent of the world's customers living outside U.S. borders.

In just the past 10 years or so, freer trade has helped raise U.S. **gross domestic product (GDP)**—a nation's total output of domestically produced goods and services within a one-year period—by nearly 40 percent. As of the end of fiscal year 2013, the U.S. manufacturing sector expanded at its fastest pace in more than two years, attributed to stronger domestic demand and improved economies among U.S. global trade partners. Europe's economy has been experiencing a steady recovery from the global recession that started in 2008. China's drop from double-digit growth leveled off in 2013—to rates that are still two to three times those of other leading economies.[11]

Figure 1.3 About half of the global benefits from freer trade in goods would go to people in developing countries, such as this Angolan fruit trader.

Figure 1.4 American-designed fashion goods are marketed throughout the world.

Emerging markets, the former growth leaders during the global recession, cooled off, due to a slowdown in foreign investment and reduced imports among developed economies. U.S. free trade agreement partners, although making up only 10 percent of global GDP, purchase nearly half of all U.S. exports.

Large companies may account for the majority of exports, but **small and medium-sized enterprises (SMEs)** make up more than one-third of all U.S. merchandise exports. Export growth has been a strong contributor to the recovery of the U.S. economy each year, from 2009 to 2012. After recording negative export numbers for the first quarter of 2013—the first time since 2009—the sector made a small contribution to growth in the second quarter of 2013. Growing imports, rather than falling exports, were the cause of negative growth numbers for the trade component of U.S. GDP. Considering the lingering recession in Europe, and the slowdown of most emerging-market trading partners during 2013, the positive growth of U.S. exports was encouraging.[12]

When the United States engages in global trade, the real purchasing power of its consumers rises. Incomes stretch further when individuals can obtain necessary goods and services at a lower cost. A nation can create a higher GDP from its **factors of production** (land, labor, and capital) because it is not using them to produce outputs other countries can, at lower prices.

WHAT MAKES UP GLOBAL BUSINESS?

All commercial transactions—private or governmental—among individuals or firms of more than two countries are considered **global business**. A segment of global business, trade between businesses or governments in two or more countries, is known as **international trade**. For study purposes, two primary components or activities of global business can be identified as *foreign investment* and *export-import trade*.

Foreign Investment

Financial transactions involving loans or ownership of international enterprises and institutions, known as **foreign investment**, take place daily. When Abercrombie & Fitch opens a store in Madrid, a Japanese firm purchases an interest in a Korean factory, or a lawyer in Canada buys shares of stock in a U.S. company, each is participating in foreign investment.

Foreign investment in the United States is a positive contribution to the nation's GDP. The invested capital provides jobs and other stimuli to the domestic economy. Even though most economists agree that U.S. residents are better off than they would be without foreign capital, there are still critics of foreign ownership. Doubters ask: What payment will foreigners exact for our use of their capital? Will these injections of foreign capital give foreign entities control of U.S. security-sensitive companies and reduce job quality, workplace safety, or union protections? Most of these concerns can be reduced by reviewing the history of

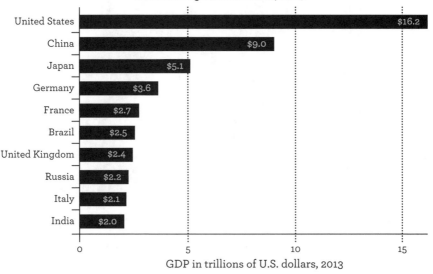

World's Largest Economies, 2013

	GDP in trillions of U.S. dollars, 2013
United States	$16.2
China	$9.0
Japan	$5.1
Germany	$3.6
France	$2.7
Brazil	$2.5
United Kingdom	$2.4
Russia	$2.2
Italy	$2.1
India	$2.0

GDP in trillions of U.S. dollars, 2013

Figure 1.5 **The world's largest economies in 2013.**

foreign investment in the United States as well as U.S. investment abroad. Foreign investment has not been synonymous with foreign control.[13]

The United States welcomes the investment and the jobs supported by the U.S. affiliates of foreign-domiciled companies. These companies either build plants and other facilities in the United States or provide additional capital to businesses that already operate domestically. Their businesses employ millions of American workers and produce goods and services for sale throughout the United States and the world.

Inbound foreign direct investment (FDI), when a foreign entity makes an investment in the United States that results in an ownership of at least a 10-percent stake in a U.S. domestic business, provides a number of benefits to the U.S. economy. These are typically high-productivity companies that are major contributors to the U.S. private sector, as it strives to innovate and build. These companies are the source of nearly 20 percent of total U.S. goods exports.[14]

Foreign Direct Investment
There are two types of foreign investment: foreign direct investment and portfolio investment of assets in a foreign country.

Foreign direct investment occurs when an investor, an individual, a company, or even a government organization gains an **equity**, or *ownership*, interest in a foreign operation. For the first time in several years, the United States ranked number one in a 2012 survey of executives on foreign investment opportunities,

Figure 1.6 This Banana Republic store in Kobe, Japan, is part of Gap's plan for global expansion.

moving ahead of China, which fell to number two. The ranking is an example of the United States' progress toward sustainable and steady growth, according to a study by the global consulting firm A. T. Kearney of more than 300 executives from 28 countries.[15]

Recently, in its global expansion, specialty retailer Banana Republic opened a store in Singapore, part of parent company Gap's expansion into Indonesia, South Korea, Turkey, and Saudi Arabia. The company's Old Navy division has announced plans for its first mainland China store, for launch during the first half of 2014.[16] These branches, along with Gap's other overseas stores, are examples of U.S. companies' FDI.

Mergers and Acquisitions

Much foreign direct investment occurs through mergers and acquisitions (M&As). An **acquisition** takes place when one company buys another. If one of the companies is headquartered in a foreign country, that acquisition becomes another example of foreign investment. Not long ago, after heavy bidding from competitors, Istithmar World, a Dubai-based private equity firm, acquired the prestigious Barneys New York fashion retail chain from the U.S. firm Jones Apparel Group. A **merger** occurs when two firms join together as owners for a specific purpose, each participating company retaining a portion of control over the new (merged) organization.

An example of a retail merger considered at the time to be "a marriage made in retail heaven" took place in 2008, when two major Japanese department stores, Isetan, Ltd. and Mitsukoshi, Ltd., decided to merge and form Isetan Mitsukoshi Holdings.[17] Note the combined names; this arrangement differs from an acquisition where the purchasing company remains dominant.

Isetan brought advanced information technology to the venture, while Mitsukoshi knew how to attract quality customers from Japan's elite. The merged company, one of Japan's leading department store operators, operates a dozen Mitsukoshi stores and about a half dozen Isetan locations throughout Japan. Mitsukoshi focuses on an older demographic, while Isetan's Tokyo-area shops offer apparel alongside food, home goods, and sundries that appeal to younger generations. Internationally, Isetan Mitsukoshi Holdings has stores in Asia, Europe, and the United States.[18]

Joint Venture

One form of merger is a **joint venture**, a direct investment in which two or more partners share ownership. In India, Walmart Stores, Inc. and India's Bharti Enterprises negotiated an agreement, a 50–50 joint venture for a wholesale operation permitting the new organization to gather goods from Indian manufacturers and farmers that would then be sold in Bharti's wholly owned subsidiary, Bharti retail stores. Walmart planned to open a retail store in India, but confusing rules and

Figure 1.7 Barneys, a well-known U.S. fashion retailer, was acquired in 2007 by Istithmar World, a Dubai-based firm.

Figure 1.8 Isetan, a 100-year-old department store in Shinjuku, Japan, sells many types of wares, ranging from the traditional (common clothing, shoes, and household items) to the esoteric (kimonos and imported food items).

political uncertainty kept Walmart and other overseas supermarket giants away from the estimated $450 billion retail market. Recent reports have indicated Walmart would drop plans to open retail stores in India and end its joint-venture with Bharti. It now plans to initiate e-commerce sales and add wholesale stores in India, to supply small shops and family-run stores. Wal-Mart is eager to sell directly to consumers there, but is waiting for new government regulations that would allow access to foreign retailers online.[19]

In another situation, Ralph Lauren, along with the Swiss luxury goods group Compagnie Richemont Financière, formed a 50–50 joint venture under the name Ralph Lauren Watch and Fine Jewelry Company to design and market luxury watches and fine jewelry to Ralph Lauren boutiques and independent jewelry stores throughout the world.[20]

Mixed Ventures

A **mixed venture** represents a commercial operation in which ownership is shared by a government and a business. In China, joint ventures with foreign companies include partnership with a Chinese government agency or company partially owned by the government. Forming joint ventures in China always involves the government. The challenge begins with the search for a potential partner. Even firms that are comfortable in global expansion elsewhere may find themselves struggling in China. Market research is in its infancy, and government statistics are not very reliable. Moreover, China has set a limit on how many joint ventures it wants per industry and the maximum per district. The accepted wisdom is that without **Guanxi** (connections usually referring to government contacts and influence) outsiders have no chance of penetrating the Chinese bureaucracy.

Guanxi implies an element of trust. A lot of business in China revolves around circles of personal and mutual trust. So for any outsiders to do business in China, they must take the time to form relationships or *guanxi*. This has been a big obstacle for many American businesses trying to enter the Chinese market.[21]

Licensing Agreements

Other forms of foreign direct investment can include licensing agreements. A **licensing agreement** is an arrangement between a company with a well-known name and a manufacturer who pays a royalty to create goods using that name. Fashion designers and organizations use licensing extensively to market their goods throughout the world; a few of these are: Christian Dior, Pierre Cardin, Marc Jacobs, Michael Kors, and Martha Stewart. Accessories such as sunglasses, shoes, handbags, or scarves bearing the Kate Spade label, for example, are often produced under licensing agreements with manufacturers (many in foreign countries) specializing in that particular accessory line.

Figure 1.9 **The Hypercity shopping mall in Mumbai, India.**

A form of licensing sometimes referred to as a **franchise** is an agreement between a company such as Ralph Lauren and a foreign organization to set up and operate that company's retail stores in foreign countries. For example, in an agreement with the Russian distribution organization Mercury, Ralph Lauren opened up two stores in Moscow. One, in a prestigious downtown shopping area, offers Lauren's highest luxury brands, Purple and Black Labels. The other, on the edge of the city, sells more sportswear.[22] Ralph Lauren is currently enjoying increased potential in the Russian market, for both its clothing and accessory lines and home collections. RL stores are located in Paris, Tokyo, Milan, and London, as well as Moscow.[23]

Figure 1.10 **Victoria's Secret is the brand most recognized by American women.**

Portfolio Investment

The second major component of foreign investment, **portfolio investment**, is a noncontrolling interest in a venture made in the form of either debt or equity. American individuals, companies, associations—even governments—can buy stocks or bonds of publicly traded foreign corporations—and they can invest in American firms. An example of portfolio investment occurs when an individual investor purchases shares of ownership in a mutual fund that invests in foreign corporations. In another example, China, Germany, and Great Britain's purchases of U.S. government bonds are financing our national debt, as well as enhancing their investment portfolios, all of which makes the United States a debtor nation, which is not necessarily a bad thing if international trade can continue to stimulate the domestic economy.

Figure 1.11 Foreign-owned assets in the United States, adjusted for inflation.

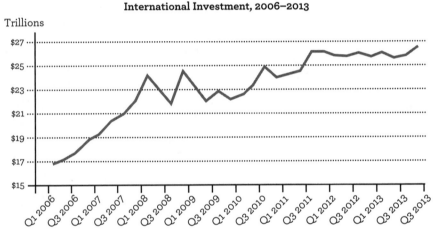

International Investment, 2006–2013

Source: U.S. Commerce Department.

Export-Import Trade

Export-import trade—the marketing (including the pricing, promotion, and physical distribution) of goods and services to countries other than their origin—is the second major division of global business. Export-import trade may seem to be complex, requiring extensive physical and financial resources, as well as language skills and extensive cross-cultural training. Fortunately, for tens of thousands of successful companies, this is not entirely true. The benefits of expanded markets and higher profit margins frequently outweigh the possible risks to export-import trade.

SPOTLIGHT ON GLOBAL TRADE 1.1
Mitumba Trade: Where Do All the Used T-Shirts Go?

What do you do with your old clothing? Give the jacket to your niece or nephew? Turn the T-shirt into a dust rag? Bundle everything and send it off to a charity? And what does your favorite organization do then, say, with your used T-shirt? The items it cannot use are sold to be offered as *mitumba*—castoff apparel from Americans and Europeans destined for markets in African nations such as Tanzania, Benin, Togo, and the Republic of Congo. Because of global entrepreneurs, many Africans, for small pocket change, can outfit themselves well—not as copies of Americans or Europeans, but with their own keen sense of local fashion. And for these consumers, shopping at the mitumba market is fun, providing the thrill of locating a treasure perhaps in the right Nike T-shirt much as an American maven's finding a jewel of a dress at Target.

When a consumer in the United States gives used clothing to, say, a nonprofit organization such as the Salvation Army, the goods it cannot use are picked up by an organization that sorts and bales clothing and ships it off to African nations such as Tanzania; in fact, the largest U.S. export to that country, by far, is used clothing. While some African nations such as Botswana and South Africa ban importing used clothing, other nations such as Tanzania and Zambia find that it provides jobs as well as consumer goods. The bales of garments coming from the United States and Europe are often 2,000 pounds in weight and need further sorting; those entering Tanzania go to a warehouse, operated by the local conglomerate METL, where they are further sorted, cleaned, pressed, and sometimes altered. They are then bundled into smaller bales and offered to individual entrepreneurs to sell in their stalls at mitumba markets. In these situations, exporting, importing, and individual entrepreneurship work hand-in-hand to provide goods in great demand.

Source: Pietra Rivoli. *The Travels of a T-Shirt in the Global Economy: An Economist Examines the Markets, Power, and Politics of World Trade.* Hoboken, NJ: Wiley, 2005.

Exports represent the *sales* of goods and services that flow out of a country, as when the U.S. handbag company Coach, or the cosmetics firm Estée Lauder, offers its goods for retail sale to foreign stores such as Bon Marché in Paris or Takashimaya in Japan. **Imports** are *purchases* of goods and services that come into a country, as when U.S. retailers purchase goods from Chanel, Gucci, or Prada. However, to be officially counted as a country's exports or imports, they must be distributed across national boundaries for the purpose of reselling them. Therefore, products brought home from a foreign vacation for personal use or as gifts for friends or relatives do not count toward a nation's **balance of trade**, the difference between a country's total imports and exports. If exports exceed imports, a favorable balance of trade, or a **trade surplus**, exists; if imports are higher than exports, a **trade deficit** exists. When a country imports more than it exports, as the United States has since the early 1970s, its currency loses value (known as currency devaluation), inflation rises, and consumers pay more not only for imports but also for domestic goods.

Trade balances are customarily measured bilaterally; the United States has experienced large trade deficits with both Japan and China over the past five years. A nation's total **balance of payments** is a record of all export-import trade and other financial transactions including investments and gold with the rest of the world during a one-year period. It provides a snapshot of a nation's economic health used by government institutions, banks, and other agencies to maintain economic stability.

GLOBALIZATION SPURS POSITIVE CHANGES IN PRODUCTION AND MARKETING PROCEDURES WORLDWIDE

Globalization of both *markets* and *production* enables firms or individual entrepreneurs opportunities to safely market or produce goods and services in the vast majority of countries around the world. The interdependency that has resulted from globalization allows consumers and marketers to source products from virtually any country or to sell their goods and services to targeted audiences on a global basis via eBay, plus millions of B2B (business-to-business) or B2C (business-to-consumer) websites.

Elimination or major reductions of tariffs and other trade barriers provide our exports increased access to most foreign markets. Improved information technologies in the form of home computers and small business networks have resulted in better-informed consumers who now demand higher-quality, innovative, and more cost-competitive imported products. Consumers now have smart phones with mobile capabilities that can access product information to ensure greater choices and lower prices for commodities, fashions, and even purchases of new homes or automobiles.

Figure 1.12 Through its majority stake in the store chain Massmart, Walmart has expanded its presence in Africa to include more than 350 stores in South Africa and 11 other sub-Saharan countries.

Information Technologies

Thanks to "smart" technologies, it is easier, faster, and less expensive to research potential export markets or import sources, and to move information, products, services, people, and ideas around the world. The microprocessor has enabled developments in communications and information processing technology—especially the Internet—so companies can conduct research before investing in the people, time, energy, and money necessary for a successful import or export effort.

In Walmart's 2012 Annual Report, the company acknowledges the important role technology plays in helping it stay customer-focused. "We have growing online businesses in 10 countries and are well positioned in markets that offer the greatest growth potential—the U.S., the U.K., Brazil and China," according to Michael T. Duke, Walmart President and Chief Executive Officer.[24]

Figure 1.13 Popular American household products, such as Tide laundry detergent, command prominent shelf space in Asian supermarkets.

Communications Breakthroughs

The way in which we communicate has also energized globalization. Although the fax is still used by businesses today, the majority of international communications now take place via email, text messaging, or social media. With mobile technology, it is now possible for individuals, corporations—even government officials—to be accessible virtually anywhere in the world, at any time of the day, for a telephone call, email, or text message.

CHALLENGES TO GLOBALIZATION

Globalization has its critics, however. They point to unequal sharing of benefits among all nations of the world, with a disregard for human rights and exploitation in developing nations as cause for economic and social unrest that may result in the eventual breakdown of a fragile global economic system.

One antiglobalization argument is that U.S. global companies create jobs overseas at the expense of domestic jobs. Would American public interest be better served if government policy stopped supporting global companies and focused instead on domestic employment and U.S. competitiveness? Should the United States protect its home markets with higher trade barriers, such as **tariffs** (taxes on specific imports to compensate for cheaper labor costs of our foreign competitors) or **quotas** (limits on quantities of specific goods from certain countries, usually over a one-year period)? Economists, government leaders, and journalists will be debating globalization for many years to come, as it is a complex matter and, as yet, simple answers will not satisfy any side. Most do agree that the benefits of increased globalization can be costly to individuals and nations, but also that society as a whole—which stands to benefit—should share in the costs of those who may lose.

One of the primary goals of this textbook is to present the essentials of global trade—through entrepreneurial export-import activities—that offer the potential of achieving world peace and prosperity.

Summary

Globalization, the increasing interdependency of nations and businesses, has a profound effect throughout the world. For the United States, trade with foreign countries can help provide domestic jobs, increase the standard of living by providing a wide assortment of goods and services, and raise the nation's overall production as measured by its GDP. Trade supports 38 million jobs in the United States—more than one in five American jobs.

Global business is made up of two primary components: foreign investment and international trade. There are two types of foreign investment: foreign direct investment and portfolio investment. Foreign direct investment occurs when an individual, organization, or government gains ownership interest or equity in a foreign operation. Joint ventures and mixed ventures are examples of foreign direct investment. Portfolio investment is a non-controlling interest in a foreign venture, such as the purchase of stocks or bonds of a foreign company.

The trade component of global business is concerned with exporting or importing. Exports are goods or services offered to foreign businesses, such as when handbags from the U.S. firm Coach, or cosmetics from Estée Lauder, are offered for retail sale in foreign stores, for example, the Bon Marché in France or Takashimaya in Japan. Imports are foreign goods that are brought into a country for sale, as when U.S. retailers buy from European vendors such as Chanel, Gucci, and Prada.

The difference between a country's total exports and imports is indicated in its balance of trade. When the value of exports exceeds that of imports, a nation has a balance of trade surplus; when imports exceed exports, it experiences a balance of trade deficit. Typically, trade balances are measured between two nations. For example, today China sells more goods to the United States than it buys; therefore, it has a huge trade surplus, while the United States has a large trade deficit with China. The record of all of a nation's financial transactions with the rest of the world, including exports and imports, investments, and gold, makes up its balance of payments.

Export-import trade is important to the United States because it fuels economic growth, maintains domestic employment, tends to raise living standards, and supplies consumers with a wide range of goods and services. The sum total of the goods and services produced within the borders of any country, during a one-year period, is that country's gross domestic product.

Export growth has been a strong contributor to the recovery of the U.S. economy from 2009 to 2013. Imports also make a significant contribution to the U.S. economy, resulting in lower prices and more choices for American families trying to stretch their budgets and for U.S. manufacturers seeking lower prices for raw materials or component parts in order to stay competitive.

Exporting and importing have become more prevalent because of enhanced communications and technologies, more favorable legislation, increased use of the Internet by businesses and ultimate consumers, and the globalization of markets. Current challenges include the threat to safety, resulting in the need for greater security in product manufacture and distribution, and the advent of more complex legislative procedures.

While globalization has certainly benefited many nations and their citizens, its critics believe the exploitation of the poorer countries must be addressed and eliminated, for the future of world peace and prosperity.

KEY TERMS, CONT'D

> SMALL AND MEDIUM-SIZED ENTERPRISES (SMES)

> TARIFFS

> TECHNOLOGICAL INNOVATION

> TRADE DEFICIT

> TRADE SURPLUS

Review Questions

1. Describe three or four benefits of globalization.

2. What are three reasons that globalization and export-import business are important to the United States?

3. Describe the two major components of global business with an example of each.

4. Explain the relationship between a nation's exports and imports and its balance of trade.

Discussion Questions and Activities

1. From your own experience, provide three examples of foreign direct investment in the United States. Visit your library and, consulting references, identify three foreign-owned companies operating in the United States. Should the United States encourage such investment? If yes, what benefits come from these investments? If no, what drawbacks exist?

2. Using the Internet, locate at least three major mergers or acquisitions between U.S. and foreign corporations over the past five years.

3. The U.S. steel industry was in dire straits toward the end of the past century, until the major Japanese steel companies formed joint ventures with most of the U.S. steel giants. Cite three reasons why you agree or disagree with this idea, considering the strategic importance of the steel industry as the primary supplier of U.S. military aircraft, tanks, weapons, and ammunition.

4. Using an Internet search engine, such as AOL, Yahoo, or Google, search "Product Licensing" and determine the world's largest consumer products licensor. Why, at many major domestic trade shows, are vendors of licensed products given increasingly larger amounts of floor space? Cite three licensed products that you own. (*Hint:* consider logo products licensed by professional or collegiate sports teams.)

5. For more than 25 years, the United States has had annual trade deficits, with imports exceeding exports by more than $471.5 billion in 2013. What steps in importing and/or exporting might be taken to reverse this economic dilemma? What are the risks of allowing the trade deficit to grow each year? Research recent literature on the United States trade deficit to determine the pros and cons of the growing imbalance of trade.

Chapter 1 Case

H&M Cleans Up Its Act

A few years ago the Swedish fast-fashion house, Hennes & Mauritz, known as H&M, ran into trouble in New York City when it became known that unsold inventory from its stores there had been shredded and put out with the trash. New Yorkers were furious to see new clothing destroyed when people in many parts of the world are desperately poor, many living on less than $2 a day.

H&M is a global chain with 2,900 stores throughout Europe, the United States, and Asia. Word of the waste traveled quickly, and management knew it had to act swiftly to repair its image. Starting in its home country Sweden, the company now asks customers to recycle their old clothing in plastic bags. For each bag of worn items in any condition brought to an H&M store, customers received a coupon for the Swedish equivalent of about $8 to be used on a purchase of $47 or more. H&M then sold the old clothes to a Swiss firm that resold items in good condition and converted others into stuffed toys or cleaning rags. H&M management also drew up plans to expand this activity to its stores worldwide.

The program has had other benefits: it recycles cotton that is increasingly expensive and in demand, and it lessens the burden on crowded landfills when clothing can be recycled instead of thrown away. In this instance, efforts to increase product life and sustainability mesh with corporate profitability.

Source: Katarina Gustafsson, "H&M's Love for Old Clothes," *Bloomberg Businessweek,* July 1–7, 2013, pp. 22–23.

Questions

1. What is your opinion of the recycling program H&M initiated in its stores? Cite some of the plusses and minuses that you see.

2. How effective do you think this program is today? Describe the programs of other export or import businesses you are aware of that are conducting programs to increase sustainability or green initiatives while boosting goodwill.

3. What kinds of sustainability or green initiatives could a small export or import business initiate?

References

1. "Nautica at 30," WWD Milestones, *Women's Wear Daily*, February 7, 2013, Sec. II, pp. 1–34. Retrieved June 1, 2013, from http://www.wwd.com /wwd-publications/wwd -milestones/2013–02–07.

2. John Murphy, "The State of World Trade 2013 . . ." U.S. Chamber of Commerce, May 1, 2013. Retrieved August 7, 2013, from https://www.us chamber.com/speech /state-world-trade-2013 -outlook-american-jobs -economic-growth -and-global-leadership -remarks.

3. "U.S. Exports Reach $2.3 Trillion in 2013," Export-Import Bank of the United States, Release dated February 6, 2014. Retrieved February 7, 2013, from http://www .exim.gov/newsandevents /releases/2014/US-Exports -Reach-2-Trillion-in-2013 .cfm.

4. Op. cit., Murphy, "The State of World Trade 2013."

5. Ibid.

6. Ibid.

7. "The History of American Business." Retrieved August 30, 2013, from http://history business.org/2753-tariffs .html?newsid=2753&seour l=tariffs.

8. Ibid.

9. "The Bretton Woods Conference, 1944," U.S. Department of State, Office of the Historian. Retrieved August 14, 2013, from http://2001-2009 .state.gov/r/pa/ho/time /wwii/98681.htm

10. Op. cit., Murphy, "The State of World Trade 2013."

11. Ibid.

12. Ibid.

13. "U.S. Inbound Foreign Direct Investment," Executive Office of the President, Council of Economic Advisors, June 2011. Retrieved August 20, 2013, from http://www .whitehouse.govsites /default/files/microsites /cea_fdi_report.pdf

14. Ibid.

15. Daniel Bases and Manuela Badway, "U.S. Tops Confidence Survey on Foreign Investments, Displaces China," Reuters, Wed., June 26, 2013. Retrieved Aug. 15, 2013 from http://www.reuters .com/article/2013/06/26 /us-fdi-survey-idUSBRE95 P05X20130636. p.1

16. "Gap Inc. Announces 2014 Launch of Old Navy in Mainland China," Gap, Inc., press release, August 22, 2013. Retrieved August 29, 2013, from www.gapinc .com/content/gapinc/html /media/pressrelease/2013 /,ed_pr_ON_China_Gap _Taiwain.html. p.1.

17. "Isetan Mitsukoshi Holdings Ltd. Company Information." Retrieved August 31, 2013, from http://www.imdhs.co.jp /english/company /philosophy.html# Philosophy01

18. Ibid.

19. "Confusing Rules Deter Foreign Supermarkets from India," *AFP News*, Mumbai, September 11, 2013. Retrieved September 13, 2013, from http://www .hindustantimes.com /business-news/confusing -rules-deter-foreign -supermarkets-from-india

/article1-1120473.aspx p.1; Laurie Burkitt, "Wal-Mart Enlists Web in India Plan," *Wall Street Journal*, April 9, 2014, p. B4.

20. Ralph Lauren Watch and Jewelry Co. Retrieved August 31, 2013, from http://www.ralphlauren watches.com/en-us/Pages /Craftsmanship.aspx

21. "What Is Guanxi?" World Learner Chinese.

Retrieved September 13, 2013, from http://www .worldlearnerchinese .com/content/what -guanxi.

22. "Our Flagships—Ralph Lauren Stores." Retrieved August 30, 2012, from http://flagships.ralph lauren.com/.

23. "The Real Potential of Russia's Luxury Market and the Challenges of Doing Business in Russia for Luxury Brands," April 21, 2012. Retrieved August 22, 2013, from http://www .cpp-luxury.com/the-real -potential-of-russias -luxury-market.

24. Walmart Annual Report 2012. Retrieved August 30, 2013, from http://stock.walmart.com /annual-reports.

Figure 2.1 Designer Michael Kors.

CHAPTER 2
GLOBALIZATION AND TRADE LIBERALIZATION

MICHAEL KORS. Perhaps no other American designer has received the kind of publicity showered on Michael Kors. Well known among television viewers for his years judging *Project Runway*, Kors is renowned in the fashion industry as recipient of some of its highest honors, among which are the Council of Fashion Designers Association's (CFDA) Designer of the Year awards for Womenswear (1999), Menswear (2003), and the Lifetime Achievement Award (2010). Awards aside, his classic, often timeless styles are worn by some of the world's most celebrated women, such as First Lady Michelle Obama, actresses Jennifer Aniston and Nicole Kidman, and tennis champion Serena Williams. Today, many customers across the globe can find Kors products in nearby shops and boutiques.

Born in 1959, Kors grew up in Merrick, New York. At first he wanted to become an architect. He changed his mind and opened, in his mother's basement, a boutique called Iron Butterfly that featured his designs. Realizing he needed further education, he attended New York's Fashion Institute of Technology for two terms, before setting off on his own again. He convinced Lothar's, a French boutique in Manhattan across the street from the exclusive Bergdorf Goodman store, to let him showcase some of his creations. One day, when he was working on a window display, a Bergdorf executive, after asking him who made the clothes he was displaying, urged him to create his own line of merchandise and let her know when it was ready. A year later, Kors called her with his first collection of womenswear. His innovative yet simple looks caught on. Soon Anna Wintour, editor of *Vogue*, began featuring his designs as worn by models such as Cindy Crawford and Claudia Schiffer.

The Japanese organization Onward Kashimaya invested in Kors' line, and in 1998, the French fashion house Céline hired him as a designer, the first time a couture maison had brought on an American. After several successful seasons, Kors decided to concentrate on expanding his own lines. He continued his women's collection, created a more moderately priced line of sportswear including jeans and T-shirts known as KORS Michael Kors, and added a line of accessories entitled MICHAEL Michael Kors. In addition to supplying stores in the United States, his company opened retail outlets in Milan, Paris, Hong Kong, Seoul, Singapore, and Macau and reached a larger market. Financing its planned global growth, his company decided to go public in 2011, with a listing on the New York Stock Exchange. Today stores and boutiques bearing the Michael Kors brand conduct business in many parts of the world. Some of the more recent additions include Berlin, Amsterdam, Madrid, Edinburgh, Beijing, Warsaw, Kiev, Kuwait, Dubai, and Jakarta.[1]

The expansion of the Michael Kors organization is just one of many global businesses that have interconnected ideas and cultures, as well as production and marketing processes, in the past 30 years. This concept may be misunderstood as implying that national markets have merged into one giant global marketplace. Fortunately, they have not. Although the participants may have become increasingly interdependent, they still retain their uniqueness and individuality, no matter where they are located.

INTERNATIONAL ALLIANCES

A critical catalyst for U.S. export and import growth has been the liberalization of international trade. Multilateral trade negotiations have brought about significant reductions in tariffs and nontariff barriers along with international commitments toward future growth in trade.

The first major international trade cooperation began while World War II was still raging. In July 1944, at the **Bretton Woods Conference**—the name commonly given to the United Nations Monetary and Financial Conference, held at Bretton Woods, New Hampshire—750 delegates from all 44 allied nations, including the Soviet Union, met to prepare for rebuilding the postwar international economic system.[2]

Bretton Woods gave birth to the **International Monetary Fund (IMF)**, to promote international monetary cooperation, and to the International Bank for Reconstruction and Development (IBRD), to provide funds for rebuilding war-torn countries, both of which will be discussed in this chapter in-depth. Thus began the new era of global alliances and economic cooperation.

Figure 2.2 The scene of the birth of the International Monetary Fund and the World Bank, today Bretton Woods is a 10,000-acre ski resort in the White Mountains of New Hampshire.

INTERNATIONAL FASHION FOCUS 2.1
Hong Kong Luxury Sales Fall as Chinese Curb Spending

How does a worldwide recession affect one of the premier global fashion centers? Hong Kong may be able to maintain its image as Asia's top luxury shopping venue, but 2012 sales were off by at least 10 percent from the year before. Mainland Chinese shoppers pulled back because of a slump in exports and a contraction in manufacturing in the world's second-largest economy, according to Joseph Tung, executive director of the Travel Industry Council.

One example of this change is the plight of the invitation-only event, for deep-pocket customers, called "Luxury Week," a private 10-day fashion extravaganza, with runway shows featuring items from most of the top fashion designers, such as Calvin Klein, Diane von Furstenberg, Oscar de la Renta, Vera Wang, Zac Posen, and others. Promoters combine all that style with celebrity speakers, fashion seminars, chats with designers, and parties, and to top it off, make sure these very styles are in local stores, ready for immediate purchase.

The major activity of visitors to Hong Kong is shopping, but in 2012, shoppers from China's mainland curbed spending at Hong Kong luxury stores during the Golden Week holiday, reflecting growing pressure on the city's economy from faltering tourist demand. More than 2,000 consumers were invited to participate in the event, hoping to reinforce Hong Kong's position as a global fashion innovator.

Source: Stephanie Tong and Billy Chan "Hong Kong Luxury Sales Fall as Chinese Curb Spending," Bloomberg News, October 5, 2012. Retrieved on August 30, 2013, from http://www.businessweek.com/news/2012–10–04/hong-kong-luxury-sales-fall-as-chinese-shoppers-spend-less.

Until the early 1970s, the Bretton Woods system was effective in controlling conflict and in achieving the common goals of the leading countries that had created it, especially the United States. A number of developments, however, including the persistent printing of too much money while maintaining a peg to gold, strenuous budget deficit problems, the Vietnam War, and marginal tax rates, have been blamed for the collapse of the Bretton Woods monetary system in 1971. It was one result after the United States suspended the convertibility of dollars to gold. Most economists agree that the increasing balance of trade deficit in the United

States, and the inability of the government to ever reverse it, brought decades of continued economic strain on Bretton Woods.

The International Monetary Fund

The IMF is an organization currently consisting of 188 countries, working to foster global cooperation in trade and employment, and to promote economic growth, while reducing poverty and providing temporary financial aid to countries with balance-of-payment problems.[3]

The World Bank

The International Bank for Reconstruction and Development (IBRD), formally organized in 1945 with only 28 countries and now known as the **World Bank**, is a specialized agency of the United Nations, with headquarters in Washington, DC. The World Bank's goal is to facilitate productive investment, encourage foreign trade, and discharge international debt. Each of the 188 members of the bank must belong to the IMF. World Bank assistance tends to be long term (rather than short term as is that of the IMF) and is funded both by member-country contributions and through bond issuance.[4]

Figure 2.3 International Monetary Fund Managing Director Christine Lagarde visits a primary school in Bamako, Mali, in January 2014.

Figure 2.4 An official of the IMF meets with a group of orphaned boys from the Kaisi Children's Home in Lusaka, Zambia. Founded in 1926, the orphanage has benefited from IMF assistance.

Both the IMF and World Bank provide low-interest loans, interest-free credit, and grants to developing countries for projects and programs to, for example, build schools and health centers, provide water and electricity, fight disease, and protect the environment.

The General Agreement on Tariffs and Trade

Another one of Bretton Woods' successes, first signed in 1947, the **General Agreement on Tariffs and Trade (GATT)**, was an international agreement to encourage free trade among member states by regulating and reducing barriers to trade and by providing a common mechanism for resolving trade disputes. Barriers to trade include both *tariffs*, import taxes on traded goods, and *quotas*, limits on the quantities of goods nations may export. Originally, the GATT was supposed to become a full international organization such as the World Bank or IMF and would be called the International Trade Organization. However, the agreement was not ratified, so the GATT remained simply an agreement. While the IMF and World Bank are still functioning entities, GATT activities have been absorbed by the World Trade Organization.[5]

The World Trade Organization

Established in 1995, the **World Trade Organization (WTO)** is the only global organization providing a forum for governments to negotiate trade agreements and a place for them to settle trade disputes. Headquartered in Geneva, Switzerland, it produces and enforces many rules governing trade among its 159 members. Unlike the GATT, the WTO issues binding decisions. In recent years, 11 new members have joined the WTO: the large economies of Russia, Saudi Arabia, Vietnam, and Ukraine; the smaller economies of Tajikistan and Montenegro; and the **less-developed countries (LDCs)** of Samoa, Vanuatu, Tonga, Laos, and Cape Verde.[6]

According to its website, the WTO's objective is "to help trade flow smoothly, freely, fairly, and predictably." It does this by doing the following:

- Administering trade agreements
- Acting as a forum for trade negotiations
- Settling trade disputes
- Reviewing national trade policies
- Assisting developing countries in trade policy issues, through technical assistance and training programs
- Cooperating with other international organizations

During the past 20 years, discussions to end trade restrictions, settle trade disputes, and enforce trade laws have been accomplished through a number of successful multinational conferences sponsored by the WTO, known as "rounds."

Figure 2.5 **Officials from the World Bank arrive in Africa to assess needs there.**

The WTO has been attempting to complete negotiations on the most recent round, known as the Doha Development Round, which began in 2001, with a primary objective of addressing the needs of developing countries. The Doha talks stalled because of clashes over necessary reciprocity, primarily between China, the European Union (EU), India, and the United States.[7]

On December 7, 2013, the WTO's Bali Ministerial Conference concluded with agreement on a package of issues, known as the "Bali Package," to streamline trade, allow developing countries more options for providing food security, boost least developed countries' trade, and help general economic development. "For the first time in our history, the WTO has truly delivered," said Brazilian Roberto Azevedo, chairman of the WTO, at the conclusion of the Conference. The Bali Package is a selection of issues from the broader Doha Round negotiations. Azevedo has challenged WTO members to now turn to the rest of the round, known officially as the Doha Development Agenda.[8]

The WTO is not just about liberalizing trade; in some circumstances its rules support maintaining trade barriers, as in protecting **intellectual property rights**, patents, trademarks, and copyrights. However, it is difficult to protect these valuable business assets from unscrupulous businesses (or governments) in other countries. Violations of intellectual property rights not only deprive legitimate businesses of millions of dollars and undercut innovation but often pose serious threats to human safety and health. Imports of counterfeit apparel and toxic merchandise are discussed later in this textbook.

Although the WTO is still young, the multilateral trading system that was originally set up under GATT is more than 67 years old. These years have seen an exceptional growth in world trade. Merchandise exports grew on average by 6 percent annually. GATT and the WTO have helped to create a strong and prosperous world trading system contributing to sustained growth.[9]

The Group of Eight (G-8) and the Group of 20 (G-20)

The **Group of Eight**, known as the **G-8**, is an international forum promoting trade and economic cooperation that includes the governments of Canada, France, Germany, Italy, Japan, Russia, the United Kingdom, and the United States. Together, these countries represent about 65 percent of the world economy.[10] The group's activities include year-round conferences and policy research to promote democratic, economic, and educational reforms throughout the world. The annual summit meeting is attended by the heads of government of the member states. The European Commission—the executive branch of the European Union, which is made up of 28 commissioners, one for each country of the EU, led by a Commission President—is also represented at the G-8 meetings.

Each year, member states of the G-8 take turns assuming the presidency of the group. The holder of the presidency sets the group's annual agenda and hosts the summit for that year.

Figure 2.6 In June 2013, the WTO science ministers and heads of the G8 national academies met at London's Royal Society to discuss scientific approaches to global challenges.

Recognizing emerging nations such as China, India, and Brazil, the G-8 grew to be part of the **Group of 20 (G-20)**. The member nations account for 80 percent of global trade and two-thirds of the world's population. The G-20 summits of heads of state or government are held in addition to the G-20 meetings of finance ministers and central bank governors. After the 2008 debut summit in Washington, DC, G-20 leaders met twice a year. Since 2011, the summits have been held only once a year. At the September 2013 summit in St. Petersburg, Russia, the geopolitical crisis in the Middle East dominated the discussions, rather than the planned economic issues of growth, creation of jobs, and fighting corruption. G-20 summits are planned be held in Australia in 2014 and Turkey in 2015.[11]

In April 2014, the U.S. and Western allies canceled the G-8 Summit scheduled for Sochi, Russia in June 2014. The remaining G-7 members cut Moscow out of the G-8 international coalition to isolate Russia and warned it that they stand ready to order tougher economic penalties if Vladimir Putin presses further into Ukraine. The G-7 leaders instead planned to meet in the summer of 2014 in Brussels.[12]

REGIONAL ALLIANCES

Global organizations such as the WTO and structures such as the World Bank were created by sovereign states to ensure a stable world trade and economic environment. These formats led to regional affiliations such as **bilateral alliances**, agreements between two sovereign nations, or **multinational agreements**, those among more than two independent countries. Examples are regional trading blocks, such as the European Union (EU) and the North American Free Trade Agreement (NAFTA), and **free trade agreements (FTAs)**, which eliminate all or most trade restrictions and subsidies with various countries, and proposed new trade alliances with both Asia and Europe: the **Trans-Pacific Partnership (TPP)** and the **Transatlantic Trade and Investment Partnership (TTIP.)**

The European Union
One of the earliest—and historically most significant—examples of the new international order is the **European Union**, consisting of most of the nations of western Europe. It was established in 1993 to manage the economic and political integration of the member states. The idea actually began in 1950, in the aftermath of decades of wars and loss of life and property in Europe. A number of visionary European leaders were convinced that the only way to secure a lasting peace among their countries was to unite them economically and politically. The six original member countries (Belgium, West Germany, Luxembourg, France, Italy, and the Netherlands) agreed to give the power to make decisions about the coal and steel industries in their respective countries to an independent, supranational body called the High Authority.[13]

Membership in the EU, as of 2014, includes 28 countries: Austria, Belgium, Bulgaria, Croatia (entered in 2013), Cyprus, Czech Republic, Denmark, Estonia, Finland, France, Germany, Greece, Hungary, Ireland, Italy, Latvia, Lithuania, Luxembourg, Malta, the Netherlands, Poland, Portugal, Romania, Slovakia, Slovenia, Spain, Sweden, and the United Kingdom. The Canary Islands (Spain); Azores and Madeira (Portugal); and French Guiana, Guadeloupe, Martinique, and Réunion (France) are sometimes listed separately even though they are legally a part of Spain, Portugal, and France. Candidates for future EU membership include Iceland, Montenegro, Serbia, the Former Yugoslav Republic of Macedonia, and Turkey.[14]

The EU's original focus was on a common commercial policy for coal and steel and a common agricultural policy. Other policies were added as time went by and as the need arose. Some key policy aims have changed in the light of changing circumstances. For example, the aim of the EU's agricultural policy is no longer to produce as much food as cheaply as possible but to support farming methods that produce healthy, high-quality food and protect the environment. The need for environmental protection is now taken into account across the whole range of EU policies.

The EU was created as an economic union. The first, oldest, and largest pillar, the European Community, was founded as the European Economic Community. Creating and maintaining the EU's single market has been a prominent goal of the Community, ensuring free movement of people, goods, services, and capital.

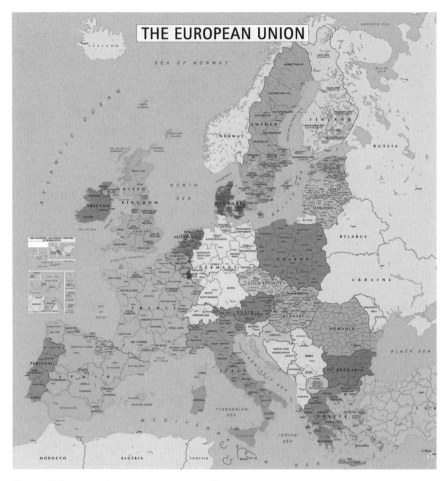

Figure 2.7 **Map of the European Union members.**

The EU is the largest U.S. commercial partner, with bilateral trade in goods and services topping $5 trillion annually.[15] The EU is also the biggest trading partner to many other countries, such as China and India.

It has taken years for the member states to remove all the barriers to trade between them and to turn their "common market" into a genuine single market in which goods, services, people, and capital can move around freely. The single market was formally completed at the end of 1992, but there is still work to be done in some areas. For example, the EU has been unable to implement a genuinely single market in financial services, which includes a single currency, known as the **euro**, for all members. Only 18 of the 28 EU member states participate in the **Eurozone**.[16] (See the Spotlight on Global Trade 2.1: History of the Euro.)

SPOTLIGHT ON GLOBAL TRADE 2.1
History of the Euro

The Eurozone is an economic and monetary union that includes 18 out of 28 EU countries. It was launched in 1999 to coordinate economic and fiscal policies, including the use of the euro (€) as its common currency. The euro began as a virtual currency for cashless payments and accounting purposes. Banknotes and coins were introduced in 2002. It is used by more than 332 million people every day.

The single currency offers many advantages, such as eliminating fluctuating exchange rates and exchange costs. The benefits of the common currency are immediately realized for anyone traveling or conducting export or import exchanges within the zone.

Member countries of the Eurozone are Austria, Belgium, Cyprus, Estonia, Finland, France, Germany, Greece, Ireland, Italy, Latvia, Luxembourg, Malta, the Netherlands, Portugal, Slovakia, Slovenia, and Spain. All European Union member states are eligible to join the Eurozone, if they meet certain monetary requirements. The United Kingdom and Denmark have negotiated exemptions, and Sweden tuned down the euro in a 2003 referendum. The small European states of Monaco, San Marino, and the Vatican City, although not EU members, have adopted the euro due to currency unions with member states. Andorra, Montenegro, and Kosovo have adopted the euro unilaterally. Croatia became an EU member in August 2012 but is not part of the Eurozone at this time.

Figure 2.8 **The euro: common currency for over 332 million people in the European Union.**

continued

continued

The euro is also used by about 150 million people in Africa whose currencies are pegged to it. It is the world's third-most traded currency. In 2013, China's yuan overtook the euro to become the second-most used currency in global trade finance after the dollar, according to the Society for Worldwide Interbank Financial Telecommunication (SWIFT).

The euro currency is printed in its member countries. The country of origin is engraved on each coin. Based on IMF estimates of gross domestic product (GDP) and purchasing power parity among the various currencies, the Eurozone is the second-largest economy in the world.

For U.S. exporters and importers, the EU and the euro have been mixed blessings. On the positive side, trade negotiations and procedures can be undertaken with one entity, the EU, which speaks for all members, rather than dealing with individual governments. But some companies and individuals have experienced an EU that has become the "fortress Europe," keeping out imports from non-EU nations and only promoting inter-EU imports and exports. This issue is expected to be resolved once the Trans-Pacific Partnership is fully implemented.

Source: European Commission, "Economic and Financial Affairs," http://ec.europa.eu /economy_finance/index_en.htm.

CE Mark of Approval

An example of the EU's exclusionary practices is the requirement that product standards and certifications must meet certain health, safety, and environmental protection stipulations, in order to receive the CE Marking. The **CE Marking** is an abbreviation for Conformité Européenne, a mandatory conformity mark on many products placed on the single market in the EU. The term initially used was "EC Mark," and it was officially replaced by "CE Marking" in 1993. "EC mark" is still in use, but it is not the official term.[17]

By affixing the CE Marking, the manufacturer, its authorized representative, or the person placing the product on the market or putting it into service asserts that the item meets all the essential requirements of all applicable EU directives, and that conformity assessment procedures have been applied. Note that the CE Marking is not a quality mark.

On the positive side, during the past 20 years, it has become increasingly easier for businesspeople, as well as tourists, to move around in Europe, as passport and customs checks have been abolished for EU citizens at most of the EU's internal borders. One consequence is greater mobility for EU citizens. Since 1987, for example, millions of young Europeans have studied abroad, many in the United States, with support from the EU. The EU's relations with the rest of the world have also become important. For example, the EU negotiates major trade and aid agreements with other countries and is developing a common foreign and security policy.[18]

The North American Free Trade Agreement

In January 1994, perhaps in response to the establishment of the EU, the United States, in cooperation with Canada and Mexico, formed the **North American Free Trade Agreement (NAFTA)**, creating, at that time, the world's largest **free trade area**—a region without trade borders or restrictions.

U.S. Trade Trends with NAFTA Partners

U.S. trade with its two NAFTA partners has more than tripled since the agreement took effect. It has increased more rapidly than trade with the rest of the world. In 2011, trilateral trade among NAFTA partners reached the $1 trillion threshold. Trade between the United States and Mexico contributed considerably to growth in North American trade, accounting for 49 percent of the increase in regional trade since NAFTA's enactment in 1994.

Between 1993 and 2012, total U.S. trade with Mexico increased by 506 percent; trade with Canada was up by 192 percent, while trade with non-NAFTA countries increased by 279 percent. In 2012, Canada was the leading market for U.S. exports, while Mexico ranked second. The two countries accounted for 32 percent of total U.S. exports in 2012. In imports, Canada and Mexico ranked second and third, respectively, behind first-place China, as suppliers of U.S. imports in 2013. The two countries accounted for 26 percent of U.S. imports.[19]

Trade Diversion

One of the strongest criticisms of NAFTA is that it causes **trade diversion**, in which member states import and export more from each other, shifting sources from one country to another, at the expense of other countries worldwide. Consider the example of Jockey Industries of Kenosha, Wisconsin. It decided to build a twin factory (known as a *maquiladora*) in Mexico to create underwear and sleepwear for its Mexican and Central American markets. Trade diversion would take place should Jockey buy its packaging materials, boxes, tape, and string from a Mexican supplier rather than from its traditional vendor in the United States.

While trade diversion has occurred in a few industries—such as textiles and apparel, where rules of origin negotiated in the agreement were specifically designed to make U.S. firms prefer Mexican manufacturers over other textile-producing nations—apparently NAFTA itself has not caused extensive across-the-board trade diversion. U.S. and World Bank studies have shown that the aggregate NAFTA imports' percentage growth was accompanied by an almost similar increase of non-NAFTA imports, suggesting that the increase in trade was not diversionary. Some economists argue that NAFTA has increased the concentration of wealth in both Mexico and the United States.[20]

Figure 2.9 The flags of the United States, Canada, and Mexico represent the countries of the North American Free Trade Agreement (NAFTA), which celebrated its 20th anniversary in January 2014.

Taking advantage of trade agreements, such as NAFTA, requires an understanding of the agreement's compliance features. In some cases, manufacturers must be willing to modify product content or even change the country of origin to obtain duty-free status for imports. **Rules of origin**—where goods are sourced, manufactured, or assembled—must comply with the regulations of countries participating in specific trade agreements.

According to the **Revised Kyoto Convention**,[21] the main trade facilitation convention (agreement) of the world customs organization, "when a product or its components is manufactured in multiple countries, the product is determined to have originated in the country where the last substantial transformation took place." Since these rules of origin often differ from country to country, a single product may be classified as having different countries of origin. (See the Spotlight on Global Trade 2.2: Fact Sheet on NAFTA Certificate of Origin for some insight into this often-misunderstood trade procedure.)

SPOTLIGHT ON GLOBAL TRADE 2.2
Fact Sheet on NAFTA Certificate of Origin

The following are frequently asked questions about NAFTA's Certificate of Origin.

What is the NAFTA Certificate of Origin?

The NAFTA Certificate of Origin is used by the United States, Canada, and Mexico to determine if imported goods are eligible to receive reduced or eliminated duty as specified by the NAFTA. For purposes of obtaining preferential tariff treatment, this document must be completed legibly and in full by the exporter and be in the possession of the importer at the time the declaration is made. This document may also be completed voluntarily by the producer for use by the exporter.

Do I need to complete the NAFTA Certificate of Origin in order to export my product to one of the other NAFTA countries?

The NAFTA Certificate of Origin is not required for shipments to another NAFTA country unless the product qualifies for preferential tariff treatment under the NAFTA rules of origin.

How do I determine where my goods are classified?

Products are classified using national tariff schedules of the country into which they are imported. All NAFTA countries are members of the World Customs Organization (WCO) and utilize the Harmonized Commodity Description and Coding System. The system is used by more than 200 countries and economies as a basis for their Customs tariffs and for the collection of international trade statistics.

The Harmonized System (HS) comprises about 5,000 commodity groups. The HS is organized into 21 sections and 96 chapters, plus general rules of interpretation and explanatory notes. The system begins by assigning goods to categories of crude and natural products, and from there proceeds to categories with increasing complexity. The first four digits are for the broadest coverage, and are referred to as the heading. When needed, the HS can assign four more digits, for a total of eight at the tariff-rate line (legal) level. Two final (non-legal) digits can be assigned as statistical reporting numbers if warranted, for a total of up to ten digits to be listed on entries.

How can I tell if my product qualifies for duty-free treatment?

Once the appropriate classification has been determined, the tariff schedules maintained by each of the NAFTA countries will indicate the related rates of duty.

All products classified under these subheadings or tariff numbers are eligible for duty-free treatment, and the NAFTA Certificate of Origin is not required.

If the rate in the "general" column is not zero, the exporter should next check the rate in the "Special/Preferential" column. The U.S. tariff schedule uses the codes "CA" and "MX" for Canada and Mexico, respectively. The Canadian tariff schedule uses the codes "US" and "MX" for the United States and Mexico, respectively.

In the case of Mexico, there is a section labeled "Tariff applied to trade partners" that uses the codes "EE.UU." and "Canada" for the preferential rate applicable to these countries. For most products, the rate applied to goods that qualify for NAFTA preferences is zero.

I can see that my product is subject to a tariff in another NAFTA country, but is eligible for duty-free treatment under the NAFTA. How do I claim the duty-free treatment?

In order to receive the preferential rate established in the NAFTA, the product must meet the applicable rule of origin. These rules, which are established in Chapter Four of the NAFTA agreement, specify the production that must occur in order for a product to be eligible for NAFTA treatment. For example, a product imported into one NAFTA country from outside North America, then shipped onward to another NAFTA country may not qualify for duty-free treatment.

The NAFTA rules of origin have been modified several times since the agreement entered into force. For the most up-to-date information on tariffs and rules of origin, please see the link provided in the Source line of this boxed text.

What language should be used to complete the NAFTA Certificate of Origin?

A uniform Certificate of Origin is used in all three countries and is printed in English, French, or Spanish. The Certificate shall be completed in the language of the country of export or the language of the importing country, at the exporter's discretion. Importers

continued

must submit a translation of the Certificate to their own customs administration when requested.

How do I complete the Certificate of Origin?

A NAFTA Certificate of Origin is not required for the commercial importation of a good valued at less than US$1,000. However, for goods to qualify for NAFTA preferential duties, the invoice accompanying the commercial importation must include a statement certifying that they qualify as originating goods under the NAFTA rules of origin. The statement should be handwritten, stamped, typed on, or attached to the commercial invoice.

Once an exporter determines that the exported good will meet the NAFTA rules of origin, a NAFTA Certificate of Origin must be completed accurately and legibly. The exporter must then send the Certificate to the importer. While the Certificate does not have to accompany the shipment, the importer must have a copy of the Certificate in hand before claiming the NAFTA tariff preference at customs. Certificates of Origin may, at the discretion of the exporter, cover a single importation of goods or multiple importations of identical goods.

In some cases, an exporter may not have the NAFTA Certificate of Origin ready at the time of export; however, the importer still has up to one year after the goods go through customs to make a claim for the NAFTA tariff preference and to apply for a refund of duties paid at the time of entry.

Who is responsible for determining if the product qualifies under NAFTA and for completing the certificate?

The Certificate of Origin must be completed and signed by the exporter of the goods. Where the exporter is not the producer, the exporter may complete the Certificate on the basis of knowledge that the good originates; reasonable reliance on the producer's written representation that the good originates; or, a completed and signed Certificate of Origin for the good voluntarily provided to the exporter by the producer.

Exporters who are not producers often request that their producers or distributors provide them with a NAFTA Certificate of Origin as proof that the final good, or an input used in the manufacture of the final good, sold to Mexico or Canada meets the rules of origin. NAFTA does not obligate a producer who is not an exporter to provide the ultimate exporter with a NAFTA Certificate of Origin. However, if the non-exporting producer does complete the NAFTA Certificate of Origin, they are subject to the same obligations regarding record keeping and other obligations as is the exporter.

How long should copies of the Certificate of Origin be retained?

In the United States, the exporter is required to retain either the original or a copy of the Certificate for five years from the date of signature. The importer is required to retain the Certificate and all other relevant documentation for five years after the importation of the goods. Mexican exporters must maintain a copy of the Certificate for 10 years. Canadian importers and exporters are required to keep the Certificate for six years from the time of the transaction for the importer and six years from the date of signing for the Canadian exporter.

Source: Office of the United States Trade Representative, retrieved on September 3, 2013, from http://www.ustr.gov/about-us/press-office/fact-sheets/2012/april/nafta-certificate -origin-frequently-asked-questions.

While most business executives and proponents of free trade concur that NAFTA has brought economic growth and rising standards of living for people in all three countries, some economists contend it has been difficult to analyze its direct benefits, because of the large number of other factors in the global economy.

TRADE LIBERALIZATION

The United States has a genuine interest in trade liberalization, as international trade is an integral part of the U.S. economy. It accounts for more than one-quarter of U.S. gross domestic product (GDP).[22]

The United States has pursued the objective of trade liberalization primarily through agreements among large numbers of countries, first in successive rounds of multilateral negotiations under the GATT and later the WTO. In recent years, however, the United States and other countries have established bilateral or multi-lateral FTAs with various countries. Chapter 3 covers U.S. FTAs and the proposed TTP and TTIP partnerships.

As a result of these alliances, since the end of World War II, a significant lowering of barriers to free trade has occurred. The move toward freer trade has, more than any other factor, facilitated the trend toward globalization of production and markets. From this perspective, many companies—of all sizes—have started to view the world as a single market, with virtually unlimited potential for success.

The stage is set, as most governments are endorsing freer trade, but it is up to the individual marketer, whether a corporate manager or entrepreneur, to capital-ize on export-import marketing opportunities.

Summary

Nations are more and more interdependent through global interactions including increased trade throughout the world. With the development of liberalized trade initiatives, export and import business has grown extensively.

The Bretton Woods Conference in 1944 established the IMF and the World Bank to assist emerging nations with economic development. The IMF provides short-term aid (such as help with balance-of-payments deficits), whereas the World Bank provides longer-term assistance (for building infrastructure such as communications systems, bridges, and highways).

Also stemming from Bretton Woods, the GATT lowered tariffs among countries; its work is now absorbed by the WTO. The WTO is responsible for creating and enforcing trade regulations among its members. Through various negotiating rounds, specific trade topics are reviewed, such as agriculture and services at the recent Doha round.

The WTO also sponsors two other international forums promoting international trade and economic cooperation. The original G-8, consisting of the major economies of the world, has expanded into the G-20, to encompass the emerging nations, whose leaders meet periodically to confer on various issues including trade.

Regional alliances also encourage international trade. One of the most significant is the EU that currently has 28 member states consisting of most western and eastern European nations, including most of the former Soviet satellites. The EU is working toward economic integration by adopting the euro as a single currency, and is aiming for political integration by developing its own constitution.

The second-largest regional alliance is NAFTA, which includes the United States and its border neighbors, Canada and Mexico. NAFTA's goal is the elimination of all trade barriers among these nations. Even though most international traders

KEY TERMS

> BILATERAL ALLIANCES

> BRETTON WOODS CONFERENCE

> CE MARKING

> EURO

> EUROPEAN UNION (EU)

> EUROZONE

> FREE TRADE AGREEMENTS (FTAs)

> FREE TRADE AREA

> GENERAL AGREEMENT ON TARIFFS AND TRADE (GATT)

> GROUP OF EIGHT (G-8)

> GROUP OF TWENTY (G-20)

> INTELLECTUAL PROPERTY RIGHTS

> INTERNATIONAL MONETARY FUND (IMF)

> LESS-DEVELOPED COUNTRIES (LDCs)

> MULTINATIONAL AGREEMENTS

> NORTH AMERICAN FREE TRADE AGREEMENT (NAFTA)

> REVISED KYOTO CONVENTION

> RULES OF ORIGIN

> TRADE DIVERSION

> TRANS-PACIFIC PARTNERSHIP (TPP)

> TRANSATLANTIC TRADE AND INVESTMENT PARTNERSHIP (TTIP)

> WORLD BANK

> WORLD TRADE ORGANIZATION (WTO)

agree that NAFTA has benefited all three economies, some critics still contend it has been difficult to analyze NAFTA's effects because of the large number of other factors in the global economy.

The United States is among the nations that continue to work toward the liberalization and elimination of trade barriers by establishing free trade agreements to increase economic growth and prosperity throughout the world.

Review Questions

1. Explain the purpose and importance of the Bretton Woods Conference.

2. What were the three major international institutions that were established as a result of Bretton Woods? Which, if any, still exist today?

3. Describe the five major activities the WTO conducts to meet its stated objective "to help trade flow smoothly, freely, fairly, and predictably."

4. Provide three examples of regional trade alliances.

5. Explain the advantages for individual countries of joining the European Union.

6. Explain why, after nearly 20 years of operation, NAFTA again became a presidential campaign issue during the 2012 election.

Discussion Questions and Activities

1. Using the Internet, research the history of the antiglobalization movement and list three major arguments of these protestors. Why are they often willing to subject themselves to arrest or injury to focus attention on their antiglobalization philosophy? Explain your position, either pro or con.

2. WTO conferences are forums for the give-and-take among most trading countries of the world as they work toward global trade liberalization. Discuss your position vis-à-vis further liberalization of U.S. export-import trade. Discuss how the United States can champion free trade while, at the same time, protect its domestic economy, including factory jobs, from unfair foreign trade practices.

3. For many years, China's entry into the WTO was blocked by most European and Western nations, including the United States. Go to the Internet and research articles explaining why China was denied access and record the promises China made to convince the voting members to finally be admitted on December 11, 2001.

Chapter 2 Case

Hall & Madden: Providing Customers with Bespoke Shirts at Department Store Prices

When Richard Hall and McGregor Madden were in their mid-20s they enjoyed traveling to major U.S. cities as part of their jobs with Proper Suit, a custom suit importer, and meeting with clients interested in professional wardrobes. Hall and Madden's work included measuring clients for suits and showing appropriate suiting fabrics. Proper Suit worked directly with fabric suppliers and manufacturers in China by ordering in small batches and obtaining finished garments quickly. Hall and Madden noticed, however, that while their clients were buying custom-tailored suits, they were still wearing designer label ready-to-wear shirts, some of which cost around $100. Why not offer custom shirts in the same price range, they thought.

Fortunately, Hall and Madden knew how to go about turning their plans into reality. The men had met in Hong Kong while both were college undergraduates. Separately each had figured that Asia held the promise of challenging career opportunities. They studied Mandarin and after graduation worked for a variety of businesses that had dealings with China. The textile and garment industries in the country particularly appealed to them as they discovered the quality of fabrics available at reasonable prices and the speed with which orders could be completed. Relying on their network connections with manufacturers in China, they decided to establish a custom shirt business with shirts designed in the United States but manufactured in China.

Hall and Madden added an innovative twist to their new venture: they set up their new company, named Hall & Madden, as an online subscription business. Paying an initial software fee, customers send in their measurements, select from an assortment of dress shirt fabrics, and order three shirts at a retail price of $150 to be delivered every three to six months. Having a supply of shirts made to fit at prices comparable or less than ready-to-wear shirts completed the well-dressed look that their customers were seeking. In its inaugural year of business, Hall & Madden saw a 500 percent subscription growth with similar growth forecasted for its next year.

Source: Corilyn Shropshire, "Cut from a Different Cloth," *Chicago Tribune*, May 15, 2013, Sec. 2, pp. 1, 4.

Questions

1. What is your opinion of the possibilities of success for this online subscription custom shirt import business?

2. Some critics believe that customers will tire of receiving three shirts periodically and will drop their subscriptions. What is your view of this possibility?

3. A major purpose of business is to grow. In what additional ways might Hall & Madden grow in the future?

References

1. Michael Kors, retrieved July 11, 2013, from http://www.vogue.com/voguedic/Michael, and July 10, 2013, from http://www.michaelkors.com.

2. *Encyclopedia Britannica Online*, s.v. "Bretton-Woods Conference." Retrieved September 27, 2013, from http://www.britannica.com/eb/article-9016387/Bretton-Wood.

3. International Monetary Fund, "About the IMF." Retrieved September 1, 2013, from http://www.imf.org/external/about.htm.

4. The World Bank, "About Us." Retrieved September 1, 2013, from http://www.worldbank.org/en/about.

5. World Trade Organization, "What Is the World Trade Organization?" Retrieved September 1, 2013, from http://www.wto.org/English/thewto_e/whatis_e/tif_e/fact1_e.htm.

6. World Trade Organization, WTO Factsheet. Retrieved September 2, 2013, from http://www.wto.org/.

7. World Trade Organization, WTO-Doha Development Agenda. Retrieved September 2, 2013, from http://www.wto.org/english/tratop/_e/dda_e/texts_intro_e.htm.

8. Shawn Donnan, "WTO Approves Landmark Global Trade Deal," *Financial Times*, December 7, 2013. Retrieved April 18, 2014, from http://www.ft.com/cms/s/0/072486ac-5f3f-11e3–8d1d00144feabdc0.html.

9. Op. cit., WTO.

10. Group of Eight. Retrieved September 1, 2013, from http://usinfo.state.gov/ei/economic_issues/group_of_8/what_is_the_g8.html.

11. "The G-20." Retrieved September 2, 2013, from www.wto.org/english/thewto_e/countries_e/org6_map_e.htm.

12. Julie Pace, "G8 Summit In Sochi Canceled, G7 Leaders To Meet In Brussels Instead," *The World Post*, March 3, 2014. Retrieved April 18, 2014, from http://www.huffingtonpost.com/2014/03/24/g8-summit_canceled_n_5023219.html.

13. "The European Union." Retrieved September 2, 2013, from http://europa.eu/about-eu/countries/index_en.htm.

14. Ibid.

15. Ibid.

16. "The Euro." Retrieved September 1, 2013, from http://ec.europa.eu/economy_finance/ the_euro/index _en.htm?cs_mid=.

17. "CE Marking." Retrieved September 3, 2013, from http://export.gov/cemark/index.asp.

18. Ibid.

19. M. Villarreal and I. Fergusson, "NAFTA at 20: Overview and Trade Effects," Congressional Research Service, February 23, 2013. Retrieved September 3, 2013, from http://www.fas.org/sgp/crs/row/R42965.pdf.

20. "NAFTA Certificate of Origin: Frequently Asked Questions." NAFTA Fact Sheet. Retrieved September 2, 2013, from http://www.ustr.gov/about-us/press-office/fact-sheets/2012/april/nafta-certificate-origin-frequently-asked-questions.

21. Ibid.

22. "The Revised Kyoto Convention Rules of Origin," World Customs Organization, 2013. Retrieved September 3, 2013, from http://tfig.unece.org/contents/revised-kyoto-convention.htm.

Figure 3.1 J. Crew storefront in Toronto, Canada.

CHAPTER 3
THE U.S. ROLE IN
GLOBAL TRADE

J. CREW ON THE LOOKOUT FOR GLOBAL GROWTH. What is J. Crew—some kind of rowing club? Not quite. Rather, it is a multichanneled international fashion organization featuring an assortment of dress and casual clothing for women, men, and children plus wedding attire at upper and more moderate prices. Customers often seek out J. Crew merchandise, which is tremendously popular among several age ranges, when they want look smart and yet avoid paying designer prices. First Lady Michele Obama is among those who have worn the brand.

Starting out with a catalog in 1983, J. Crew needed to distinguish itself from competitors such as L.L. Bean and Lands' End. Capitalizing on the relaxed country club elegance of the times, the company positioned itself as a stylish brand, somewhat similar to but lower-priced than Ralph Lauren. To enhance a leisure-time image, J. Crew opened its first store at New York's South Street Seaport in 1989, at that time one of Manhattan's hottest shopping spots. During this same period, its management had reacted to a growing demand for fashionable apparel at a lower price range by opening its first outlet stores, known as j.crew factory, consisting of the current season's goods based on favorites from the pricier collection and created exclusively for the factory store. Later a website followed. In 2006, recognizing the need for more casual clothes, particularly denim, the company unveiled Madewell, later followed by madewell.com.

Crossing the border to Canada in 2011, J. Crew established stores in Toronto, Edmonton, and Vancouver. The following year it set up an e-commerce website reaching 100 countries. Realizing that growth comes from new markets, the company has continued to look globally for additional brick-and-mortar locations.[1]

Current U.S. government trade policy is consistent with the goals of U.S. firms such as J. Crew. The United States supports international market expansion through the strengthening of export-import relationships in every region. A recent focus is on partnering with developing countries, to share the benefits of trade more broadly, while continuing to uphold American values in trade policy.[2]

Table 3.1 Top U.S. Trading Partners: 2012

Rank	Country	Exports	Imports	Total trade	Percent of total trade
	Total, all countries	1,547.1	2,275.0	3,822.2	100.0%
	Total, top 15 countries	1,049.0	1,703.0	2,752.0	72.0%
1	Canada	292.4	324.2	616.7	16.1%
2	China	110.6	425.6	536.2	14.0%
3	Mexico	216.3	277.7	494.0	12.9%
4	Japan	70.0	146.4	216.4	5.7%
5	Germany	48.8	108.5	157.3	4.1%
6	United Kingdom	54.8	54.9	109.8	2.9%
7	Korea, South	42.3	58.9	101.2	2.6%
8	Brazil	43.7	32.1	75.8	2.0%
9	Saudi Arabia	18.1	55.7	73.8	1.9%
10	France	30.8	41.6	72.4	1.9%
11	Taiwan	24.4	38.9	63.2	1.7%
12	Netherlands	40.7	22.3	63.0	1.6%
13	India	22.3	40.5	62.9	1.6%
14	Venezuela	17.6	38.7	56.4	1.5%
15	Italy	16.0	36.9	52.9	1.4%

Note: Data are goods only, on a census basis, in billions of U.S. dollars, unrevised.

Source: U.S. Census Bureau. Retrieved September 15, 2013, from http://www.census.gov/foreign -trade/statistics/highlights/top/top1212yr.html.

THE U.S. TRADE POLICY AGENDA

Since 2009, President Barack Obama's **National Export Initiative (NEI)** is credited with record-high exports in all major sectors by 2012: services exports were up 24 percent, manufacturing exports increased by 47 percent, and agricultural exports were up by 44 percent. Overall, U.S. exports of goods and services increased by more than 39 percent above the level of exports in 2009, supporting more than one million additional U.S. jobs, according to U.S. Department of Commerce data.[3]

A top priority of the NEI and U.S. trade policy overall has been to help U.S. small businesses become more involved in exporting. An example was the creation of the **Small Business Network of the Americas (SBNA)**—a network of counterpart small business centers in the western hemisphere that linked to centers throughout the United States. Through online trade platforms and business competitions, the SBNA sought to increase the opportunities for U.S. small businesses to export

Figure 3.2 Goods are ready for offloading at Busan, South Korea's second largest city and its number one trading port. Photo credit: Ric Frantz

and to strengthen international business-to-business connections throughout the hemisphere.[4]

U.S. Export-Import Trade Equals Jobs

Now more than at any period in U.S. history, Americans have been selling more U.S. goods and services to the 95 percent of consumers who live outside the nation's borders. In 2012, U.S. exports hit an all-time record of $2.2 trillion and supported 9.8 million jobs.[5] (See Figure 3.3.)

Complacent about international trade for the decades after World War II, which saw record domestic growth and prosperity, U.S. industry and government leaders have come to recognize and embrace the concept that global trade leads to economic growth, which in turn creates more and better employment opportunities at home. The larger the economic pie, the more prosperity in societies across the globe.

Countries that engage exporting and importing benefit from more efficient allocations of their resources, including the factors of production—land, labor, and capital. Without free—and fair—trade, the world's individual and corporate consumers would have fewer choices and likely higher prices for goods and services.

Jobs Supported by Exports, 2009–2012

	Total	Goods	Services
2009	8.5	6.0	2.5
2010	9.1	6.6	2.5
2011(R)*	9.7	7.2	2.5
2012(P)*	9.8	7.3	2.5

Figure 3.3 Jobs supported by exports, 2009–2012.

*Values for 2011 are revised from previous estimates; values for 2012 are preliminary.

Source: ITA calculations from BLS data, 2009 to 2010; ITA calculations from BLS, BEA, and Census data, 2011 to 2012.

Trade provides manufacturing economies of scale, bringing down the average cost of production.

The Death of American Manufacturing?

According to a U.S. Chamber of Commerce report, U.S. manufacturing output rose by 73 percent between 1993 and 2011. That fact seems to dispel any notion that American manufacturing is dying; it just isn't true. Plus, the outlook is for manufacturing output to double within the next two decades.[6]

The U.S. Chamber of Commerce noted that U.S. manufacturing-value-added has grown eightfold since 1947 in real terms. The United States remains the world's largest manufacturer, accounting for about one-fifth of the world manufacturing output, a percentage that has remained fairly steady for about four decades.

U.S. Trade Balance, Exports, and Imports—2012–2013

	2013 (Billions of $)	2012 (Billions of $)	Percent Change from Prior Year
Trade Balance	−$471.5	−$534.7	−11.8
U.S. Exports	$2,272.3	$2,210.6	2.8
U.S. Imports	$2,743.9	$2,745.2	−0.1

Figure 3.4 The U.S. trade deficit improved in 2013 over 2012, but still remains nearly a half-trillion dollars, as American consumers and businesses continue to buy from abroad much more than they sell.

Source: U.S. Census/U.S. Department of Commerce 2013.

Table 3.2 U.S. Export Trade for 2012

Rank	Country	Exports	Percent of total exports
	Total, all countries	1,547.1	100.0%
	Total, top 15 countries	1,105.4	71.4%
1	Canada	292.4	18.9%
2	Mexico	216.3	14.0%
3	China	110.6	7.1%
4	Japan	70.0	4.5%
5	United Kingdom	54.8	3.5%
6	Germany	48.8	3.2%
7	Brazil	43.7	2.8%
8	Korea, South	42.3	2.7%
9	Netherlands	40.7	2.6%
10	Hong Kong	37.5	2.4%
11	Australia	31.2	2.0%
12	France	30.8	2.0%
13	Singapore	30.6	2.0%
14	Belgium	29.4	1.9%
15	Switzerland	26.2	1.7%

Note: Data are goods only, on a census basis, in billions of U.S. dollars, unrevised.

Source: U.S. Census Bureau. Retrieved September 15, 2013, from http://www.census.gov/foreign
-trade/statistics/highlights/top/top1212yr.html.

The 2008–2009 recession hit American manufacturers hard, and producers saw a big drop in consumer demand—the first serious setback in nearly 20 years. During the preceding two decades, however, American manufacturers set new records for output, revenues, profits, profit rates, and return on investment (ROI). Perhaps the most sensitive aspect of the fallout from the prolonged recession was the loss of American factory jobs. The Chamber of Commerce report stated that U.S. manufacturing jobs peaked at 19.5 million in 1979, with a steady decline since then.

Contrary to widespread public opinion, the "lost" U.S. manufacturing jobs have *not* gone to Mexico or China. U.S. government reports conclude that less than 1 percent of factory layoffs were attributed to the movement of jobs overseas— known as **offshoring**.[7]

Instead, these jobs have been lost to global productivity. Technological change, automation, and widespread use of information technologies have enabled firms

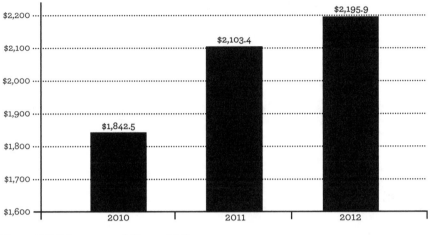

U.S. Exports in Billions of Dollars

Figure 3.5 U.S. exports in billions of dollars.

to increase output with inevitable cuts in payrolls. This productivity revolution is a complex, global phenomenon. A study by the RAND Corporation found that China lost 25 million manufacturing jobs between 1994 and 2004, 10 times more than the United States lost in the same period.[8]

Productivity equals prosperity, and the productivity of the U.S. workforce leads the world. But productivity does not necessarily equate to job creation, as U.S. manufacturers can generate more output today with fewer workers. Fortunately, the productivity advantage of the United States is not the only advantage the nation has. The recent exciting shale energy revolution, launched in 2013, will give the United States access to cheaper energy than our major global competitors for years to come.

American manufacturers were still experiencing a slow recovery at home in 2013, so export success became a key asset in their business survival. In 2012, 12 million Americans were working in manufacturing, contributing to the production of more than $1.35 trillion of U.S. *exports* in that year.

Exports generate revenue of more than $100,000 for each American factory worker, according to the U.S. Bureau of Labor Statistics and the U.S. Department of Commerce. Compared with the annual earnings of the typical U.S. manufacturing worker—about $50,000—many manufacturers today could not make their payrolls without the revenues they earn by exporting.[9]

The U.S. business community often faces an unfair playing field in global commerce, tilted against American workers and companies. The U.S. market is primarily open to imports, but many other countries impose high tariffs on U.S. exports, as well as nontariff barriers to trade in U.S. goods and services. These barriers are especially difficult for U.S. small and medium-sized companies to overcome. That is just one reason why the United States has been in the forefront of establishing free trade agreements—to open up these markets.

Table 3.3 U.S. Import Trade for 2012

Rank	Country	Imports	Percent of total imports
	Total, all countries	2,275.0	100.0%
	Total, top 15 countries	1,714.0	75.3%
1	China	425.6	18.7%
2	Canada	324.2	14.3%
3	Mexico	277.7	12.2%
4	Japan	146.4	6.4%
5	Germany	108.5	4.8%
6	Korea, South	58.9	2.6%
7	Saudi Arabia	55.7	2.4%
8	United Kingdom	54.9	2.4%
9	France	41.6	1.8%
10	India	40.5	1.8%
11	Taiwan	38.9	1.7%
12	Venezuela	38.7	1.7%
13	Italy	36.9	1.6%
14	Ireland	33.3	1.5%
15	Brazil	32.1	1.4%

Note: Data are goods only, on a census basis, in billions of U.S. dollars, unrevised.

Source: U.S. Census Bureau. Retrieved September 15, 2013, from http://www.census.gov/foreign -trade/statistics/highlights/top/top1212yr.html.

U.S. FREE TRADE AGREEMENTS

The United States has historically had positive results from its free trade agreements (FTAs) because they have opened up key markets to increased trade. U.S. exports to the most recent FTA partners—South Korea, Panama, and Colombia— have grown up to four times faster, in the five-year period after agreement, than other U.S. export relationships.[10]

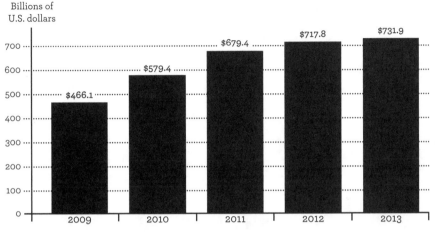

U.S. Exports to FTA Partners, 2009–2013

Billions of
U.S. dollars

- $466.1 (2009)
- $579.4 (2010)
- $679.4 (2011)
- $717.8 (2012)
- $731.9 (2013)

Figure 3.6 U.S. exports to FTA partners are up 57 percent since 2009.

With about 350 free trade agreements in force around the world, the United States is a partner in just 14, covering 20 countries. If other nations continue to negotiate trade agreements without the United States, American workers, farmers, and companies will continue to be at a competitive disadvantage. That has been the motivation behind the Obama administration's endorsement of two pending trade partnerships—the **Trans-Pacific Partnership (TPP)** and the **Transatlantic Trade and Investment Partnership (TTIP)**.[11]

New Free Trade Agreements
Every $1 billion in new exports of American goods supports more than 6,000 additional jobs here at home. Every $1 billion of services exports supports more than 4,500 jobs. The South Korea, Colombia, and Panama trade agreements have opened markets for U.S. firms, increasing trade and exports. Increasing U.S. exports through these agreements supports additional jobs for American workers who produce made-in-the-USA goods and services.[12]

U.S.–Korea Free Trade Agreement
The **United States–Korea Free Trade Agreement (KORUS)** entered into force on March 15, 2012. On the day of implementation, almost 80 percent of U.S. industrial goods exports to Korea were duty-free including aerospace and other

transportation equipment, auto parts, building products, chemicals, electrical equipment, paper products, scientific equipment, and consumer goods. Other benefits of the FTA include the following:

- Duty-free status for most U.S. agriculture exports.
- Stronger protection and enforcement of intellectual property rights in Korea.
- Increased access to Korea's $580 billion services market for highly competitive American companies.[13]

Table 3.4 U.S. Trade Surpluses in 2012

Rank	Country	Surplus
1	Hong Kong	$32.0
2	Australia	21.7
3	United Arab Emirates	20.3
4	Netherlands	18.4
5	Belgium	12.1
6	Brazil	11.6
7	Singapore	10.3
8	Chile	9.5
9	Panama	9.4
10	Turkey	6.2

Note: Data are goods only, on a census basis, in billions of U.S. dollars, unrevised.

Source: U.S. Census Bureau. Retrieved September 15, 2013, from http://www
.census.gov/foreign-trade/statistics/highlights/top/top1212yr.html.

U.S.–Colombia Free Trade Agreement

The **United States–Colombia Trade Promotion Agreement** (TPA) entered into force on May 15, 2012. On the day of implementation, more than 80 percent of U.S. industrial goods exports to Colombia became duty-free including agricultural and construction equipment, building products, aircraft and parts, fertilizers, information technology equipment, medical and scientific equipment, and wood. Other benefits of the TPA include the following:

- Duty-free status for more than half of U.S. exports of agricultural commodities to Colombia.
- Stronger protection and enforcement of intellectual property rights.
- Increased access to Colombia's $180 billion services market for highly competitive American companies.[14]

Table 3.5 U.S. Trade Deficits in 2012

Rank	Country	Deficit
1	China	-$315.1
2	Japan	-76.3
3	Mexico	-61.3
4	Germany	-59.7
5	Saudi Arabia	-37.5
6	Canada	-31.8
7	Ireland	-25.9
8	Venezuela	-21.1
9	Italy	-21.0
10	Russia	-18.6

Note: Data are goods only, on a census basis, in billions of U.S. dollars, unrevised.

Source: U.S. Census Bureau. Retrieved September 15, 2013, from http://www.census.gov/foreign-trade/statistics/highlights/top/top1212yr.html.

U.S.–Panama Free Trade Agreement

The **United States–Panama Trade Promotion Agreement** entered into force on October 31, 2012. On this day, more than 87 percent of U.S. industrial goods exported to Panama became duty-free including information technology equipment, agricultural and construction equipment, aircraft and parts, medical and scientific equipment, environmental products, pharmaceuticals, fertilizers, and agro-chemicals.

Other benefits of the TPA include the following:

- Duty-free exports for more than half of U.S. agricultural products.
- Stronger protection and enforcement of intellectual property rights in Panama.
- Increased access to Panama's $20.6 billion services market, including in priority areas such as financial, telecommunications, computer, distribution, express delivery, energy, environmental, and professional services.
- Significant infrastructure opportunities in the ongoing $5.25 billion Panama Canal expansion project, as well as through the almost $10 billion in other extensive infrastructure projects, including construction of a highway between Colon and Panama City, the expansion and modernization of the Tucumen International Airport, and a mega-port project for container ships on the Pacific side of the Panama Canal.[15]

Proposed New Trade Partnerships

The two proposed trade partnerships for the United States, one across the Atlantic—the TTIP—and the other across the Pacific—the TPP—have the same founding objective: to stimulate U.S. and global employment and economic growth through an expansion of world trade.

The Trans-Pacific Partnership (TPP)

The Asia-Pacific region stands out as one of the world's fastest-growing economic regions, with two billion Asians joining the middle class in the past 20 years and another 1.2 billion expected to join by 2020. According to the International Monetary Fund (IMF), the world economy is expected to grow by more than $21 trillion from 2014 to 2018, with almost half of that growth in Asia.[16]

The TPP is the best way for American firms to access the world's most promising and exciting markets, which are projected to import nearly $10 trillion worth of goods in 2020. The U.S. objective is to commit to a comprehensive, high-standard, and commercially sound trade and investment agreement among Asia-Pacific nations, currently including Australia, Brunei, Chile, Malaysia, Mexico, New Zealand, Canada, Peru, Singapore, Vietnam, and most importantly, Japan

Figure 3.7 President Obama discusses the U. S.–led Trans-Pacific Trade Partnership with Thailand's former Prime Minister Yingluck Shinawatra, in Bangkok, Thailand.

and potentially Korea. Existing U.S. trade agreements with the Americas—Canada, Mexico, Peru, and Chile—would likely be integrated into the new TPP.[17] The United States has a lot at stake in these negotiations: the goal is to increase exports by almost $600 billion and help create more than 3 million American jobs by the year 2020.

The Transatlantic Trade and Investment Partnership (TTIP)

The view across the Atlantic is equally promising. The European Union (EU) is America's largest commercial partner, and together they generate about half of all global gross domestic product (GDP). U.S. companies make foreign direct investments (FDIs) that total more than $2 trillion in the EU—more than 20 times the U.S. investment in China.[18]

According to the Office of the U.S. Trade Representative Fact Sheet on the TTIP, the proposed partnership could boost economic growth in the United States and Europe and add to the more than 13 million American and European jobs now supported by transatlantic trade and investment.[19]

KEY U.S. TRADE RELATIONSHIPS

Momentum in the global economy is shifting back to the developed world, away from the emerging economies that had led growth since the financial crisis. During the first half of 2013, for the first time since mid-2007, the advanced economies—including the United States, Japan, and Europe—contributed more to growth in the $74 trillion global economy than the emerging nations— including China, India, and Brazil—according to a report in the *Wall Street Journal*.[20]

The rate of growth for world trade in 2012 and the first half of 2013 slowed to 2.0 percent, from 5.2 percent during 2011. The abrupt drop was mainly attributed to slow growth in the developed economies and continuing uncertainty over the future of the euro. Europe's economic slowdown adversely affected global import demand. High unemployment in developed countries reduced imports and stunted export growth in both developed and developing countries. The slow economic recovery in the United States during the first half of 2013 was not enough to offset the continuing weakness in the EU. Even core euro-area economies felt the impact of the region's downturn in 2013.[21] (See the Spotlight on Global Trade 3.1: The BRICS and TIMPs Have Arrived.)

U.S.–Canada Trade

Canada was the largest bilateral trading partner of the United States in 2013 with more than $632 billion in goods crossing their borders. U.S. exports to Canada were $300 billion and imports were $332 billion, resulting in a U.S. goods deficit of $32 billion in 2013.[22]

SPOTLIGHT ON GLOBAL TRADE 3.1
The BRICS and TIMPs Have Arrived

"Emerging Markets" is the popular term used to describe growth markets—the world's most dynamic and fast-growing economies. Some of these markets have already made significant contributions to the global economy, while others offer potential for growth in the coming decades. Goldman Sachs Asset Management, one of the world's largest investment-banking organizations, describes a "growth market" as "an economy outside the Developed World that is at least 1 percent of the current global GDP."[1]

Using this definition, the emerging markets would include each of the BRICS countries—Brazil, Russia, India, China, and South Africa—as well as Mexico, Korea, Turkey, and Indonesia. Goldman Sachs Global Investment Research projects that "by the year 2050, [emerging] markets will represent nearly half (46 percent) of global GDP, representing a 2,100 percent increase in real GDP since the year 2000."[2]

From 2001 to 2010, the BRIC nations (South Africa was added in 2013) were the best economic performers of the emerging markets, growing at nearly twice the rate of the global economy. But the momentum in the global economy shifted in 2013, back to the developed economies—away from the emerging economies that had led growth since the 2008 global financial crisis. In 2013, the outlook brightened for the developed economies, as the recovering United States began producing a slow but deliberate growth. Europe's economy experienced a slight growth in 2013, but no acceleration was predicted for the next 18 months.[3]

A 2013 Associated Press survey of the opinions of private, corporate, and academic economists concluded that weak global growth would make it more difficult to overcome some of the world's most serious economic challenges in the following few years. According to the survey, historically high unemployment in Europe, a slow recovery in consumer and business spending in the United States, big government debt levels in Europe and Japan, and unstable economies in some of the emerging markets completed a somber picture for global economic stagnation.[4]

After a two-decades-long recession, Japan recovered in 2013 to be the fastest-growing large developed country, primarily because of a weak currency, the yen, which made imports much more expensive than domestically made items. That encouraged a consumer-led boost to the economy, along with the Japanese government's large spending incentives. Some economists worried, however, that spark of growth might be short-lived when the nation's higher "consumption tax" took effect in 2014.[5]

Although many emerging market economies have been the world's fastest-growing, this has not been so in recent years. China's expected GDP growth of 7.5 percent for 2013 was its slowest since 1990—although still much greater than the U.S. pace of less than 3 percent that year. Although indications in 2013 pointed to a China recovery, its slowdown has been felt by Latin American and Southeast Asian countries that were suppliers to China's manufacturers. As a result, economists expect slower—but still strong—GDP growth for the smaller emerging economies in those regions in 2014 and beyond.[6]

Brazil, Latin America's largest economy, with GDP growth of only 1 percent in 2012, after dropping from 7.5 percent in 2010, has also stagnated because of China's reduced demand for manufacturing products, such as iron ore.[7] India's economic mismanagement has resulted in a dramatic drop in its currency and wider current-account deficits. Consumers can't spend and businesses can't invest because of the banks holding back on credit.[8]

A new group of emerging markets in Turkey, Indonesia, Mexico, and the Philippines, or the TIMPs, has caught the attention of investors and exporters. Whereas the BRICS were more commodity-driven, the TIMPs are considered more consumer-oriented. The TIMPs also have lower debt than the developed world and have improved their credit ratings.[8]

Emerging market growth will depend on growing the middle classes in those nations. More spending on autos, clothing, dining out, and higher-end grocery purchases will contribute to GDP growth. The Asian Development Bank predicts that consumer spending in Asia will reach $32 trillion by 2030, up from only $4.3 trillion in 2008.[9] It is definitely a regional market U.S. exporters should be exploring.

References

1. "The Rise of Growth Markets," Goldman Sachs, March 2012. Retrieved September 18, 2013, from http://www.goldmansach.com/our-thinking/focus-on/growth-markets/dataviz/index.html.

2. Ibid.

3. Lisa Gibbs, "Emerging Markets Lose a Step," *CNNMoney*, May 28, 2013. Retrieved June 7, 2013, from http://money.cnn.com/2013/06/01/investing/emerging-markets.moneymag/.

4. Christopher S. Rugaber, "AP Survey: Sluggish Global Economic Recovery Ahead," *Associated Press*, September 17, 2013. Retrieved September 19, 2013, from http://bigstory.ap.org/article/ap-survey-sluggish-global-economic-recovery-ahead.

5. Ibid.

6. Alex Frangos, Sudeep Reddy, and John Lyons, "Emerging World Loses Growth Lead," *Wall Street Journal*, August 11, 2013. Retrieved September 16, 2013, from http://online.wsj.com/news/articles/SB10001424127887324769704579006833569484924.

7. Ibid.

8. Op. cit., Gibbs, "Emerging Markets Lose a Step."

9. Ibid.

The United States and Canada share the world's largest and most comprehensive trading relationship, which supports millions of jobs in each country. Canada is the single-largest foreign supplier of energy to the United States. Recognition of the commercial viability of Canada's oil sands has made it the world's third-largest holder of oil reserves after Saudi Arabia and Venezuela, and it is the only non-OPEC (Organization of the Petroleum Exporting Countries) member in the top five.[23]

The U.S. and Canadian economies are closely intertwined; they are each other's largest trading partner. The United States is the largest foreign investor in Canada, and the United States is the most popular destination for Canadian investment. The two countries share the world's longest open border, with 90 percent of Canada's 33 million people living within 100 miles of the U.S. border.

Canada and the United States operate an integrated electricity grid that meets jointly developed reliability standards, and they provide all of each other's electricity imports. Canadian uranium helps fuel U.S. nuclear power plants.

Figure 3.8 Ambassador Bridge crossing, between Detroit, Michigan, and Windsor, Ontario, Canada.

The North American Free Trade Agreement (NAFTA) among the United States, Canada, and Mexico has reduced trade barriers and established agreed-on trade rules. The agreement has resolved long-standing bilateral issues and liberalized rules in several areas, including agriculture, energy, financial and investment services, and government procurement. The Regulatory Cooperation Council seeks to further stimulate trade by increasing regulatory transparency and cooperation between the United States and Canada and eliminating unnecessary regulatory differences and redundant actions that hinder cross-border trade and investment.[24]

Approximately 80 percent of Canadian exports go to the United States while the U.S. share of Canada's total imports is about 55 percent. U.S. exports to Canada exceed U.S. exports to the entire EU, even though the EU has 15 times Canada's population. The two-way trade that crosses the Ambassador Bridge between Michigan and Ontario equals all U.S. exports to Japan.[25]

U.S.–Mexico Trade

To the south, on the other major U.S. border, Mexico is the third-largest single-country trading partner of the United States and has been among the fastest-growing U.S. export markets, since the signing of NAFTA in 1994. NAFTA has built

Figure 3.9 The U.S. and Mexico border crossing at San Diego and Tijuana. More than 6 million jobs in the United States depend on trade with Mexico.

both a strong trade relationship and a more equitable set of trade rules as Mexico's barriers have been reduced or eliminated.

U.S. imports from Mexico include manufactured goods, oil and oil products, silver, fruits, vegetables, coffee, and cotton. U.S. exports to Mexico totaled $226 billion in 2013, while the United States imported $280.5 billion worth of Mexican products, for a trade deficit of $54.5 billion.[26]

U.S. relations with Mexico are important and complex. The two countries share a 2,000-mile border, and bilateral relations between the two have a direct impact on the lives and livelihoods of millions of Americans, whether the issue is trade and economic reform, homeland security, drug control, immigration, or the environment. The scope of U.S.–Mexican relations goes beyond diplomatic and official contacts. It includes extensive commercial, cultural, and educational ties, with more than $1.25 billion of two-way trade and about one million legal border crossings each day.

Approximately one million American citizens live in Mexico. U.S. tourists to Mexico numbered more than 20.3 million in 2012, making Mexico the top destination for U.S. travelers. Mexican tourists to the United States were about 13.4 million in 2011, and they spent some $9.2 billion.[27]

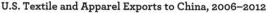

U.S. Textile and Apparel Exports to China, 2006–2012

Value of Exports,
USD millions

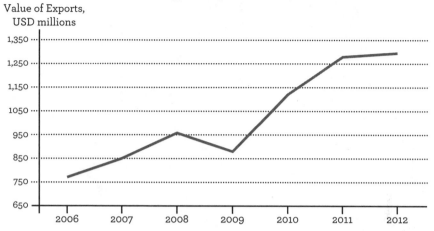

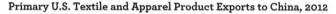

Primary U.S. Textile and Apparel Product Exports to China, 2012

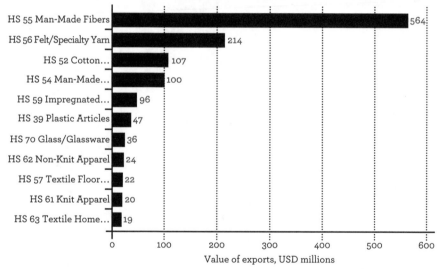

HS 55 Man-Made Fibers — 564
HS 56 Felt/Specialty Yarn — 214
HS 52 Cotton... — 107
HS 54 Man-Made... — 100
HS 59 Impregnated... — 96
HS 39 Plastic Articles — 47
HS 70 Glass/Glassware — 36
HS 62 Non-Knit Apparel — 24
HS 57 Textile Floor... — 22
HS 61 Knit Apparel — 20
HS 63 Textile Home... — 19

Value of exports, USD millions

Figure 3.10 The supply chain for textiles and apparel has become increasingly global, including North America, Latin America, Europe, Africa, and the Asia-Pacific region.

Source: Office of Textiles and Apparel (OTEXA), U.S. Dept. of Commerce

U.S.–China Trade

More than 7,000 miles across the Pacific, China is the second-largest single-country trading partner of the United States. Two-way trade between China and

Figure 3.11 China is the third-largest market for U.S. exports. Many U.S. exports are sold in department stores and high-end shops on the 700-hundred-year-old Wangfujing Street in Beijing, China.

the United States has grown from $33 billion in 1992 to more than $562 billion in 2013. The United States is China's largest export market. The U.S. goods trade deficit with China was $318.4 billion in 2013, up $3.3 billion from 2012. U.S. goods exports in 2013 were $122 billion. Corresponding U.S. imports from China for the year were $440.4 billion.[28]

The U.S. approach to its economic relations with China has had two main elements: the United States sought to integrate China fully into the global, rules-based economic and trading system and to expand U.S. exporters' and investors' access to the Chinese market. Direct investment into China from the United States climbed 7.1 percent in 2013, to $3.4 billion. In July 2013, the two countries announced measures to strengthen macroeconomic cooperation, promote open trade and investment, enhance global cooperation and international rules, and foster financial stability and reform.[29]

U.S.–Japan Trade

Japan is the world's third-largest economy and fourth-largest export market for the United States. The country is the second-largest foreign investor in the United States, behind only the United Kingdom, with more than $200 billion in Japanese

Figure 3.12 The Ginza in Tokyo, Japan, is a famous shopping district by day and entertainment center by night. In addition to $10 cups of coffee, you can find almost every leading brand of global fashion and apparel.

investment. Japan's economic recovery in recent years has been based on a new fiscal stimulus package that features a sharply weaker yen, which makes imports more expensive. This means Japanese consumers are more likely to buy cheaper homemade goods, slowing the demand for imports, but still boosting growth and trade. In 2013, the United States exported $65 billion in goods and services to Japan but imported nearly $138.5 billion from the island nation. The resulting U.S. trade deficit with Japan, totaling more than $73 billion in 2013, was second only to China's $318 billion.[30]

Japan has become one of Asia's most successful democracies and largest economies. The U.S.–Japan alliance is the cornerstone of U.S. security interests in Asia and is fundamental to regional stability and prosperity.[31]

Japan provides military bases as well as financial and material support to U.S. forward-deployed forces, which are essential for maintaining stability in the region. During the past decade, the alliance has been strengthened through revised defense guidelines, which expand Japan's noncombatant role in a regional contingency, and the renewal of the agreement on host nation support of U.S. forces stationed in Japan.[32]

Table 3.6 U.S. Export-Import Trade with Key Partners for 2012

Country	Exports	Imports	Trade balance
Canada	$292,539.7	$323,936.5	–$31,396.8
Mexico	215,931.2	277,569.8	–61,638.6
China	110,483.6	425,578.9	–315,095.3
Japan	69,955.0	146,392.2	–76,437.2
European Union	265,359.6	381,207.6	–115,848.0

Note: All figures are in millions of U.S. dollars on a nominal basis, not seasonally adjusted. A negative sign in the trade balance column indicates a trade deficit.

Source: U.S. Census Bureau. Retrieved (and consolidated) January 24, 2013, from http://www.census.gov/foreign-trade/balance/.

U.S.–EU Trade

The U.S. economic relationship with the European Union is one of the largest and most complex in the world, generating an estimated goods and services trade flow of about $2.7 billion a day in 2012, and representing an estimated 50 percent of world GDP and nearly one-third of world trade flows. The enormous volume of trade and investment is a key pillar of prosperity in the United States and Europe. The transatlantic economy is a powerful link between companies and producers, and businesses and employment opportunities.

In 2012, the United States exported $463 billion in goods and services to the EU, estimated to support more than 2.2 million U.S. jobs. U.S. exports of agricultural products to EU countries totaled $9.9 billion that year. In 2011, the United

Figure 3.13 London's pedestrian-only Carnaby Street is famous for the shops and cafes that line its wide walkways.

Figure 3.14 U.S. President Barack Obama speaks during an event on food security in Dakar, Senegal, June 28, 2013.

Figure 3.15 This Indian spinning mill factory produces yarn from organic and fair trade cotton.

States supplied 11 percent of all EU goods imports and 29 percent of all EU private services imports, and purchased 17 percent of all EU goods exports and 24 percent of all EU services exports.[33]

In his 2013 State of the Union address, President Barack Obama announced his intention for the United States to negotiate a TTIP with the EU. The TTIP is a bold vision based on many potential areas of shared opportunity and has the potential to become an historic agreement. It would be different from any trade agreement the United States has ever negotiated.

The EU has 62.7 percent of the FDI stock in the United States. The United Kingdom, the Netherlands, Germany, and France have the largest FDI in the United States. The United States and the EU encourage multilateral liberalization in a globalized world. In the G-8, G-20, the World Trade Organization (WTO), and the Organisation for Economic Cooperation and Development (OECD), the United States and the EU work together to promote an open, transparent, and nondiscriminatory trade and investment climate worldwide.[34]

NEW CHALLENGES FOR WORLD TRADE

"The future of world trade, and the global trading system, will be shaped by a range of economic, political, and social factors, including technological innovation, shifts in production and consumption patterns, and demographic change," according to the *World Trade Report 2013*, published by the WTO. "One element clearly stands out in the report, and that is the importance of trade for development," stated former WTO Director-General Pascal Lamy.[35]

According to Ambassador Ron Kirk, former U.S. trade representative,

> the trade policy of the Obama administration addresses trade-related environmental issues affecting everyone on the planet. We will continue to open up markets and advance environmental issues at the same time. We will pursue a balanced and comprehensive approach to a trade policy that advances U.S. interests and reflects our values. Because of these efforts, U.S. producers are selling more goods around the world stamped with 'Made in America,' and trade is supporting more jobs here at home.[36]

Figure 3.16 The Grand Bazaar, Istanbul, Turkey.

Summary

Global trade has been an important contributor to growing the U.S. economy and supporting more jobs for more American workers. The nation's trade policy agenda for 2013 and beyond expressed a commitment to use every possible available policy tool— or to develop new ones, if necessary—to achieve an ultimate goal of trade liberalization that would support economic growth and jobs.

The NEI is credited with record high exports in all major sectors in 2012; services exports were up 24 percent over 2009 (the date NEI was established); manufacturing exports increased by 47 percent, and agricultural exports were up by 44 percent. According to the U.S. Department of Commerce, U.S. exports of goods and services have increased by more than 39 percent over the level of exports in 2009, supporting more than one million additional U.S. jobs.

Media reports of American manufacturing jobs being "lost" or gone to Mexico or China have just not been true. U.S. government and U.S. Chamber of Commerce reports have concluded that less than 1 percent of factory layoffs have been attributed to the movement of jobs overseas. The U.S. Chamber of Commerce noted that 12 million American manufacturing jobs contributed to the production of $1.3 trillion worth of U.S. exports last year. Exports generate revenue of more than $100,000 for each American factory worker.

Free Trade Agreements (FTAs) have opened up key markets to increased U.S. global trade. But of the approximately 350 free trade agreements in force around the world today, the United States is a partner in only 14, covering 20 countries. That has been the motivation behind the implementation of three recent FTAs—with South Korea, Colombia, and Panama—and two pending trade partnerships— the Trans-Pacific Partnership (TPP) and the Transatlantic Trade and Investment Partnership (TTIP).

Results from the three new FTAs have been quick and impressive:

- Highly competitive American companies now have increased access to Korea's $580 billion services market.
- The U.S.–Colombia FTA gave more than half of U.S. exports of agricultural commodities to that nation duty-free status and increased access to Colombia's $180 billion services market.
- More than 87 percent of U.S. industrial goods exports to Panama became duty-free under the U.S.–Panama FTA, as did American access to the country's $20.6 billion services market.

The two proposed trade partnerships for the United States, one across the Atlantic—the TTIP—and the other across the Pacific—the TPP—have the same founding objective: to stimulate U.S. and global employment and economic growth through an expansion of world trade. The United States has a lot at stake in these negotiations: increased exports by almost $600 billion, and supporting more than 3 million American jobs expected by the year 2020.

With momentum in the global economy shifting back to the developed world, away from the emerging economies that had led growth since the financial crisis, U.S. trade policy is to strengthen key trade relationships with other developed countries.

Review Questions

1. List the top three ranking U.S. international trade relationships in terms of: total trade, U.S. exports to, and U.S. imports from.

2. To what extent do U.S. small and medium-sized businesses participate in world trade?

3. State the purpose of free trade agreements. Why is the United States interested in lowering trade barriers?

4. Explain the history and purpose of the proposed TPP and TTIP trade partnerships. How would the United States benefit from them?

Discussion Questions and Activities

1. Access the Web site *Everything International* at http://faculty.philau.edu /russowl/russow.html. This site provides links to a wide variety of international business, education, and research Internet sites. In the past 25 years, over twenty million viewers have accessed this site. More than 200 libraries, colleges, universities, schools, businesses, and government agencies use it as a resource and recommend it to their members and customers. What lessons do think would apply to global business successes or failures?

2. Go to the CIA's World Factbook Web site (https://www.cia.gov/library /publications/the-world-factbook/) and read the "Guide to Country Comparisons" and "The World Factbook User Guide" for an idea of what kind of country-specific information can be obtained from this research resource. Then return to the main menu and click on the *About* link for the "History of the World Factbook."

3. Divide the class into two groups; one should debate the pros of "free trade" and the other should present the case for "fair trade." Research websites on free trade versus fair trade to prepare for the debate.

Chapter 3 Case

Target Bumps across the Border

For years, Canadian customers have crossed their southern border to take advantage of the styles and prices offered by Target stores in the United States. Customers from Vancouver, British Columbia, in the West, to the Niagara Falls area in the East, have shopped the trendy stateside discounter and returned jubilantly to Canada with goods not available at home.

Although Target had never operated stores outside of the United States, management was familiar with the tastes of Canadian customers because of their frequent cross-border shopping expeditions. What could be so difficult, management wondered, about extending the company's reach up north? Consequently, instead of building stores from the start, as Walmart has done in its global expansion, Target bought a group of shuttered discount stores formerly belonging to the Canadian department store chain Hudson's Bay Company. This way, Target could start operating in Canada almost immediately. In three months Target opened 48 stores across Canada, with plans of opening 124 within the year. Quite a change of pace for a company that formerly averaged an opening of 20 stores annually!

Target's traditional strong point is promotion, creating a stir among consumers for its specialized products, offering fashion brands bearing designer names such as Jason Wu, Phillip Lim, Shaun White, and Nate Berkus. In Canada, the clothing lines of Kate Young and Roots marketed through exclusive agreements with Target struck a positive note with customers who eagerly bought those goods. The company's strength in building demand sometimes has fallen flat as when Target failed to anticipate the popularity of its Missoni promotion and lost sales because inventories were not sufficient.

Lack of inventory planning was highly evident in many of the Canadian Target stores as when customers in Calgary found empty shelves that should have been stocked with electronics and racks that ought to have displayed men's apparel. In Toronto, Target stores had sold out of basic items such as clothing and milk. In Target's defense, management had no record of previous customer purchases on which to plan stock for its new stores. In addition, it takes time for retailers to build consistent and reliable supply chains equipped to handle reorders promptly and deliver merchandise swiftly.

Source: Thomas Lee, "Ambitious Canadian Timeframe Giving Target Growing Pains," *Minneapolis Star Tribune,* May 29, 2013. Retrieved May 31, 2013, from http://www .startribune.com/printarticle?id=209281601.

Questions

1. What is your opinion of Target's purchasing a group of defunct Canadian stores instead of building its own stores from the ground up? What advantages did this purchase give Target? What disadvantages?

2. What are Target's corporate strengths mentioned in the case? What are its weaknesses?

3. How might Target capitalize on its strengths in Canada? What should it do to improve its weaknesses?

4. From what you know about the Target Corporation, how well do you believe it will succeed in its Canadian venture?

References

1. "J. Crew on the Lookout for Global Growth." Retrieved July 17, 2013, from http://www.jcrew.com/.

2. "President's 2013 Trade Policy Agenda," Office of the U.S. Trade Representative, March 1, 2013. Retrieved July 18, 2013, from http://www.ustr.gov/about-us/press-office/press-releases/2013/march/president.

3. "National Export Initiative (NEI)." Retrieved July 17, 2013, from http://export.gov.

4. "Fact Sheet: Small Business Network of the Americas," White House Office of the Press Secretary, April 13, 2012. Retrieved September 2, 2013, from http://www.whitehouse.gov/the-press-office/2012/04/13/fact.

5. "U.S. Trade and Exports Support 9.8 Million American Jobs," Tradeology: The Official Blog of the International Trade Administration, February 26, 2013. Retrieved July 20, 2013, from http://blog.trade.gov/2013/02/26/u-s-trade-and-exports-support-9-8-american-jobs-2/.

6. John Murphy, "The State of World Trade 2013 . . ." U.S. Chamber of Commerce, May 1, 2013. Retrieved August 7, 2013, from http://www.uschamber.com/press/speeches/2013/state-world-trade.

7. Ibid.

8. Ibid.

9. Ibid.

10. "Benefits of Free Trade Agreements," U.S. Department of State. Retrieved August 14, 2013, from http://www.state.gov/e/eb/tpp/bta/fta/c26474.htm.

11. "Joint Statement on U.S.-EU Negotiations for a Transatlantic Trade and Investment Partnership," Council on Foreign Relations, February 13, 2013. Retrieved August 15, 2013, from http://www.cfr.org/trade/joint-statement-us-eu-negotiations-transatlantic.

12. Op. cit., "President's 2013 Trade Policy Agenda."

13. "The U.S.–Korea Free Trade Agreement (KORUS)," Export.gov. Retrieved September 10, 2013, from http://export.gov/FTA/korea/index.asp.

14. "The U.S.–Colombia Trade Promotion Agreement," Export.gov. Retrieved September 10, 2013, from http://export.gov/FTA/colombia/index.asp.

15. "The U.S.–Panama Trade Promotion Agreement," Export.gov. Retrieved September 11, 2013, from http://export.gov/fta/panama.

16. The Trans-Pacific Partnership: Building on U.S. Economic and Strategic Partnerships in the Asia-Pacific, Fact Sheet. U.S. Department of State, September 5, 2013. Retrieved September 9, 2013 from http://www.state.gov/r/pa/pl/2013/214166.htm.

17. "Everything You Need to Know About the Trans-Pacific Partnership." Retrieved on February 20, 2014, from http://www.washingtonpost.com/blogs/wonkblog/wp/2013/12/11/everything-you-need-to-know-about-the-trans-pacific-partnership.

18. "Fact Sheet: United States to Negotiate

Transatlantic Trade and Investment Partnership with the European Union," Office of the U. S. Trade Representative, February 13, 2013. Retrieved on September 9, 2013, from http://www.ustr.gov/about -us/press-office/fact -sheets/2013/february /US-EU-TTIP.

19. Op. cit., "Joint Statement on U.S.-EU Negotiations," Council on Foreign Relations.

20. Alex Frangos, Sudeep Reddy, and John Lyons, "Emerging World Loses Growth Lead," *Wall Street Journal*, August 11, 2013. Retrieved Sept. 16, 2013, from http://online.wsj.com.

21. "Trade to Remain Subdued in 2013 After Sluggish Growth in 2012 as European Economies Continue to Struggle," WTO 2013 press releases, April 10, 2013. Retrieved August 24, 2013, from http://www.wto.org /english/news_ea.

22. "U.S.–Canada Trade," U.S. Census: Foreign Trade Statistics/ Highlights, February 6, 2014. Retrieved February 20, 2014, from http://www .census.gov/foreign -trade/statistics/highlights /top/top1312yr.html.

23. "U. S. Relations with Canada." Embassy of the United States Ottawa, Canada. Retrieved on February 20, 2014, from http://canada.usembassy .gov/canada-us-relations /trade.html.

24. "Joint Statement from 2012 NAFTA Commission Meeting," Office of the United States Trade Representative, April 2012. Retrieved September 9, 2013, from http://www.ustr.gov/about -us/press-office/press releases/2012/april/.

25. "Ambassador Bridge: Bridge Facts." Retrieved on February 20, 2014, from http://www .ambassadorbridge.com /intlcrossing/bridgefacts .aspx.

26. "U.S.–Mexico Trade," U.S. Census: Foreign Trade Statistics/ Highlights, February 6, 2014. Retrieved February 20, 2014, from http://www .census.gov/foreign-trade /statistics/highlights /top/top1312yr.html.

27. "U.S. Relations with Mexico," U.S. Department of State, September 5, 2013. Retrieved September 9, 2013, from http://www.state.gov/r /pa/ei/bgn/35749.htm.

28. "U.S.–China Trade," U.S. Census: Foreign Trade Statistics/ Highlights, February 6, 2014. Retrieved February 20, 2014, from http://www .census.gov/foreign-trade /statistics/highlights /top/top1312yr.html.

29. "U.S. Relations with China," U.S. Department of State, August 16, 2013. Retrieved September 9, 2013, from http://www .state.gov/r/pa/ei/bgn /1890, and *Reuters*, January 16, 2014. Retrieved on February 20, 2014, from http://www .reuters.com/article/2014 /01/16/us-china-economy -fdi-idUSBREA0F0EI2014 0116.

30. "U.S.–Japan Trade," U.S. Census: Foreign Trade Statistics/ Highlights, February 6, 2014. Retrieved February 20, 2014, from http:// www.census.gov/foreign -trade/statistics /highlights/top /top1312yr.html.

31. "U.S. Relations with Japan," U.S. Department of State, January 31, 2014. Retrieved February 21, 2014, from http://www .state.gov/r/pa/ei/bgn /4142.htm.

32. Ibid.

33. "EU-USA Trade in Goods Statistics," European Commission, March 13, 2013. Retrieved September 5, 2013, from http://www.census.gov /foreign-trade/balance /c0003.html.

34. "Fact Sheet: United States to Negotiate Transatlantic Trade and Investment Partnership with European Union," Office of the U.S. Trade Representative, February 13, 2013. Retrieved September 10, 2013, from http://ustr.gov/about -us/press-office/fact -sheets/2023/february/.

35. "World Trade Report 2013," World Trade Organization Publications. Retrieved September 15, 2013, from http://www.wto.org /english/res_e /publications_e/wtr13 _e.htm.

36. Op. cit., "President's 2013 Trade Policy Agenda."

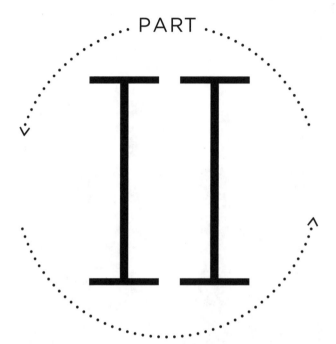

PART

II

U.S. Exporting Policies and Procedures

Figure 4.1 An advertisement for U.S. fashion house Coach at the Shanghai Pudong International Airport in Shanghai, China.

CHAPTER 4
BASICS OF EXPORTING

COACH GOES GLOBAL. How does a company expand from a small leather goods manufacturer to a worldwide fashion accessories lifestyle behemoth with annual sales approaching $5 billion? This is just what Coach succeeded in accomplishing over the past three-quarters of a century.

Famous for its leather handbags, eyewear, men's and women's accessories, business cases, fragrances, watches, and jewelry, Coach has grown over the years from a family-run business, to a division of Sara Lee Corp., to a publicly held corporation. Its products, bearing the horse-and carriage logo, are recognized throughout the world, but particularly in Britain, Japan, China, Vietnam, South America, and only recently in continental Europe. However, the expansion was not always smooth.

Its first international move was to Britain, where Coach opened a shop in 1988. It soon closed because the company failed to understand potential customers through sufficient marketing research. Management painfully discovered that customers did not recognize the brand, and that the available product assortment was skimpy. In addition, at that time an unfavorable exchange rate between the dollar and the British pound pushed Coach prices to the sky. Coach pulled back from Britain in favor of concentrating on Japan. Having learned a lesson from its UK experience, this time the company did its research thoroughly. Working with a Japanese partner, Coach was quick to recognize that Japanese consumers appreciated known brand names, style, and quality, and it emphasized those product features in its promotions. The result today has been that the Coach brand in Japan ranks second only to Louis Vuitton in sales.

Coach saw that its greatest growth potential was in Asia and so partnered with local businesses to establish stores in mainland China, Macau, and Hong Kong. Later as customers became familiar with the brand and sales grew, Coach bought out the local owners, preferring to control marketing and supply chains itself, as a goodly assortment of its products are manufactured in Asia. Today, Coach has expanded there, for example into Vietnam. It also has returned to Britain as well as venturing into South America and Europe, including Spain and France among other countries. The company's success, it well learned, rests on ascertaining and meeting the demand of customers, wherever they may be.[1]

WHAT IS EXPORTING?

As you can tell, Coach places great marketing emphasis on selling goods overseas. This process, **exporting**, is distributing a product, service, technology, or idea that originates in one country and is sent beyond its borders to distributors or end-users in another country. Every day people and businesses around the globe use **products** or goods and services that were produced in the United States and exported to their country. American-made goods can be found in Japanese kitchens (Kellogg's Corn Flakes), French offices (Parker Pens), Mexican construction projects (U.S.-made steel and cement components), and Chinese camp sites (L.L. Bean). Harley-Davidson motorcycles, Hanes hosiery and underwear, Holiday Inns, and McDonald's and Kentucky Fried Chicken franchises are influencing lifestyles in nations worldwide.

Why have these and many other U.S. firms ventured into foreign markets when they may still have untapped opportunities in the United States? With 95 percent of the world's population living outside the United States, even small-to-medium-sized firms now acknowledge that exporting must be an important consideration when planning their future business strategies. With domestic competition intense and foreign imports growing rapidly in most industry sectors, a global marketing strategy may be necessary not only for increased sales and profits but also for business survival.

REASONS FOR EXPORTING

Exporting is beneficial to the country as well as to the company. Creating more jobs, stimulating economic growth from higher employment, and adding tax revenues are some of the reasons U.S. federal and state governments vigorously promote exporting. Exports also help reduce the U.S. deficit in the International Trade Account (the difference between a nation's exports and imports). Record annual U.S. trade deficits in excess of $700 billion were recorded in 2011 and 2012, as imports rebounded from the prolonged recession much faster than did exports.[2]

Successful exporters may wonder why only about 65,000 firms—10 percent of all businesses—are active in foreign trade, according to the U.S. Department of Commerce estimates. Success stories emphasize that increased sales and expanded profits can result from exporting, but many corporate managers still regard international marketing as mysterious, time consuming, and too expensive for them. Global trade consultants believe that fear of the unknown and ignorance of export policies and procedures are the real reasons keeping firms from trying to export.

On the other hand, successful participants in exporting extol its benefits, which include the following:

- **Increased revenues and profits.** Expanded markets can lead to more sales and profits—usually over a reasonable period of time. Foreign accounts may take more time and money to sign up, but they usually are more reliable and loyal for the long term. For example, U.S. specialty department stores realize they are operating domestically in mature markets, so they are increasingly looking to overseas expansion.

- **Countercyclical marketing.** A U.S. business can use world markets to combat domestic market influences such as economic downturns and seasonal purchases. The various phases of the business cycle (stability, growth, decline, and recovery) describe the state of the economy at a given time. Should the economy in the United States see a downturn, some of the other world markets may lag behind for several months to a year. Putting more emphasis on exports could level out the peaks and valleys of the nation's economic health. In the case of the changing seasons and the effect of weather, companies producing seasonal products (bathing suits, skis, and boats) look south of the equator for markets during the U.S. winter months.

- **Extended product life cycles.** If domestically marketed products become technologically obsolete, or fall out of fashion with their target market, chances are good that a developing market (more than half of the world's economies) would welcome imports of less expensive, older models of electronics such as cell phones and computers.

- **Diversification.** Even though the United States is the world's largest market, **consumer demand**, the amount consumers are willing to buy, still fluctuates according to the economic climate. Selling to foreign markets enables firms to balance market changes. This applies for product diversification as well.

  For example, Gap, Inc. announced in 2013 its plans to begin franchising Old Navy stores internationally, including opening its first franchise-operated Old Navy store in the Philippines in 2014. Franchising Old Navy stores is a key step in the company's international expansion as it works to grow its share of the global retail apparel market.[3]

- **Enhanced company image.** Export marketing tells customers that a company understands how important it is to be truly global in today's competitive climate. This creates a new perception for a company. It also provides the appearance of a well-established firm with 21st-century management. The Judith Ripka fine jewelry company is one example of an organization whose owners count on international distribution to enhance its image in the global luxury goods market. As Ripka's president, Charles Jayson, puts it, "In terms of global expansion, there's a global shift taking place and we have to follow the money."[4]

- **Reduced unit costs.** New exporters often find foreign-based orders will lower cost-per-unit for their entire output. By utilizing excess manufacturing capacity or reducing existing inventories, exporters can take advantage of these economies-of-scale.

Figure 4.2 The Milan store is the first one in Europe for Juicy Couture.

In spite of these significant advantages to exporting, many U.S. firms still do not export, for the following reasons:

- They have no need to expand; the U.S. market is still large enough for their anticipated growth.
- They perceive the mysteries of foreign marketing—different language, etiquette, new business customs—as too difficult or time-consuming to deal with.

- Exporting requires a greater use of resources (people, money, and time) than does domestic marketing.
- Exporting is more complex, and sometimes more costly, particularly in coping with payment and financing procedures.[5]

SPOTLIGHT ON GLOBAL TRADE 4.1
Exploding Exporting Myths

In order to take the mystery and confusion out of global marketing, some of the many myths surrounding exporting need to be exposed. Before you begin, please know that each one is false.

- **Myth #1:** Exporting is only for large-staffed, well-known, and well-financed companies that can hire experienced staffs, conduct marketing research, modify products, and increase production to satisfy demand.
- **Myth #2:** Export success depends on a large export department.
- **Myth #3:** Exporting is too risky, especially for smaller or medium-sized companies unable to absorb losses from nonpayment.
- **Myth #4:** Exporting regulations are too complex, with punishments for violations too common and severe.
- **Myth #5:** Violations of patents, copyrights, and trademarks are so common that new exporters risk losing their property rights.
- **Myth #6:** Only experts know how to navigate today's myriad of international trade laws, policies, and procedures. How-to-export tutorials and procedural guides are not readily available.

Taken as a group, the above myths, if true, would be strong disincentives for entering the export business. To repeat, however: *all the myths cited are false.* According to U.S. Department of Commerce studies, companies of all sizes are engaging in export; in fact 60 percent of all successful exporting companies have 100 or fewer employees. What matters is the effective planning, research, pricing, and delivery of a product wherever the demand may be profitably served.

Source: Harvey R. Shoemack, "Essentials of the Export-Import Business," an online course at Oakton Community College, Des Plaines, IL, September 2013.

Figure 4.3 Fine jewelry is popular all over the world. Gold bracelets and similar jewelry by Judith Ripka are found in the company's stores and boutiques in the United States, Canada, the Caribbean, and Russia, among other locations.

CHALLENGES TO EXPORTING

Of course, challenges do accompany the benefits of exporting but, with careful planning and preparation, they are often surmountable. Some of these challenges include the fact that exporting frequently requires a substantial investment in travel and research, possibly hiring new staff, and perhaps modifying products or packaging. Moreover, the commitment of top management is crucial, not just early on, but for the long haul. It takes not willingness alone, but sustained effort, resources, and time to establish and maintain relationships in foreign markets. This means learning cultural differences, as an automobile manufacturer failed to do when, deciding to market its small automobile in Spanish-speaking countries, it named the car Nova—easily translated into "doesn't go." In addition to knowing the language, learning cultural differences also means being available to overseas customers, dealing with extensive paperwork, and being aware of and alert to local existing and potential competition.

DECIDING TO EXPORT

The decision to export should be based on practical reasons, supported by current and accurate statistical market research. Emotional rationalizations—such as the company owner or chief executive officer (CEO) suggesting exporting as a means for traveling the world with a business write-off—are usually poorly planned and unrealistically funded, thus quite often destined to fail. Such actions may actually discourage firms from continuing efforts to sell in foreign markets, when good planning and research could have built a substantial profit center for the company.

Is Our Product Exportable?

The company's key question—do we have an exportable product?—is followed swiftly by others, such as do we have adequate resources of personnel, time, and money, and are we backed by management's long-term commitment to succeed in international marketing? In attempting to export T-shirts to China, the sportswear company American Apparel knew that although its product is exportable, the company could not register the name "American Apparel" there because Chinese copyright laws forbid including the name of a country in a brand name.[6]

To be exportable, a product must meet the following criteria:

- Be legally exportable from the United States, according to the **Export Administration Regulations (EARs)** rules of the U.S. Department of Commerce for specific product and country classifications (see Chapter 5 for export controls and procedures)
- Be easily imported into the targeted foreign market country, without unreasonable taxes or administrative expense
- Be exempted from any market-related restrictions, such as size of unit, nature of the product (e.g., ice cream melts if not kept frozen), or modification costs
- Possess unique qualities that provide a competitive edge over foreign or international products (design, quality, or technology, because a low price is no longer a guarantee of success in international business)
- Satisfy an existing and growing demand for the product's category and specific characteristics
- Enjoy no existing prejudice against imports from the United States[7]

Exporting Goods versus Exporting Services

Exporting goods (such as Michael Kors apparel) differs from exporting services (management consulting on textile technologies) because each operates in a unique environment. Marketing tangible goods requires packaging, customs, and physical delivery. Exporting services requires empowering staff—that is, enabling export project managers to create marketing plans, travel between headquarters and overseas assignments, obtain work permits, and maintain cross-cultural communications in the language of the designated market.

SPOTLIGHT ON GLOBAL TRADE 4.2
Making the Export Decision

The product a company intends to export must meet certain marketability requirements. Answers to the questions below call for research of current data concerning each potential market. Assessing a product's export potential should yield useful answers.

1. What need does the product fulfill?
2. Does the need exist abroad?
3. Is a profitable market share attainable, or is the need already being met?
4. Is the proposed export competitive in features, benefits, and pricing?
5. Can the product stand alone or does it require basic or supplemental products to operate? (Example: what use are computers without software to run them?)
6. Does the product require modifications? (Example: since the Japanese drive on the left side of the street, their automobile factories mount the steering wheel on the right; to market their automobiles in the United States, the factories must mount the steering wheel on the left.)
7. If so, will the cost of modification make the product too expensive for the targeted export market?
8. Is the product easily packaged and shipped?
9. Are there legal/governmental export restrictions or nontariff barriers to trade and/or investment?
10. Are there industry-specific controversies that might create barriers for export? (Example: could certain chemicals be converted for use as chemical or biological weapons?)

Do We Have Sufficient Resources?

After a company determines that its products or services are exportable, it must ask if the export activity is compatible with corporate objectives and operations management. Management needs to address the following questions:

- What are the firm's export marketing goals? Are they realistic?
- Are the exporting goals consistent with overall corporate strategic planning?
- Can current company resources of personnel, production capacity, and finances support increased demands?
- Does the corporate Business Plan include an Export Marketing Strategy that also provides a roadmap to foreign marketing success?
- Adequate personnel resources are essential for successful exporting. Since market development involves frequent and lengthy foreign travel on the part of key marketing or sales executives, can these managers be spared without compromising domestic productivity?

Many foreign company executives will judge a company's level of commitment by the caliber and experience of managers sent to their country. Will top managers be able to spend the time necessary for domestic meetings to plan export marketing strategies, as well as travel overseas to meet with prospective distributors, agents, or joint venture partners?

The bottom line is always about money. Overseas travel, meals, and lodging are usually much more expensive (and more so with a weak dollar), as is participation at foreign trade shows (highly recommended—but go as a visitor first, then possibly become an exhibitor). If top management is not fully committed, and proper funding not allocated, chances for success are diminished.[8]

ARE WE PREPARED TO EXPORT?

What makes a business export-ready? Simply stated, the business has an exportable product (from a legal and marketing point of view), as well as the capacity, resources, and management commitment to compete on an international scale. The trick is to figure out whether or not this is true of your company—and, if it isn't yet, how to make it happen.

The first step is to think about the knowledge and resources your business already has. To begin, consider the following:

Your expectations—do you have

- Clear and achievable export objectives?
- A realistic idea of what exporting entails?
- An openness to new ways of doing business?
- An understanding of what is required to succeed in the international marketplace?

Human resources—do you have

- The capacity to handle the extra demand associated with exporting?
- Top management committed to exporting?
- Efficient ways of responding quickly to customer inquiries?

- Personnel with culturally sensitive marketing skills?
- Ways of dealing with language barriers?

Financial and legal resources—can you

- Obtain enough capital or lines of credit to produce the product or service?
- Find ways to reduce the financial risks of international trade?
- Find people to advise you on the legal and tax implications of exporting?
- Deal effectively with different monetary systems?
- Ensure protection of your **intellectual property** (patents, trademarks, and copyrights)?

Competitiveness—do you have

- The resources to do market research on the exportability of your product or service?
- Proven, sophisticated market-entry methods?
- A product or service that is potentially viable in your target market?[9]

GETTING STARTED IN EXPORTING

Although many government agencies have questionnaires to help determine export-readiness status, there is no clear-cut definition of being export-ready. However, export service providers have determined some aspects that firms need to be aware of when becoming export-ready; such guidelines help prepare for global market entry. In most cases, they are extensions and adaptations of existing marketing-related programs companies are already implementing to serve their domestic markets.[10]

Key factors to consider for becoming export-ready include the following items.

Export-Readiness Evaluation

To check for export-readiness, start with a company SWOT (strengths, weaknesses, opportunities, threats) assessment. Add the company's level of management commitment. If sufficient commitment is not present, don't go any further. Most firms can experience some success in establishing international sales and distribution during the first year, but becoming established often can be a much longer process, requiring more dedication and perseverance than that needed to market domestically.

Market Entry Options

Investigate the characteristics and size of the markets you are thinking of entering. Methods and approaches to market research are covered later in this chapter. Initially, exporters may be able to serve up to a dozen foreign markets with existing sales and marketing staff. Many firms considered to be successful exporters serve fewer than 30 overseas markets. Europe, the Pacific Rim countries, Latin America, and a few other select countries easily represent more than 30 potential markets for most products.[11]

Table 4.1 Comparison of Foreign Market Entry Modes

Mode	Conditions favoring this mode	Advantages	Disadvantages
Exporting	• Limited sales potential in target country; little product adaptation required • Distribution channels close to plants • High target country production costs • Liberal import policies • High political risk	• Minimizes risk and investment • Speed of entry • Maximizes scale; uses existing facilities	• Trade barriers and tariffs add to costs • Transport costs • Limits access to local information • Company viewed as an outsider
Licensing	• Import and investment barriers • Legal protection possible in target environment • Low sales potential in target country • Large cultural distance • Licensee lacks ability to become a competitor	• Minimizes risk and investment • Speed of entry • Able to circumvent trade barriers • High return on investment	• Lack of control over use of assets • Licensee may become competitor • Knowledge spillovers • License period is limited
Joint Ventures	• Import barriers • Large cultural distance • Assets cannot be fairly priced • High sales potential • Some political risk • Government restrictions on foreign ownership • Local company can provide skills, resources, distribution network, brand name, etc.	• Overcomes ownership restrictions and cultural distance • Combines resources of two companies • Potential for learning • Viewed as insider • Less investment required	• Difficult to manage • Dilution of control • Greater risk than exporting and licensing • Knowledge spillovers • Partner may become a competitor
Direct Investment	• Import barriers • Small cultural distance • Assets cannot be fairly priced • High sales potential • Low political risk	• Greater knowledge of local market • Can better apply specialized skills • Minimizes knowledge • Spillover • Can be viewed as an insider	• Higher risk than other modes • Requires more resources and commitment • May be difficult to manage the local resources

Source: "A Comparison of Market Entry Strategies," reprinted with permission from *The Global Entrepreneur*, by James Foley, Dearborn Financial Publishing Inc., 1999.

Market Entry Strategies

There are numerous entry strategies available to consider, but three are basic to most successful exporting companies. These include stocking distributors, piggybacking, and export management companies.

Stocking Distributors

The majority of export sales are accomplished through distributors. Distributors are generally responsible for all aspects of marketing and distribution of imported product in their country. **Stocking distributors** purchase products in stocking quantities, have a sales and support staff similar to the U.S. operation, and warehouse and ship products to customers.

Piggybacking

For new-to-export companies, successful international marketing may come through **piggybacking**, in this instance meaning seeking out and tying in with other noncompetitive, complimentary product line exporters in their industry. Thus, through practice, the new exporter can learn the industry specifics of overseas distribution. Start by introducing the proposed export idea to your existing distributors. They may be interested in helping you establish relationships with their own distributors, so they become a stronger factor in their own markets.

Export Management Companies

Private firms can serve as the export department for several producers of goods or services, either by taking title or by soliciting and transacting export business on behalf of its clients in return for a commission. **Export management companies (EMCs)** work on a salary or retainer plus commission basis. Others, known as *export trading companies (ETCs)*, can be very helpful to the firm that either doesn't want to do the actual exporting itself, or wants to serve countries not considered to be primary markets. ETCs usually take title to the goods they export.[12]

There is no single, correct way for a firm to market internationally. A combination of the above, plus a company's unique strategies, can lead to a successful formula for most firms. In many instances, teaming up with another organization, in particular one possessing local market knowledge and resources, can ease entry into a foreign market.

INTERNATIONAL FASHION FOCUS 4.1
Maine Comes to China: The L. L. Bean Story

What do people in the country of China and the state of Maine have in common? For one thing, it seems that consumers in both places have similar tastes in sportswear and sporting goods. These like interests led L. L. Bean, headquartered in Freeport, Maine, to open its first store in China in 2008. By the end of 2012, L. L. Bean had opened a total of 62 stores in China and expected that number to grow.

"Throughout China there is a growing interest in participating in outdoor and recreational activities," noted Chris McCormick, president and CEO of the Maine retailer. "L. L. Bean is a natural fit within this market. This is an area we have been studying for some time as we've considered ways to expand our international presence and diversify our business. China provides many opportunities with its growing marketplace."

Located in an open-air mall, L. L. Bean's first store in China, at 3,000 square feet, resembled the layout of the flagship headquarters store in Freeport. The interior offered a weathered woodsy New England atmosphere, with company photos and displays illustrating outdoor recreation activities. Product lines include outerwear and sportswear for men, women, and children; footwear; luggage; and hiking and camping equipment.

L. L.Bean opened its first international retail store in Tokyo, Japan, in 1992 and by 2013 operated 20 retail stores and outlets in several cities in Japan. The company's research findings plus the partnering agreement help pave the way to expanding its customer base, increasing sales, and gaining profits in Asia.

Source: www.LLBean.com.

DETERMINING YOUR EXPORT POTENTIAL

Is your company too small to export? Probably not, particularly if you have a website that may bring in customers from other countries without additional promotion on your part. To succeed in international markets, you don't have to be a big-name firm with lavish resources and an entire department devoted to exporting. In the United States alone, more than 60,000 small and medium-sized companies are currently engaged in exporting. Each of these accounts for anywhere from occasional sales to $5 million in exported goods and services each year.

Can your product find a worthwhile market outside of the United States? Getting this right is crucial—if there's no demand for what you are offering, obviously you'd be unwise to proceed.[13]

DEVELOPING AN EXPORT MARKETING PLAN

Before deciding to allocate personnel and resources to an export effort, make the effort to invest your energies in preparing an Export Marketing Plan. Think of the plan not only as a road map to profits, but also as a test for deciding whether or not you should venture into international trade. Many individual entrepreneurs and businesses have unearthed reasons (competitive, financial, or marketing) for postponing or canceling a proposed expansion into global marketing—after finding themselves unable to justify the action by analyzing the firm's Export Marketing Plan.

As you will discover, foreign markets can differ greatly from those at home. Some of these differences include: climate and other environmental factors such as local infrastructure (transportation, highways, and bridges; communications); social and cultural traditions and practices; local availability of raw materials or product alternatives; lower wage costs; varying amounts of purchasing power; the availability of foreign exchange, and government import controls.

Once you have decided that your company is able to overcome those potential barriers and is committed to exporting, the next step is to develop a marketing plan. A clearly written marketing strategy offers six immediate benefits:

- Because written plans display strengths and weaknesses more readily, they are a great help in formulating and polishing an export strategy.
- Written plans are not easily forgotten, overlooked, or ignored by those charged with executing them. If deviation from the original plan occurs, it is likely because of a deliberate choice.
- Written plans are easier to communicate to others and are less likely to be ignored by those charged with executing them.
- Written plans allocate responsibilities and provide for an evaluation of results.
- Written plans are essential when seeking financial assistance. They indicate to potential lenders that you are serious in your export venture.
- Written plans give management a clear understanding of what will be required and thus help ensure the commitment to exporting. Actually, a written plan signals that the decision to export has already been made.

This last advantage is particularly important. Building an international business takes time—months, if not years—before an exporter begins to see a return on its investment of time and money. Budgeting for these commitments is an essential element of export marketing planning. By committing to the specifics of a written plan, top management can make sure that the firm sets out to finish what it begins, and that the hopes that prompted its export efforts will be realized.

As you can tell from Table 4.2, when developing a business/marketing plan, the first step is to create a company profile, a description of the company and its products, plus its mission and goals. This type of plan serves to guide any marketing business, domestic or global. In planning to enter international trade, a subsequent step is to create an Export Marketing Plan indicating export commitment, resources, and strategies (see Table 4.3). To provide adequate data on export potential, the next step is to conduct relevant market research.[14]

Table 4.2 **Basic Business/Marketing Plan**

Preparing a Basic Business/Marketing Plan is an absolute prerequisite for export business success. The major sections of the plan should include the following:
- Individual or company profile
- Market research data
- Sales/marketing objectives
- Marketing strategy/timetable (what, when ,who, and how)
- Resources inventory (people, money, and time)

Source: Harvey R. Shoemack, "Essentials of the Export-Import Business," an online course at Oakton Community College, Des Plaines, IL, September 2013.

Table 4.3 Sample Outline for an Export Marketing Plan

Table of Contents Introduction: Why This Company Should Export (Executive Summary—one or two pages maximum)
Part I–Export Policy Commitment Statement
Part II–Situation/Background Analysis • Product • Operations • Personnel and Export Organization • Resources of the Firm • Industry Structure, Competition, and Demand
Part III–Marketing Components • Identifying, Evaluating, and Selecting Target Markets • Product Selection • Pricing • Distribution and Delivery • Promotion • Terms and Conditions • Internal Organization and Procedures • Sales Goals: Profit and Loss Forecasts
Part IV–Tactics: Action Steps • Primary Target Countries • Secondary Target Countries • Indirect Marketing Efforts
Part V–Export Budget: Pro Forma Financial Statements
Part VI–Implementation Schedule • Follow-up • Periodic Operational and Management Review   (Measuring Results Against Plan)
Addenda: Background Data on Target Countries and Markets • Basic Market Statistics: Historical and Projected • Background Facts • Competitive Environment

Source: Harvey R. Shoemack, "Essentials of the Export-Import Business," an online course at Oakton Community College, Des Plaines, IL, September 2013.

INITIATING MARKET RESEARCH

The purpose of overseas **market research**, data concerning consumers, is to collect information about the marketplace abroad that results in planned marketing activities with the goal of generating new revenues. Results of such research can reveal useful information such as the largest market for a company's product, its fastest-growing markets, market trends and outlook, market conditions and practices, and competitive firms and products.

Research data that is already compiled by other sources such as the government, trade associations, or the Internet (such as the per-capita income of a given country) is known as **secondary data**. Original data that is collected firsthand via surveys, personal interviews, or focus groups (such as consumers' ideas on a new product concept) is called **primary data**. Most companies find they need to use both sources to achieve the results they are seeking.

Gathering data from secondary sources is less expensive than collecting primary data, and a company may decide to begin its research here, consulting various sources such as trade statistics for a country or product. However, secondary sources have their limitations: available figures may be old, out-of-date, distorted, or not otherwise relevant. Nevertheless, some secondary data may be quite useful, and here is an easy place to begin research. In fact, utilizing secondary data may be the only step the company needs to take, provided its distributors have more advanced research capabilities.

In conducting primary research, a company collects data directly from the foreign marketplace through interviews, observation, and surveys with representatives and potential buyers. Although primary market research is time consuming and expensive, it has the advantage of being tailored to the company's needs and provides answers to specific questions.[15]

SPOTLIGHT ON GLOBAL TRADE 4.3
Export Questionnaire

This questionnaire highlights the characteristics common to successful exporters. It should help you to assess your export readiness, as well as identify areas where your business needs to strengthen and improve its export activities.

1. Does your company have a product or service that has been successfully sold in the domestic market?   Yes   No
2. Does your company have or is it preparing an international marketing plan with defined goals and strategies?   Yes   No

3. Does your company have sufficient production capacity that can be committed to the export market?   Yes   No
4. Does your company have the financial resources to actively support the marketing of your products in the targeted overseas markets?   Yes   No
5. Is your company's management committed to developing export markets and willing and able to dedicate staff, time, and resources to the process?   Yes   No
6. Is your company committed to providing the same level of service given to your domestic customers?   Yes   No
7. Does your company have adequate knowledge in modifying product packaging and ingredients to meet foreign import regulations and cultural preferences?   Yes   No
8. Does your company have adequate knowledge in shipping its product overseas, such as identifying and selecting international freight forwarders and freight costing?   Yes   No
9. Does your company have adequate knowledge of export payment procedures, such as developing and negotiating letters of credit?   Yes   No
10. Do you have access to Internet marketing capabilities, including social media?   Yes   No

Scoring: Add up the number of "yes" answers

- 1 or 2 yes   You may be on the right track, but you have a long way to go.
- 3 or 4 yes   A good beginning, but you still have work to do.
- 5 or 6 yes   You are well on the way to being a successful exporter.
- 7 or 8 yes   You are almost there; you just need to fine-tune your plans.
- 9 or 10 yes   You are ready to export.

Source: Basic Guide to Exporting: Export Questionnaire. Retrieved on September 9, 2013, from http://export.gov/begin/assessment.asp.

Where to Begin

Because of the cost of primary market research, most firms rely heavily on second-ary data sources. Here are three sources exporters find useful.

The Library and the Internet

Start exploring your global market potential with library and Internet research. To stay alert to current world events that influence the international marketplace, monitor the Internet. Watch for announcements of specific projects, or visit likely markets. For example, a thawing of political hostilities often leads to the opening of economic channels among countries.

Analyze Web-based and economic statistics sites. General country-specific information—critical to any export plan—may be found on the CIA World Fact-book website at https://www.cia.gov/library/publications/the-world-factbook /index.html. Demographic and general economic statistics, such as population size and composition, per capita income, and production levels by industry, can be important indicators of the market potential for a company's products. Trade sta-tistics are generally compiled by product category and by country. These statistics provide U.S. firms with information concerning product shipments during certain time periods. Review international market reports, locate potential overseas trade contacts, and prepare a list of services that can help you. You may even be able to form your own export team—those private and government sources that can assist you in each step of your export development process.

International Marketing Experts

There are several ways of obtaining advice from the experts in a given field. These include the following:

- Contact experts at the U.S. Department of Commerce, the Small Business Administration, and other government agencies.
- Attend seminars, workshops, and international trade shows.
- Hire an international trade and marketing consultant.
- Talk with successful exporters of similar products.
- Contact trade and industry association staff.
- Enroll in a college-level course in exporting and importing and/or international trade.

Gathering and evaluating secondary market research data can be complex and sometimes tedious; however, many websites, publications, and people can add information to the knowledge you seek.

Figure 4.4 Essential country-specific information may be found in the CIA World Factbook.

A Step-by-Step Approach

As you can tell from Tables 4.4 and 4.5, screening and selecting target markets calls for locating relevant data. The following approach to research may be useful; it involves screening potential markets, assessing the targeted markets, and drawing conclusions.

Table 4.4 **Nine Factors in Target Market Selection**

Location	Political climate	Distribution channels
Culture	Socioeconomic factors	Market size
Government regulations	Infrastructure	Competition

Source: Harvey R. Shoemack, "Essentials of the Export-Import Business," an online course at Oakton Community College, Des Plaines, IL, September 2013.

Screen Potential Markets

- **Step 1:** Obtain statistics indicating product exports to various countries. Published statistics provide a reliable indicator of where U.S. exports are currently being shipped. The U.S. Census Bureau Foreign Trade Data website, http://www.census.gov/indicator/www/ustrade.html, provides these statistics every month.
- **Step 2:** Identify five or more large and fast-growing markets for the firm's product. Look at the growth over the past three years. Has it been consistent? Did the market grow even during a recession, or did it resume with economic recovery?
- **Step 3:** Identify some smaller but rapidly emerging markets that may provide ground-floor opportunities. If the market is just beginning to open up, there may be fewer competitors than in established markets. Given a lower starting point here, growth rates should be substantially higher to qualify as potential markets.
- **Step 4:** Target three to five of the most statistically promising markets for further assessment. Consult with the Department of Commerce's U.S. Export Assistance Center (USEAC; www.doc.gov), business associates, freight forwarders, and others knowledgeable concerning export to further evaluate these targeted markets.

Assess Targeted Markets

- **Step 5:** Examine trends for company products as well as related items that could influence demand. Calculate the overall product consumption and the amount accounted for by imports. U.S. government sources include the official U.S. Department of Commerce export website (http://export.gov/); the National Trade Data Bank (NTDB) (login/password required, in-library use only) and the National Technical Information Service (NTIS) (www.ntis.gov/); Industry Sector Analysis (ISA); and the Country Commercial Guides (CCGs) (www.bis.doc.gov). These are among the sites that give economic backgrounds and market trends for each country. Demographic information (such as population size, composition, and age) can be obtained from the *World Population (Census) and Statistical Yearbook*, United Nations, as well as the CIA *World Factbook*.
- **Step 6:** Discover sources of competition, including the extent of domestic industry production and the major foreign competitors in each target market by using ISAs and competitive assessments. This information is available from the NTDB and the NTIS.

- **Step 7:** Analyze factors affecting the marketing and use of the product in each market, such as end-use sectors, channels of distribution, cultural idiosyncrasies, and business practices. Again, the ISAs and the Customized Market Analyses (CMAs) offered by the Department of Commerce are useful.
- **Step 8:** Identify any foreign barriers (tariff or nontariff) for the product to be exported, plus any U.S. barriers such as export controls (see Chapter 5).
- **Step 9:** Take advantage of any U.S. or foreign government incentives that promote exporting your particular product. Attending a foreign trade show can result in comprehensive market data to affirm or cancel plans to enter that market.[16]

Draw Conclusions

The data gathered from taking the preceding steps should provide enough information to determine your next move. However, further data sources are available in the Appendix at the end of this chapter.

Table 4.5 **Market Screening: How to Select Foreign Markets**

Initial screening: • Basic needs potential • Foreign trade and investment
Second screening: Economic and financial forces/environments
Third screening: • Political forces/environments • Legal forces/environments
Fourth screening: Sociocultural forces/environments
Fifth screening: Competitive forces/environments
Final selection: • Personal visits to foreign market country • Attendance at trade shows in the country • Locally conducted market research (if necessary)

Source: Harvey R. Shoemack, "Essentials of the Export-Import Business," an online course at Oakton Community College, Des Plaines, IL, September 2013.

FORMULATING PROACTIVE STRATEGIES: COMMUNICATION AND TRADE SHOWS

Once you have determined your plan, you will need to consider how you are going to present your company and product information to interested parties overseas, and in turn, how you can obtain information from them. Many firms today use a website as one way to accomplish this. For instance, your website can be a virtual

Figure 4.5 Première Vision textile trade show in Paris brings buyers from all over the world.

catalogue of your products or services, but it should also include an international sales program that provides the standard terms and conditions for selling your products overseas.

You will probably want to also develop international distributor support programs for advertising and promotion, sales and marketing, and after-sales service. These include items such as translation, price quotations, discount structures, warranties, services, parts, and training.

When you have made your commitment, assessed your ability to serve international markets, developed an international marketing plan, and created your communication tools, you are considered to be export-ready. Now you can use the numerous federal and state agency programs for exporters. As mentioned earlier, a great place to start is with **trade shows**, periodic wholesale markets for buyers and sellers in related industries. Trade shows are a key method for exposing your company and its products to prequalified trade prospects and buyers. International trade shows are the single best method for contacting distributor prospects and are widely attended. For example, Germany hosts more than 200 trade shows each year (an average of two per week). While many companies new to export cannot afford to attend trade shows overseas, most domestic trade shows have a foreign component. In fact, one of the more popular programs offered by the U.S. Department of Commerce is its Foreign Buyers Program that promotes and brings international visitors to many domestic trade shows.

By this time, you are ready to get some orders. What do you do with them?[17]

FOLLOWING THROUGH WITH AN ORDER

Suppose you are a novice exporter exhibiting your products at the appropriate industry trade show. You have collected attendees' business cards, and after the show one of these prospects sends you an order inquiry and request for a quotation.

You respond with a **pro forma invoice**, a form describing the merchandise including its specifications, packaging, per unit price, and payment terms. Your prospect responds with a purchase order, including payment information. Based on the terms of the sale, the prospective importer arranges for financing with its bank. Simultaneously, you plan for order fulfillment if inventory is sufficient, or production, if necessary.

The importer's bank, after verifying its client's credit-worthiness, prepares the necessary documents and informs your bank that the financial requirements have been satisfied. When your bank advises you that export payment is in place, the order is prepared for exporting (crating, if necessary), and you engage a freight forwarder or directly contact a shipping company to pick up the export shipment. New-to-export companies or individual exporters are strongly encouraged to utilize the services of established freight forwarders. Their fees-for-services can usually be built into the export price, and they provide not only security but also peace of mind.

When the shipping company receives the goods, it provides you with a receipt known as a **bill of lading (B/L)**. If the shipment is by air, the proper form is an **air waybill**. Both forms provide a full description of the shipment's contents. The exporter then prepares the required documents that may include an insurance policy, consular invoice, and other permits or certificates specified in the terms of sale. These documents go to your bank (or to your freight forwarder who also can coordinate all documentation). Your bank sends the importer's bank copies of all documents, including the bill of lading receipt from the shipping company. The importer's bank negotiates—reviews—the final documents for errors or omissions. Once satisfied that everything is in order, the importer's bank then transfers (usually electronically) payment to your bank, according to the terms of sale. Various international payment methods are presented in Chapter 9 of this text. Meanwhile, the goods are en route.

All export documents are ultimately forwarded to the importer (or to their customs broker) who must present transmitted copies of the original bill of lading in order to claim the goods at the importer's port-of-entry.[18]

Your first export transaction is complete. May it lead to many more!

KEY TERMS

> AIR WAYBILL

> BILL OF LADING (B/L)

> CONSUMER DEMAND

> EXPORT ADMINISTRATION REGULATIONS (EARs)

> EXPORT MANAGEMENT COMPANIES (EMCs)

> EXPORTING

> INTELLECTUAL PROPERTY

> MARKET RESEARCH

> PIGGYBACKING

> PRIMARY DATA

> PRODUCTS

> PRO FORMA INVOICE

> SECONDARY DATA

> STOCKING DISTRIBUTORS

> TRADE SHOWS

Summary

Today, exporting is a necessity for many businesses seeking to grow their markets and remain competitive. Exporting is beneficial to a country as well as to its businesses, because it helps lower unemployment and trade deficits.

To be successful, an exporting organization contemplating establishing overseas channels needs a commitment from top management, including a long-term willingness to invest resources in the venture. An exportable product must meet certain criteria, particularly those of creating a competitive edge and satisfying existing demand.

Some of the challenges potential exporters need to face include determining the company's readiness to export and its export potential. Once a decision is reached, several overseas market entry options are available. Developing a basic Business/ Marketing Plan and an Export Marketing Plan geared to the particular foreign market are the next essential steps. To make the plans effective, the findings gained from conducting market research serve as the foundation for developing overseas marketing strategies.

Two useful places to begin research are the local library and the Internet. Other sources include consulting the U.S. Department of Commerce and relevant trade associations and enrolling in college courses in international trade. A step-by-step approach culminates in attending trade shows and then participating as an exhibitor.

Review Questions

1. Why is exporting important to U.S. businesses both large and small?

2. Explain four reasons for businesses to export.

3. Name three or four of the concerns top management must resolve in ascertaining that a business is export-ready.

4. Cite five factors to consider in determining a company's export potential.

5. Explain several reasons why a written Export Marketing Plan is important.

Discussion Questions and Activities

1. Why is it necessary to consider a venture into export as requiring a long-term commitment from top management?

2. If a major company executive likes to travel, what could be the advantages of that person's assuming the responsibility for managing the export venture? What could be the disadvantages of such an arrangement?

3. Why is it important for a company to do market research when creating an Export Marketing Plan? What would be the advantages and disadvantages of engaging an independent firm to conduct the research?

4. What are some of the benefits of attending relevant trade shows before attempting to participate in one?

Chapter 4 Case

Basics of Exporting:
Health and Beauty Aids for Africa

Consumer demand for health and beauty aids, that is, cosmetics and fragrances, has been emerging in Africa, which is not only the world's second-largest continent but has many growing economies. To meet an increasing fashion interest in Nigeria, the MAC division of Estée Lauder cosmetics decided to offer its products in the oil-rich capital Lagos, as well as in the nations of Botswana and Zambia. Earlier, MAC had conducted preliminary research in its Strasbourg-St. Denis store in Paris whose clients were mainly African. Here the company was able to add six or so deeper colors to its foundations product line. It also learned of cultural differences and consumer preferences in the three areas: Nigerians seek out trendy fashions and luxury goods, while customers in Botswana and Zambia are more conservative.

The French health and beauty aids company L'Oréal entered the African market by purchasing a Kenyan manufacturer of skin and hair care goods marketed to East Africa. Its product lines are easily recognized because of L'Oréal's ownership of Softsheen Carson, which markets products to 25 countries and runs an Institute for Ethnic Hair and Skin Research in Clark, New Jersey.

Procter and Gamble (P & G) has concentrated on the huge East African market, consisting of 170 million people. Here it has been marketing Old Spice, Safeguard soap, and some Oil of Olay items. P & G also introduced its antibacterial soap recently by promoting hand washing as a health measure. Too many African children die of pneumonia and diarrhea, and routine hand washing is estimated to cut the risk in half. The many people who live in the 49 nations comprising East Africa speak different languages, use different forms of money, and have different customs. Instead of marketing to individual countries, companies such as P & G concentrate on the region's growing urban areas.

Source: Pete Born and Bambina Wise, "Oh Africa!" WWD Beaut Inc. *Women's Wear Daily*, January 2013, pp. 30–33.

Questions

1. Suppose you are thinking about expanding your successful ethnic cosmetics company by entering emerging markets in Africa. You market a line of fragrances and makeup that could become popular in a number of African countries. From the information given in the case, how would you go about deciding which markets to investigate?
2. Cite the criteria in the chapter that would aid you in your search.

References

1. "Coach at 70, Chronicling the Journey from Local Leather Shop to Global Fashion Powerhouse," http://www.coach.com. *WWD Milestones*, September 26, 2011, pp. 1–44.

2. "U.S. Trade Overview 2012," Department of Commerce, June 2013. Retrieved September 2, 2013, from http://www.trade.gov/mas/ . . . /tg_ian_002065.pdf.

3. "Old Navy to Open in Philippines," *Women's Wear Daily*, September 5, 2013. Retrieved September 7, 2013, from http://www.wwd.com /retail-news/specialty -stores/old-navy-to-open -in-philippines-7112157 /print-preview/.

4. Caroline Tell, "Judith Ripka Seeks to Expand Worldwide Presence," *Women's Wear Daily*, August 25, 2008, p. 9.

5. "Introduction to Exporting," Basic Guide to Exporting, Chapter 1. Retrieved September 10, 2013, from https://new .export.gov/basic-guide /1-world-is-open.

6. Lisa Movius, "Role Reversal: American Apparel Heads to China," *Women's Wear Daily*, August 21, 2008, p. 14.

7. "Export Basics," Basic Guide to Exporting, 2012 ed. Retrieved September 5, 2013, from http:// export.gov/basicguide /eg_main_043070.asp.

8. Harvey R. Shoemack, Introduction to the Export-Import Business, Northbrook, IL: International Marketing Center. Unpublished work. N/D, pp. 2, 3.

9. Ibid.

10. "Developing an Export Strategy," Basic Guide to Exporting, Chapter 2. Retrieved September 7, 2013, from https://new .export.gov/basic-guide /2-export-strategy.

11. Ibid.

12. Op. cit., Shoemack, Introduction to the Export-Import Business.

13. Ibid.

14. "Developing a Marketing Plan," Basic Guide to Exporting, Chapter 3. Retrieved September 8, 2013, from http://export.gov/basic guide/eg_main_043075 .asp.

15. "Market Research," Export.gov—Market Research Index. Retrieved September 9, 2013, from http://export.gov/mrkt research/eg_main _018209.asp.

16. Op. cit., Shoemack, Introduction to the Export-Import Business.

17. "Export Advice," Basic Guide to Exporting, Chapter 4. Retrieved September 7, 2013, from http://export.gov/basic guide/eg_main_043077 .asp.

18. Op. cit., Shoemack, Introduction to the Export-Import Business.

Appendix: Basic Resource Links Data

Further information may be secured from additional government and private resources available to help companies new to export:

- *Private services.* The number of private resources is too great to list here, but the following are few of the essentials every exporter needs:
  - An international banker to receive payment from export sales
  - A foreign freight forwarder for shipping and documenting your exports
  - An attorney for reviewing intellectual property rights
  - Agent-distributor contracts.

  Companies will also find the services of an accountant, insurance agent, and export packer to be useful. These, and other resources, can be accessed through the Internet or off-line *Yellow Pages*, by other firms already exporting and using these services, or by most export assistance service providers.
- *Government services.* Two key agencies are generally available to provide export promotion services to companies across the nation. The first is the State Trade Office. Second, almost all states have an international group within their Department of Economic Development (some states refer to this agency as their Department of Commerce). They will provide numerous trade promotion services for firms ready to develop their global market potential. They do this by helping with global marketing and making overseas contacts.
- *Federal government agencies.* Commercial Service is a Commerce Department agency that helps U.S. companies, particularly small and medium-sized businesses, conduct sales in international markets. The agency's network includes 107 U.S. Export Assistance Centers throughout the country and more than 150 offices overseas. Each U.S. Export Assistance Center is staffed by professionals from the Small Business Administration (SBA), the U.S. Department of Commerce, the U.S. Export-Import Bank, and other public and private organizations. The U.S. Commercial Service facilitated more than $54 billion in U.S. exports and assisted over 18,500 clients in 2011.

  State and federal export promotion agencies can be contacted via their websites. They offer a wide range of export promotion services and educational programs.
- *Other agencies.* As companies begin their search for resources, they may find other agencies that provide special services that help with export development. These include the Service Core of Retired Executives (SCORE), Small Business Development Centers (SBDC), state or

city chambers of commerce, local or regional economic development agencies, university and community college extension and outreach offices, and special organizations that focus on specific areas of international activities.

There is a catch-22 to be aware of when using these services. They are promoted as services to assist firms that are prequalified as export-ready. They can identify and contact international intermediary prospects (distributors, agents, and representatives) in a given foreign country, but it is important firms are prepared to respond quickly and effectively to inquiries they generate. Companies must be ready to support those willing to represent them in the foreign market.

Exporting Links
Automated Export System
https://aesdirect.census.gov/

Bureau of Industry and Security
www.bis.doc.gov

Bureau of the Census
www.census.gov

Defense Threat Reduction Agency
www.dtra.mil

Export.gov—U.S. Commercial Service, International Trade Administration (ITA)
http://www.trade.gov/cs/

Foreign Corrupt Practices Act
http://www.justice.gov/criminal/fraud/fcpa/

International Trade Data System
www.itds.gov

Market Access and Compliance
http://trade.gov/mac/

Directorate of Defense Trade Controls
www.pmddtc.state.gov

Office of Foreign Assets Control (OFAC)
www.treas.gov/ofac

Schedule B Export Codes
www.census.gov/foreign-trade/schedules/b/

The Chemical Weapons Convention
www.cwc.gov

The Advocacy Center
www.export.gov/advocacy

Office of Trade Agreements Negotiations and Compliance
http://tcc.export.gov/

Trade Information Center
www.export.gov

U.S. Customs and Border Protection
www.cbp.gov

U.S. Department of Commerce
www.doc.gov

U.S. International Trade Administration
www.ita.doc.gov

U.S. International Trade Commission
www.usitc.gov

U.S. Trade Representative
www.ustr.gov

ATA Carnet
www.atacarnet.com

Incoterms
www.iccwbo.org/incoterms/id3045/index.html

National Association of Foreign Trade Zones
www.naftz.org

Overseas Private Investment Corporation
www.opic.gov

China's Export Controls
www.nti.org/db/china/excon.htm

Introduction To Commerce Department
Export Controls

U.S. DEPARTMENT OF COMMERCE
BUREAU OF INDUSTRY AND SECURITY
OFFICE OF EXPORTER SERVICES

Figure 5.1 **The Bureau of Industry and Security publishes a guide to U.S. export regulations and how to use them.** Source: Bureau of Industry and Security, U.S. Department of Commerce.

CHAPTER 5
U.S. EXPORT CONTROLS AND PROCEDURES

INTRODUCTION TO U.S. EXPORT CONTROLS. A Texas doctor who was also a college professor illegally exported vials of a deadly bacterium to Tanzania, but he claimed to the FBI that the shipment of his plague had been stolen. As a result of the government's investigation and his subsequent export control violation trial, the doctor was convicted on 47 counts of a 69-count indictment, fired from his college, and sentenced to two years in prison.[1]

In another criminal case, the U.S. Department of Commerce's **Bureau of Industry and Security (BIS)** announced in 2013 that Computerlinks FZCO, Dubai, United Arab Emirates, agreed to pay a $2.8 million civil penalty following allegations that it committed three violations of the Export Administration Regulations related to the transfer to Syria of devices designed to monitor and control Internet traffic. In addition to the civil penalty, which is the statutory maximum, the company has agreed to submit to independent, third-party audits.

"The Computerlinks FZCO settlement reflects the serious consequences that result when companies evade U.S. export controls. It is the result of an aggressive investigation and prosecution by BIS of the unlawful diversion of U.S. technology to Syria," said Under Secretary for Industry and Security Eric L. Hirschhorn. "It is vital that we keep technology that can repress the Syrian people out of the hands of the Syrian government."[2]

These cases are examples of how U.S. export control laws help protect the United States and its trading partners by keeping certain goods and technologies away from unfriendly countries and terrorists. This chapter provides an overview of complex and lengthy policies and procedures of U.S. export control laws and offers suggestions for exporters to follow in maintaining compliance with these laws.

Many of the U.S. executive branch agencies are responsible for regulating exports from the United States. The U.S. Department of Commerce is responsible for controlling goods and technology that are capable of being used for commercial purposes, but that also present foreign policy or national security concerns when used for military applications.

Broad export controls are maintained by BIS against countries that have been designated by the U.S. Secretary of State to be state sponsors of terrorism. In some cases, such countries are subject to partial or complete embargoes, maintained on a multilateral or unilateral basis. As a result, many exports to these countries—even of ordinary commercial items including portable digital music players, such as iPods, and digital cameras that are not typically controlled to other countries—may require authorization from the U.S. government. BIS or the Department of the Treasury's Office of Foreign Assets Control (OFAC)—or in some cases both agencies together—work to implement the licensing requirements and enforce these controls. Trade with these destinations should be undertaken with extreme caution.[3]

THE EXPORT ADMINISTRATION REGULATIONS

BIS is the primary government agency responsible for implementing and enforcing the **Export Administration Regulations (EARs)**, which regulate the export and reexport of most commercial items. The **Export Enforcement Arm (EEA)** of BIS protects U.S. national security, foreign policy, and economic interests by educating potential exporters on how to improve their compliance practices. Its job is to intercept illegal exports, investigate violations, and help prosecute violators of export control laws.[4]

The U.S. government prosecutes intentional violations of U.S. export control laws by assessing substantial fines and even prison terms for criminal violators. Even if no criminal charges are claimed, administrative (civil) penalties, such as fines and a denial of export privileges, can be assessed for other EAR violations. Offenders may be subjected to *both* criminal and administrative penalties. Criminal penalties can amount to 20 years of imprisonment and $1 million per violation. Administrative monetary penalties can amount to $11,000 per violation and $120,000 per violation in cases involving items controlled for national security reasons. Fines for export violations can amount to $1 million per violation in criminal cases, $50,000 per violation in administrative cases, and up to $120,000 per violation in certain cases involving national security issues.[5]

BIS enforcement efforts continue to focus on transactions that impose the most serious threat to U.S. national security, such as proliferation networks. In FY2013, BIS's Office of Export Enforcement's criminal investigations resulted in the criminal conviction of 52 individuals and businesses for export violations, as compared to 27 convictions in FY2012. The penalties for these convictions came to $2,694,500 in criminal fines, more than $18 million in forfeitures, and more than 881 months of imprisonment, compared to $4,786,500 in criminal fines, more than $5 million in forfeitures, and more than 187 months of imprisonment in FY2012.[6]

Criminal and administrative violations may result in the offending individual or organization being prohibited from receiving U.S. exports, and others may receive goods only if they have been licensed. The BIS website (http://www.bis .doc.gov/) features a link to actual investigations of export control and antiboycott violations, titled "Don't Let This Happen to You!" In recent years individuals have been convicted three times more often than companies, which is one reason behind our emphasis on individual responsibility.

Primary responsibility for compliance with the EARs falls on the **principal parties in interest (PPIs)** in a transaction. Generally, the PPIs in an export transaction are the U.S. seller and foreign buyer. However, in most export-control cases, BIS negotiates settlement in administrative cases before they get to a formal administrative hearing. The settlements are the result of **voluntary self-disclosures (VSDs)**, that is, the individual or company voluntarily admitting to export law violations. These voluntary admissions of administrative errors are viewed by BIS as significant mitigating factors when negotiating settlements of administrative cases. To encourage VSDs, in appropriate cases, fines and other administrative penalties could be significantly reduced if BIS became aware of the violations as a result of voluntary disclosure.[7]

The EARs place legal responsibility on anyone who has information, authority, or functions relevant to carrying out export business subject to the regulations. Included are exporters, freight forwarders, carriers (ships, planes, rail, and truck), consignees (those parties receiving the exports), and any other relevant party. The EARs apply not only to parties within the United States, but also to individuals and companies in foreign countries who are involved in transactions subject to the EARs.

REASONS FOR EXPORT CONTROLS

According to the Commerce Department, certain export controls are necessary for three major reasons: national security, foreign policy, and short supply.[8]

National Security Controls

National security (NS) export controls are placed on exports of certain strategic commodities or technology that "would make a significant contribution to the military potential of any other country or combination of countries which would prove detrimental to the national security of the United States," and are for national security reasons.

Foreign Policy Controls

Foreign policy (FP) export controls are placed on some commodities "where necessary to further significantly the foreign policy of the United States or to fulfill its declared international obligations."[9] Foreign policy controls may be commodity-oriented (crime control, and regional stability) or country specific (Iran, North Korea, Cuba, and other embargoed countries).[10]

Short Supply Controls

Controls that are used "where necessary to protect the domestic economy from the excessive drain of scarce materials and to reduce the serious inflationary impact of foreign demand (example: petroleum products)" are known as **short supply (SS) controls**.[11]

Other controls include antiterrorism (AT), suspected terrorist-enabling products; missile technologies (MT), such as specifications on missile delivery systems; nuclear proliferation (NP) products or technologies that further nuclear expansion; chemical and biological (CB) weapons; crime control (CC); regional stability (RS); computers (XP); and the United Nations (UN) controls.[12]

THE EARS AND DUAL-USE ITEMS

Note that EARs do *not* control all goods, services, and technologies. Other U.S. government agencies regulate more specialized exports. For example, the U.S. State

Department has authority over defense articles and defense services. A list of other agencies involved in export controls can be found on the State Department website (http://www.state.gov/strategictrade/resources/c43182.htm).[13]

The exports regulated by BIS are often referred to as **dual-use items**. They may have a commercial application but also a potential military or proliferation use, as a weapon of mass destruction, conventional arms, or **end-use violations** by terrorists.[14]

Nearly all U.S. exporters trade in items that are subject to the export control laws administered by BIS. Controlled items tend to be sophisticated hardware, software, or technologies. However, purely commercial items without an obvious military use, such as the chemical ingredients used in ballpoint pens, may be precursors to chemical weapons and are also subject to EARs.

It is essential for potential exporters, before processing a transaction, to consider exactly what they are selling, to whom it will go, and how it will ultimately be used. They must be certain their exports will not adversely affect national security or U.S. foreign policy interests.

Most of the dual-use export control system is spelled out on the EAR website (http://www.bis.doc.gov/index.php/regulations/export-administration-regulations -ear?tmpl=component&print=1&page=/). The following information presents a general understanding of the U.S. regulations and how to use them. It is designed for those firms and individuals who are new to exporting and, in particular, new to export controls.[15] However, since the regulations are still complex to novices, they will likely turn to a licensed **freight forwarder**—an independent service organization that, for a fee, expedites export shipments by providing information and assistance on U.S. export regulations and documentation, shipping methods, freight costs, and major foreign import regulations.

The BIS website provides a link to the EARs, the bureau's regulations governing exports of dual-use items. The site also provides discussions of certain key regulatory policy areas, including policies governing exports of high-performance computers, exports of encryption products, deemed exports, U.S. antiboycott regulations, special regional considerations, the multilateral export control regimes, and the technical advisory committees.

The BIS website on EARs also includes answers to frequently asked questions, detailed step-by-step instructions for determining if a transaction is subject to the regulations, how to request a commodity classification or advisory opinion, and how to apply for a license. Using the government website or the assistance of a freight forwarder cannot substitute for consulting the EARs.[16]

NEW DUAL-USE EXPORT CONTROL INITIATIVE

At the 2013 annual BIS Export Control Forum in Washington, DC, the U.S. government announced a new Export Control Reform Initiative to protect and enhance U.S. national security interests. By fundamentally reforming the export control system, the government ensured that dual-use export control policies and practices support the National Security Strategy while facilitating U.S. economic and technological leadership.[17]

Export Control Reforms
The conference discussed recent changes made to the **Automated Export System (AES)** as a result of the Initial Implementation Rule for Export Control Reform. The main topic was the evolution of AES to reflect changes to the Foreign Trade Regulations of the Bureau of the Census. The changes are of particular interest to exporters who are shipping items subject to the EARs, including changes to BIS's AES filing and post-departure filing requirements. These new procedures may affect software providers and companies with in-house programs that interface with AES.

Changes to many of the EARs license exceptions will become effective October 15, 2014. They facilitate the realignments in the Commerce Control List and the International Traffic in Arms Regulations of the Department of State. The new "600 series" of Export Control Classification Numbers within the EARs allows for identification, classification, and control of items transferred from the U.S. Munitions List to the Commerce Control List.[18] Details of these export control reforms can be found on the BIS website.

Countries around the world face unprecedented security challenges from threats of terrorism to proliferation of nuclear, biological, and chemical weapons and advanced conventional weapons to instability. The security issue is further affected by an unprecedented economic challenge from the increasing worldwide diffusion of high technology and globalization of markets. In this country, U.S. government policies must ensure that the dual-use export control system is precisely focused to meet those challenges.

"Export control reform is a crucial piece of our national security agenda. We must continue to prevent key products and technologies from falling into the wrong hands. The core mission of our export control system is not being compromised in any way by these new reforms. In fact, these reforms are increasing our security by allowing greater interoperability with our allies," remarked Commerce Secretary Penny Pritzker at the 2013 Update Conference on Export Controls and Policy.[19]

Foreign End-Users
The dual-use export control system increasingly focuses on foreign end-users of U.S. high-technology products. This program encourages growth in trade to reliable foreign customers, while denying access to sensitive technologies to proliferators, international terrorists, and other foreign parties acting contrary to U.S. national security and foreign policy interests.[20]

Keeping track of foreign end-users involves the end-user process, which is intended to facilitate legitimate exports to civilian end-users and reliable foreign companies, while also imposing additional scrutiny of exports to foreign parties with a record of activities contrary to U.S. foreign policy and national security interests.

U.S. Competitiveness

To sustain U.S. global economic competitiveness and innovation—keys to the nation's domestic economic recovery and long-term national security—the U.S. government's export control agencies constantly reassess policies to ensure that the most sensitive items are regulated as well as to ensure that other items are available for trade. The current focus on U.S. competitiveness includes the government's systematic review of the list of controlled dual-use items, the revision of controls on intra-company transfers and encryption products, and the review of reexport controls.

Transparency

U.S. exporters need sufficient information to support both domestic security and competitiveness goals. There must be enough clear communication between the government and potential exporters to enable compliance. In order to ensure the public is knowledgeable about the Commerce Department's policies and practices, the Department publishes its advisory opinions and lists of foreign parties warranting higher scrutiny. The government's transparency fosters public awareness.

A number of industry associations, as well as individual companies, work closely with government agencies to implement these reforms to ensure that dual-use exports are controlled and security threats are addressed, while also maintaining the economic competitiveness of our country.

In addition to the U.S. export control policy for dual-use items, BIS is also charged with the development, implementation, and interpretation of the anti-boycott provisions of the Export Administration Act. The provisions encourage, and in some cases require, U.S. businesses to refuse to participate in foreign boycotts that the United States does not sanction, such as the Arab boycott of Israel. Domestic companies and any of their foreign operations are required to report receipt of boycott-related requests.[21]

The EARs impose responsibilities on all parties to an export transaction: manufacturers/exporters, freight forwarders, transport carriers (ship, air, rail, and truck), and consignees (those receiving the exported goods).

EXPORT LICENSING REQUIREMENTS

As discussed in Chapter 1, any item sent from the United States to a foreign destination is an export. Items include commodities, software or technology, clothing, building materials, circuit boards, vehicles and parts, blueprints, design plans, retail software packages, and technical information.

How an item is transported outside of the United States does not matter in determining export license requirements. For example, an item can be sent by regular mail or hand-carried on an airplane. A set of technical diagrams can be sent via fax to a foreign destination, software can be uploaded to or downloaded from an Internet site, or technology can be transmitted via email or during a telephone conversation. Regardless of the method used for the transfer, the transaction is considered an export for export control purposes.[22]

An item is also considered an export even if it is only leaving the United States temporarily; if it is leaving the United State but is not for sale, such as a trade show exhibit; or if it is going to a wholly owned U.S. subsidiary in a foreign country. Even a foreign-origin item exported from the United States, transmitted or transshipped through the United States, or being returned from the United States to its foreign country of origin is considered an export. Finally, release of technology or source code subject to the EARs to a foreign national in the United States is considered to be an export to the home country of the foreign national under the EARs. An employee's innocent review of technical drawings, while sitting on a park bench at lunch, may result in those drawings being considered an export, should a foreign national sit down next to the employee and casually look at the materials. If so, the incidental action would require compliance with all EARs regarding exports to the country of the foreign national.[23]

HOW TO DETERMINE IF YOU NEED A COMMERCE EXPORT LICENSE

According to the U.S. Commerce Department's export controls, a relatively small percentage of total U.S. exports and reexports, dual-use in particular, require an **export license**, which would come from BIS. License requirements depend on an item's technical characteristics, the destination, the end-user, and the end-use. The exporter-of-record must determine whether an export requires a license. When making that determination, consider the following questions:

- What are you exporting?
- Where is your export going?
- Who will receive your export?
- What will be the end-use of your export?[24]

What Are You Exporting?

A key in determining whether an export license is needed from the Commerce Department is researching whether your intended export has a specific **Export Control Classification Number (ECCN)**, the alpha-numeric code that identifies the level of export control for all export "items, including products, technology, and software that are exported from the United States."[25] All ECCNs are listed in the **Commerce Control List (CCL)**, which includes items subject to the Commerce Department's export licensing authority. The CCL does not include those items exclusively controlled for export or reexport by another department or agency of the U.S. government. In instances where agencies other than the Commerce Department administer controls over related items, entries in the CCL contain a reference to these controls. BIS maintains the CCL within the EARs. The CCL is available on the Government Printing Office website (http://www.gpo.gov) and the Commerce Department website (http://www.bis.doc.gov/index.php/regulations /commerce-control-list-ccl).[26]

BIS also maintains the **Commerce Country Chart (CCC)**, which can be found in Supplement No. 1 to part 738 of the EARs. It contains licensing requirements based on destination and reasons for export controls. In combination with the CCL, the CCC allows you to determine whether an export license is required for certain items to be exported to specific countries.[27]

Classifying Your Item

The proper classification of your item is essential to determining any licensing requirements under the EARs. You may classify the item on your own, ask your freight forwarder, or submit a classification request and BIS will determine the ECCN for you.[28]

Commerce Control List Categories

When reviewing the CCL to determine if your item is specified by an ECCN, you will first need to determine in which of 10 broad categories of the CCC your item is included and next consider to which of the five specific product groups your exports apply.

For example, assume that you have lie detectors—polygraph or psychological stress analysis equipment—that are used to help law enforcement agencies. What is your ECCN? Start by looking in the CCL under the category of electronics (Category 3) and the product group that covers equipment (Product Group A). Then read through the list to find whether your item is included. In this example the item is 3A981 (see Figures 5.2 and 5.3).

If your item falls under Commerce Department jurisdiction and is not listed on the CCL, it is designated as **EAR99**. These items generally consist of low-technology consumer goods and do not require a license in many situations. However, if your proposed export of an EAR99 item is to an embargoed country, to an end-user of concern, or in support of a prohibited end-use, a license is required and you will most likely have difficulty in obtaining one.[29]

Where Are Your Exports Going?

Restrictions vary from country to country. The most restricted destinations are embargoed countries and those countries designated as supporting terrorist activities. As of this writing embargoed countries include Cuba, Iran, Sudan, Taliban-controlled Afghanistan, and Syria. There are U.S. export restrictions on some products, for example nuclear devices, that are worldwide.

Figure 5.2   Commerce Control List Categories

0 = Nuclear materials, facilities, and equipment (and miscellaneous items)
1 = Materials, chemicals, microorganisms, and toxins
2 = Materials processing
3 = Electronics
4 = Computers
5 = Telecommunications and information security
6 = Sensors and lasers
7 = Navigation and avionics
8 = Marine
9 = Aerospace and propulsion

Figure 5.3   Five Product Groups

A. Systems, equipment,
   and components
B. Test, inspection,
   and production equipment
C. Material
D. Software
E. Technology

Note: All ECCNs are listed in the Commerce Control List (CCL) (Supplement No. 1 to Part 774 of the EAR) which is available on the government printing office website. The CCL is divided into ten broad categories, and each category is further subdivided into five products.

Source: http://www.bis.doc.gov/index.php/regulations/commerce-control-list-ccl.

The EARs describe embargoed destinations and refers to certain additional export controls imposed by the **Office of Foreign Assets Control of the Treasury Department (OFAC)**. The agency administers and enforces economic and trade sanctions based on U.S. foreign policy and national security goals against targeted foreign countries, terrorists, international narcotics traffickers, and those engaged in activities related to the proliferation of nuclear, biological, and chemical weapons.[30]

The OFAC administers a number of U.S. economic sanctions and embargoes that target geographic regions and governments. Comprehensive sanctions programs currently include Burma (Myanmar), Cuba, Iran, Sudan, and Syria. Other noncomprehensive programs include the Western Balkans, Belarus, Côte d'Ivoire, Democratic Republic of the Congo, Iraq, Liberia (Former Regime of Charles Taylor), Persons Undermining the Sovereignty of Lebanon or Its Democratic Processes and Institutions, Libya, North Korea, Somalia, and Zimbabwe, as well as other programs targeting individuals and entities located around the world.

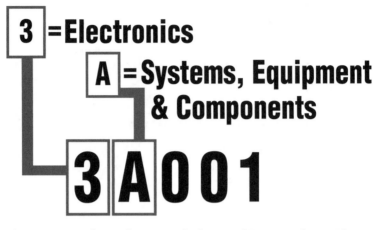

Figure 5.4 According to the Bureau of Industry and Security website, "A key for exporters to determine whether an export license is needed from the U.S. department of Commerce is to reference the CCL for a specific Export Control Classification Number (ECCN). An alpha-numeric code, the ECCN describes a particular item or type of item, and shows the export controls the U.S. government has placed on that item. If an item is subject to U.S. Department of Commerce jurisdiction and is not listed on the CCL, it is designated as EAR99. Those items are usually low-technology consumer goods that do not usually require a license to be exported."

Source: Export Control Basics at http://www.bis.doc.gov/exportingbasics.htm.

The OFAC acts under presidential wartime and national emergency powers, as well as authority granted by specific legislation, to impose controls on transactions and may freeze foreign assets under U.S. jurisdiction. Many of the sanctions are based on United Nations and other international mandates, are multilateral in scope, and involve close cooperation with allied governments.[31]

How to Cross-Reference the ECCN with the Commerce Country Chart

Once you have classified potential export items, the next step is to determine whether you need an export license based on the "reasons for control" of the item and the country of ultimate destination.[32]

Begin this process by cross-referencing the ECCN with the CCC, which identifies the reasons for export controls by country. When used together, they define the items subject to export controls based solely on the technical parameters of the item and the country of ultimate destination.

Below the main heading on the CCC, you will find the "Reason for Control" (NS for national security, AT for antiterrorism, CC for crime control, etc.). Below the titles, the columns on the CCC indicate the specific licensing requirements for exports identified by your ECCN as they apply to different countries.

Reason for Control

Country	Chemical & Biological Weapons			Nuclear Nonproliferations		National Security		Missile Tech	Regional Stability		Firearms Convention	Crime Control			Anti-Terrorism	
	CB 1	CB 2	CB 3	NP 1	NP 2	NS 1	NS 2	MT 1	RS 1	RS 2	FC 1	CC 1	CC 2	CC 3	AT 1	AT 2
Guyana	X	X		X		X	X	X	X	X	X	X		X		
Haiti	X	X		X		X	X	X	X	X	X	X		X		
Honduras	X	X		X		X	X	X	X	X	X	X		X		
Hong Kong	X	X		X		X		X	X	X			X		X	
Hungary	X					X		X	X							
Iceland	X			X		X		X	X							

Figure 5.5 **The Commerce Country Chart identifies reasons for U.S. export controls by matching the ECN number with the export target country.**

Source: http://www.bis.doc.gov/index.php/policy-guidance/country-guidance.

If there is an "X" in the box based on the reason(s) for control of your item and the country of destination, a license is required, unless a **license exception** excluding that item from licensing is available. The EARs set forth the license requirements and licensing policy for most reasons for control.[33]

If there is no "X" in the control code column(s) specified under your ECCN and country of destination, you will not need an export license unless you are exporting to an end-user or end-use of concern.

Who Will Receive Your Export?

Part of any firm's export control compliance is to review several lists of individuals and entities to whom and to which no exports are permitted—no matter what the product may be. These lists of parties-of-concern[34] (http://www.bis.doc.gov/index .php/policy-guidance) should be reviewed before each export transaction and recommended even before going through the trouble of applying for an export license. Violators of the EARs may be placed on one of the following lists:

- Entity List
- Denied Persons List
- Treasury Department's Specially Designated Nationals and Blocked Persons List
- Debarred List
- Unverified List

Placement on a list can apply even to goods or services that don't normally require a license. It is a violation of the EARs to participate in an export transaction subject to the EARs with a denied party.

Certain individuals and organizations may only receive goods if they have been licensed, even items that do not normally require a license based on the ECCN and CCC or the "catch-all" EAR99 designation. The EARs provide that BIS may inform exporters, individually or through amendment to the EAR, that a license is required for exports or reexports to certain prohibited parties. The EAR maintains lists of such parties of concern, including the following:

Entity List

The **Entity List**, established in February 1997, informs the public of parties whose activities imposed a risk of diverting exported and reexported items into programs related to nuclear, biological, and chemical weapons. (See Figure 5.6.) Since then, the grounds for listing a person, company, or even a country on the Entity List have

Supplement No. 4 to Part 744 - Entity List

This Supplement lists certain entities subject to license requirements for specified items under this part 744 of the EAR. License requirements for these entities include exports, reexports, and transfers (in-country) unless otherwise stated. This list of entities is revised and updated on a periodic basis in this Supplement by adding new or amended notifications and deleting notifications no longer in effect.

Country	Entity	License Requirement	License Review Policy	Federal Register Citation
Afghanistan	Abdul Satar Ghoura, 501, 5th Floor, Amanullah Sancharaki Market Opp Chaman E Huzuri, Kabul, Afghanistan; *and* Flat No. 41 Block No. 24 Macroyan 3, Kabul, Afghanistan.	For all items subject to the EAR. (See §744.11 of the EAR.)	Presumption of denial.	76 FR 71867, 11/21/2011.
	Afghan-German Construction Company, Golaye Park, Shari Naw, Kabul, Afghanistan, *and* Dasht Qala, Takhar Province, Afghanistan.	For all items subject to the EAR. (See §744.11 of the EAR.)	Presumption of denial.	77 FR 25055, 4/27/12.
	Assadullah Majed, 42S WD 18476 22167 Kabul, Afghanistan; *and* A2 Ground Floor, City Computer Plaza, Shar-e-Naw, Kabul, Afghanistan.	For all items subject to the EAR. (See §744.11 of the EAR.)	Presumption of denial.	76 FR 71867, 11/21/2011.

Figure 5.6 The Entity List is just one of several lists a potential exporter or importer is required to check to be sure their customer or "end-user" of their item is not in violation of the U.S. Export Administration Regulations, which would prohibit the transaction.

Source: U.S. Bureau of Industry and Security. Retrieved March 3, 2014, from http://www.bis.doc.gov/index.php/regulations/export-administration-regulations-ear.

expanded to include entities sanctioned by the State Department for which United States foreign policy goals are served by imposing additional license requirements on exports and reexports to them.[35]

Publishing this list puts exporters on notice of export license requirements that apply to exports to these parties. While this list will assist exporters in determining whether an entity poses proliferation concerns, it is not comprehensive. It does not relieve exporters of the responsibility to determine the nature and activities of their potential customers using BIS's *Guidance and Red Flags.*[36]

Denied Persons List

U.S. firms may not participate in an export or reexport transaction subject to the EARs with a person whose export privileges have been denied by BIS. A list of those firms and individuals, the **Denied Persons List**, is available on the BIS website (http://www.bis.doc.gov/dpl/thedeniallist.asp). Note that some denied persons are located within the United States. If approached by a person whose export privileges have been denied, you must not make the sale and should report the situation to BIS's Office of Export Enforcement.[37]

Treasury Department's Specially Designated Nationals and Blocked Persons List

The Treasury Department's **Specially Designated Nationals and Blocked Persons List** is maintained by the OFAC. It is comprised of individuals and organizations that represent restricted countries or those known to be involved in terrorism and narcotics trafficking.[38]

The Unverified List

The **Unverified List** is composed of firms for which BIS was unable to complete an end-use check. The list is available on the BIS website (http://www.bis.doc.gov /enforcement/unverifiedlist/unverified_parties.html). Firms on the unverified list present a "red flag" that exporters have a duty to inquire about before making an export to them.[39]

What Will Be the End-Use of Your Export?

Some end-uses are prohibited while others may require a license. For example, you may not export to certain entities involved in the proliferation of nuclear, biological, and chemical weapons and the missiles to deliver them without specific authorization, no matter what your item is.[40]

EXPORT AUTHORIZATION

There is no such thing as an "exporter's license." Authorization to export is determined by the transaction: what the item is, where it is going, who will receive it, and how it will be used. The majority of U.S. commercial exports do *not* require a

SPOTLIGHT ON GLOBAL TRADE 5.1
Things to Look for in Export Transactions

Exporters can avoid EAR violations by watching out for the following **Red Flags**. Also helpful is the BIS website, *Know Your Customer Guidance*, at http://www.bis.doc.gov/index.php/component/content /article/23-compliance-and -training/47-know-your-customer-guidance.

Red Flags

- The customer or its address is similar to one of the parties found on the BIS list of denied persons.
- The customer or purchasing agent is reluctant to offer information about the end-use of the item.
- The product's capabilities do not fit the buyer's line of business, such as an order for sophisticated computers for a small bakery.
- The item ordered is incompatible with the technical level of the country to which it is being shipped, such as semiconductor manufacturing equipment being shipped to a country that has no electronics industry.
- The customer is willing to pay cash for a very expensive item when the terms of sale would normally call for financing.
- The customer has little or no business background.
- The customer is unfamiliar with the product's performance characteristics but still wants the product.
- Routine installation, training, or maintenance services are declined by the customer.
- Delivery dates are vague, or deliveries are planned for out-of-the-way destinations.
- A freight-forwarding firm is listed as the product's final destination.
- The shipping route is abnormal for the product and destination.
- Packaging is inconsistent with the stated method of shipment or destination.
- When questioned, the buyer is evasive and especially unclear about the whether the purchased product is for domestic use, for export, or for reexport.

If you have a reason to believe a violation is taking place or has occurred, you may report it to the Department of Commerce by calling its 24-hour hotline number at 1–800–424–2980, or if you prefer, request a form to submit a confidential tip.

Source: Bureau of Industry and Security. Retrieved January 13, 2014, from http://www.bis.doc.gov/index.php/compliance-a-training/export-management-a-compliance/freight-forwarder-guidance/23-compliance-a-training/51-red-flag-indicators.

license. The three types of export authorization are no license required, license, and license exception.[41]

No License Required (NLR)

Most exports from the United States do not require a license, and are therefore exported under the designation **No License Required (NLR)**. Except in those relatively few transactions when a license requirement applies because the destination is subject to embargo or because of a proliferation end-use or end-user, no license is required when:

- The item to be shipped is not on the CCL (that is, its EAR99).
- The item is on the CCL but there is no "X" in the box on the CCC under the appropriate reason for control column on the row for the country of destination.

In each of these situations, you would enter "NLR" on your export documents.

License

If your item requires a **License** to be exported, you must apply for one to BIS. If your application is approved, you will have an export license number and expiration date to use on your export documents. A BIS-issued license is usually valid for two years.

License Exception

If a license is normally required for your transaction, a **License Exception** may be available. License exceptions, and the conditions on their use, are set forth in the EAR. If an export is eligible for a license exception, use the designation of that license exception (example, LVS, GBS, and TMP) on the export documents.

APPLYING FOR AN EXPORT LICENSE

If an export license is required, exporters must prepare a Form BIS-748P, Multipurpose Application Form and submit it for review and approval. The application form can be used for requesting authority to export or reexport, or to request BIS to classify your item for you. Requirements for submitting a license are detailed in the EAR.

The best and fastest way to submit an export application form is to use the online **Simplified Network Application Process Redesign (SNAP-R)**,[42] http://www.bis.doc.gov/index.php/licensing/simplified-network-application -process-redesign-snap-r. SNAP-R includes enhanced security, the ability to attach supporting documentation electronically, user access rights, and the ability for BIS licensing officers to view work items and supporting documents electronically. Exporters can also request a Form BIS-748P from the U.S. Department of Commerce Office of Exporter Services. Exporters must be certain to follow the instructions on the form carefully. In most cases, technical brochures and support documentation must also be included.

Export License Application Processing

BIS conducts a complete analysis of the license application along with all documentation submitted in support of the application. The bureau reviews the item, its destination, and its end-use, and considers the reliability of each party to the transaction. In addition to the review, applications are often sent for interagency review by the Departments of State, Energy, and/or Defense.

License Status

For the status of pending export license applications and commodity classification requests, exporters can contact the **System for Tracking Export License Applications (STELA)**. STELA is an automated voice response system that will provide up-to-the-minute status on any pending license application or commodity classification. Provide the number of your license application in order to determine licensing status.[43]

How to Avoid Delays

The fastest way to submit an export application is over the Internet, using SNAP-R. If submitting a hard copy application through the mail, exporters should take care to avoid common errors that often account for delays in processing. These are as follows:

- Failing to sign the application
- Failing to submit a typewritten application
- Inadequately responding to the section of the application where the specific end-use of the products or technical data is to be described
- Answering vaguely or entering "unknown" (this may even cause a rejection of the application)
- Inadequately responding to the section of the application "Description of Commodity or Technical Data"

Exporters must be specific and are encouraged to attach additional material that thoroughly explains the product.

SPOTLIGHT ON GLOBAL TRADE 5.2
Summary of Steps to Process an Export

- Determine if the export is under U.S. Department of Commerce jurisdiction. If the export items are not listed on the Commerce Control List (CCL), and no other U. S. government agency claims control, the goods can usually be shipped under the no license required (NLR) authority.
- Classify intended exports according to the Commerce Control List (CCL) and the Export Control Classification Number (ECCN). Unlisted items, if still subject to Commerce Department jurisdiction, will be designated EAR99; generally low-technology consumer goods do not usually require a license. The ECCN is used to identify the reasons for control (see the polygraph example in the "Commerce Control List Categories" section).
- Cross-reference the ECCN controls against the Commerce Country Chart (CCC) to see if a license is required. If none is required, the goods can be shipped under the authority, no license required. If yes, determine if a license exception is available before applying for a license.
- Check that no illegal or restricted end-users or end-uses are involved with your export transaction. If restricted end-users or end-uses are involved, determine if you can proceed with the transaction or must apply for a license.

Export your item using the correct ECCN and the appropriate symbol (NLR, license exception, or license number and expiration date) on your export documentation, such as the **Electronic Export Information (EEI)**, formerly known as the Shipper's Export Declaration (SED).

Source: U.S. Bureau of Industry and Security. Retrieved January 13, 2014, from http://www .bis.doc.gov/index.php/forms-documents/doc . . . /142-eccn-pdf, p 9.

EXPORT DOCUMENTS

The following documents are commonly used in exporting, but which of them are necessary in a particular transaction depends on the requirements of the U.S. government and the government of the importing country. Documentation required for export shipments varies widely according to the country of destination and the type of product being shipped. Determining what additional documentation is necessary can be a frustrating process.

Exporters can complete and file all required paperwork in-house or choose to appoint an experienced freight forwarder to expedite the formidable amount of paperwork that exporting requires. The following sections list common documents and information resources to help with this process. They are divided into the following subsections:

- Common export documents
- Transportation documents
- Export compliance documents
- Certificates of origin
- Other certificates for shipments of specific goods
- Other export-related documents
- Temporary shipment documents
- Export license

Common Export Documents
Commercial Invoice
A **commercial invoice** is a bill for the goods from the seller to the buyer. These invoices are often used by governments to determine the true value of goods when assessing customs duties. Governments that use the commercial invoice to control imports will often specify its form, content, number of copies, language to be used, and other characteristics.

Export Packing List
Considerably more detailed and informative than a standard domestic packing list, an **export packing list** lists seller, buyer, shipper, invoice number, date of shipment, mode of transport, and carrier. The list also itemizes quantity, description, the type of package—such as a box, crate, drum, or carton—the quantity of packages, total net and gross weight (in kilograms), package marks, and dimensions, if appropriate. A packing list may serve as a conforming document, but it is not a substitute for a commercial invoice. U.S. and foreign customs officials may use the export packing list to check the cargo.

Pro Forma Invoice
A **pro forma invoice** is an invoice prepared by the exporter before shipping the goods, informing the buyer of the goods to be sent, their value, and other key specifications. It also can be used as an offering of sale or price quotation.

Transportation Documents
Airway Bill
Air freight shipments require **airway bills**. Airway bills are shipper-specific (i.e., USPS, FedEx, UPS, DHL, etc.).

Bill of Lading
A **bill of lading (B/L)** is a contract between the *owner of the goods* and the *carrier* (as with domestic shipments). For vessels, there are two types: a straight bill of lading, which is nonnegotiable, and a negotiable or shipper's order bill of lading. The latter can be bought, sold, or traded while the goods are in transit. The customer usually needs an original as proof of ownership to take possession of the goods.

Electronic Export Information Filing
Electronic Export Information (EEI), formally known as the Shipper's Export Declaration (SED), is the most common of all export control documents. It is used for compiling official U.S. export statistics and for enforcement of U.S. export laws.[44]

The EEI is required for shipments above $2,500 and for shipments of any value requiring an export license. It has to be electronically filed via the **AESDirect** online system, which is a free service from the U.S. Census and Customs Bureaus. See "AES Frequently Asked Questions" at http://www.census.gov/foreign-trade /aes/documentlibrary/mandatoryaesfaqs.html.

The EEI is required for shipments to Puerto Rico, the U.S. Virgin Islands, and the former Pacific Trust Territories even though they are not considered exports (unless each "Schedule B" item in the shipment is under $2,500). Shipments to Canada do not require an EEI except in cases where an export license is required. (Shipments to third countries passing through Canada do need an EEI.)

Numerous videos are available from the BIS website (http://www.bis.doc.gov) on AES Direct, including *Registering for AESDirect*, *Filing a Shipment in AESDirect*, *Response Messages from AES*, *Proof of Filing Citations*, and *AESDirect—The Shipment Manager*.

Export Compliance Documents
Export Licenses
An **export license** is a government document that authorizes the export of specific goods in specific quantities to a particular destination. This document may be required for most or all exports to some countries or for other countries only under special circumstances. Examples of export license certificates include those issued by BIS (dual-use articles), the State Department's Directorate of Defense Trade Controls (defense articles), the Nuclear Regulatory Commission (nuclear materials), and the U.S. Drug Enforcement Administration (controlled substances and precursor chemicals).

Several videos are available on export licenses from the BIS website, including *Export Compliance Introduction, Exporting Commercial Items: ECCNs and EAR99, The Commerce Control List and Self-Classification,* and *Exporting EAR99 Items: Screening Your Transaction, Lists to Check and Red Flags.*

Destination Control Statement

A Destination Control Statement (DCS) is required for exports from the United States for items on the CCL that are outside of EAR99 (products for which no license is required) or controlled under the International Traffic in Arms Regulations (ITAR). A DCS appears on the commercial invoice, ocean bill of lading, or airway bill to notify the carrier and all foreign parties that the item can be exported only to certain destinations. For more information, watch relevant videos on the BIS website, such as *Export Compliance Introduction* and *Exporting Commercial Items: ECCNs and EAR99.*

Certificates of Origin
Generic Certificate of Origin

The Certificate of Origin (CO) is required by some countries for all or only certain products. In many cases, a statement of origin printed on company letterhead will suffice. The exporter should verify whether a CO is required with the buyer and/or an experienced shipper/freight forwarder or the Trade Information Center.

Some countries (e.g., numerous Middle Eastern countries) require that certificate of origin be notarized, certified by the local chamber of commerce, and legalized by the commercial section of the consulate of the destination country. For certain Middle Eastern countries, the National U.S.-Arab Chamber of Commerce may also provide such services.

For textile products, an importing country may require a certificate of origin issued by the manufacturer. The number of required copies and language may vary from country to country.

Certificate of Origin for Claiming Benefits under Free Trade Agreements

Special certificates of origin may be required for countries with which the United States has free trade agreements (FTAs). The BIS website features a webinar on FTAs. The site offers potential exporters more information on how to claim certificates of origin.

Some certificates, including those required by the North American Free Trade Agreement (NAFTA) and the FTAs with Israel and Jordan, are prepared by the *exporter*. Others, including those required by the FTAs with Australia and the Dominican Republic-Central America-United States Free Trade Agreement (CAFTA-DR) countries Chile and Morocco, are the *importer's* responsibility.

Certificate of Origin for Goods Not Manufactured in the United States

Certificates of origin for goods not manufactured in the United States can be obtained from the U.S. Chamber of Commerce. The U.S. Chamber of Commerce uses **EZCertOrigin**, a service provided by ICS Consulting, LLC, to process all requests submitted for certificates of origin (both U.S. and non-U.S.). Its website (https://www.ezcertorigin.com/Instructions.aspx) is the place to obtain the required forms and detailed instructions on how to fill them out.[45]

The fee for each certificate (as of April 25, 2014) is as follows:

- $150.00 for U.S. Chamber of Commerce contributing members (include U.S. Chamber member ID number).
- $500.00 for non-U.S. Chamber of Commerce members
- $5.00 per copy of each additional certificate
- $5.00 per invoice signed by the U.S. Chamber of Commerce

Other Certificates for Shipments of Specific Goods

Additional certificates are needed for different purposes. Check with an importer or freight forwarder, or contact the Trade Information Center at http://export .gov/logistics/eg_main_018121.asp#TopOfPage for further information.

Certificate of Analysis

A certificate of analysis can be required for seeds, grain, health foods, dietary supplements, fruits and vegetables, and pharmaceutical products.

Dangerous Goods Certificate

Exports submitted for handling by air carriers and air freight forwarders classified as dangerous goods need to be accompanied by the Shipper's Declaration for Dangerous Goods required by the International Air Transport Association (IATA). The exporter is responsible for accuracy of the form and ensuring that requirements related to packaging, marking, and other required information by IATA have been met.

For shipment of dangerous goods, it is critical to identify goods by proper name and to comply with packaging and labeling requirements, which vary depending on the type of product shipper and the country to which the shipment is sent. More information on labeling/regulations is available from the International Air Transportation Association or Department of Transportation— HAZMAT websites: http://www.iata.org/publications/dgr/Pages/hazard-labels .aspx and https://hazmatonline.phmsa.dot.gov/services/publication_documents /measure_up.pdf.

For ocean exports, hazardous material regulations are contained in the International Maritime Dangerous Goods regulations. For details, see their website: http://www.unzco.com/regre/maritimere.htm.

Pre-Shipment Inspections

The governments of a number of countries have contracted with international inspection companies to provide **pre-shipment inspections** that verify the quantity, quality, and price of shipments imported into their countries. The purpose of pre-shipment inspections is to ensure that the price charged by the exporter reflects the true value of the goods, to prevent substandard goods from entering the country, and to deflect attempts to avoid payment of customs duties. Requirements for pre-shipment inspection are normally spelled out in letter-of-credit or other documentary requirements. Inspections companies include Bureau Veritas, SGS, and Intertek. Some countries require pre-shipment inspection certificates for shipments of used merchandise.

Insurance Certificate

Insurance certificates are used to assure the consignee that insurance will cover the loss of or damage to the cargo during transit. These can be obtained from the freight forwarder or publishing house. An airway bill can serve as an insurance certificate for a shipment by air. Some countries may require insurance certification or notification.

Photo-Sanitary Certificate

All shipments of fresh fruits and vegetables, seeds, nuts, flour, rice, grains, lumber, plants, and plant materials require a federal photo-sanitary certificate. The certificate must verify that the product is free from specified epidemics and/or agricultural diseases. Additional information and forms are available from Animal and Plant Health Inspection Service (APHIS) on its website: http://www.aphis.usda .gov/import_export/index.shtml.

Radiation Certificate

Some countries, including Saudi Arabia, may require a radiation certificate for some plant and animal imports. The certificate states that the products are not contaminated by radioactivity. See the Wisconsin International Trade Team's website: http://datcp.wi.gov/uploads/Business/pdf/ExportRegulatoryCertificates.pdf.

Halal Certificate

Required by most countries in the Middle East, a **Halal certificate** states that fresh or frozen meat or poultry products were slaughtered in accordance with Islamic law. Certification by an appropriate chamber and legalization by the consulate of the destination country is usually required.

Other Export-Related Documents

Consular Invoice

Required in some countries, a **consular invoice** describes the shipment of goods and shows information such as the consignor, consignee, and value of the shipment.

If required, copies are available from the destination country's embassy or consulate in the United States. The cost for this documentation can be significant and should be discussed with the buyer.

Canadian Customs Invoice

Although not required by regulation, a Canadian customs invoice is a preferred document by Canadian Customs and customs brokers. It is issued in Canadian dollars for dutiable and taxable exports exceeding $1,600 Canadian dollars. Detailed invoice requirements can be obtained at the Canadian Customs website: http://www .canadacustomsinfo.com/canada-customs-invoice-form-cil.

Dock Receipt and Warehouse Receipt

A **dock receipt** and **warehouse receipt** are used to transfer accountability when the export item is moved by the domestic carrier to the port of embarkation and left with the ship line for export.

Import License

Import licenses are the responsibility of the importer and vary depending on destination and product. However, including a copy of an import license with the rest of the export documentation may in some cases help avoid problems with customs in the destination country.

Shipper's Letter of Instruction

The shipper's letter of instruction is issued by the exporter to the forwarding agent and includes shipping instructions for air or ocean shipment.

Temporary Shipment Documents
ATA Carnet

An **ATA Carnet**, also known as a "Merchandise Passport," is a document that facilitates the temporary importation of products into foreign countries by eliminating tariffs and value-added taxes (VATs) or the posting of a security deposit normally required at the time of importation. This form is often used by importers exhibiting samples of machinery or other products at a trade show in the U.S. If the show items are eventually sold, the importer would be responsible for paying any import taxes at that time. How to apply for a Carnet can be found on the Export.gov website: http://export.gov/logistics/eg_main_018129 .asp.[46]

Customs Certificate of Registration

Customs Certificate of Registration Form 4455 may be used (often in conjunction with a temporary import bond or ATA Carnet) for goods that are leaving the United States on a temporary basis for alteration, repair, replacement, and processing.

Export License

An export license is a U.S. government document required for dual-use exports or exports to embargoed countries. These licenses, granted by BIS, are transaction-based—not based on the individual exporter, although they are the applicants to the license. As such, there is no such thing as an "exporter's license." However, most export transactions do not require specific approval from the U.S. government, as they are classified as NLR. Before shipping products, exporters should be sure they understand the concept of dual-use and the basic export control regulations.

Significant changes to the U.S. Export Control System were made under the President's **Export Control Reform (ECR) Initiative**, announced October 15, 2013, in a White House Fact Sheet.[47]

In addition to the U.S. export control policy for dual-use items, BIS is also charged with the development, implementation, and interpretation of the antiboycott provisions of the Export Administration Act. The antiboycott provisions encourage, and in some cases require, U.S. traders to refuse to participate in foreign boycotts that the United States does not sanction. They are also required to report receipt of boycott-related requests.[48]

Summary

A U.S. Commerce Department agency, BIS, is charged with the development, implementation, and enforcement of federal export regulations or the EARs. These regulations control the export and reexport of most, but not all, commercial and noncommercial goods, services, and technologies. Other U.S. government agencies, including the U.S. Departments of State, Homeland Security, Treasury, Defense, and Energy, also play critical roles in export control and nonproliferation activities both within the United States and outside its borders.

The primary reasons for export controls are national security, foreign policy, and short supply. The key questions to ask in determining whether or not a commerce export license is required are: *What are you exporting? Where are your exports going? Who will receive your exports? What will be the end-use of your exports?*

There is no such thing as an "exporter's license." The majority of U.S. commercial exports do *not* require a license. The three types of export authorization are: no license required (NLR), license, and license exception. One of three options must be selected and referenced on all export documentation. Only the "license required" designation requires written authorization from BIS. NLR and license exception are assumed grants of authority to export—but subject to commodity and country restrictions outlined in the EARs.

Classification, by Export Control Classification Number (ECCN), as listed on the CCL, will describe the export controls placed on that item. Most U.S. export controls pertain to dual-use commodities, software, and technology. Dual-use items are those that have predominantly commercial uses, but also have military or proliferation applications that make their export contrary to U.S. national security, foreign policy, or

KEY TERMS

> AESDirect

> AIRWAY BILLS

> ATA CARNET

> AUTOMATED EXPORT SYSTEM (AES)

> BILL OF LADING (B/L)

> BUREAU OF INDUSTRY AND SECURITY (BIS)

> COMMERCE CONTROL LIST (CCL)

> COMMERCE COUNTRY CHART (CCC)

> COMMERCIAL INVOICE

> CONSULAR INVOICE

> DENIED PERSONS LIST

> DOCK RECEIPT

> DUAL-USE ITEMS

> EAR99

> ELECTRONIC EXPORT INFORMATION (EEI)

> END-USE VIOLATIONS

> ENTITY LIST

> EXPORT ADMINISTRATION REGULATIONS (EARs)

> EXPORT CONTROL CLASSIFICATION NUMBER (ECCN)

> EXPORT CONTROL REFORM (ECR) INITIATIVE

> EXPORT ENFORCEMENT ARM (EEA)

> EXPORT LICENSE

> EXPORT NATIONAL SECURITY (NS) CONTROLS

> EXPORT PACKING LIST

economic interests. Perhaps the easiest method of export application is the Simplified Network Application Process Redesign (SNAP-R).

At the 2013 annual BIS Export Control Forum in Washington, DC, the U.S. government announced a new Export Control Reform Initiative to protect and enhance U.S. national security interests. The new program includes revised procedures concerning foreign end-users, U.S. competitiveness, and transparency.

U.S. exporters cannot export to just anyone. A number of regulatory procedures prohibit this, including the Lists of Parties of Concern, which includes the Entity List; the Treasury Department's Specially Designated Nationals and Blocked Persons List; the Unverified List, and the Denied Persons List.

The U.S. export control agency for dual-use items, BIS, is also charged with the development, implementation, and interpretation of the antiboycott provisions of the Export Administration Act.

Review Questions

1. Describe the primary purpose for U.S. export controls.

2. What is meant by "dual-use items?"

3. What are the four questions that must be answered before determining the need for a commerce export license?

4. What are the functions of the Commerce Control List, the Export Control Classification Number, and the Commerce Country Chart?

5. Explain the three forms of export authorization, and identify the only form that requires written authorization from the BIS.

6. Can U.S. individuals or firms export to whomever they wish? If not, what restrictions are imposed and are they consistent with our democratic system?

Discussion Questions and Activities

1. Go to the primary U.S. government website for export controls, http://www.bis .doc.gov, and review the following brochures: "Don't Let This Happen to You," and "Introduction to the Commerce Department's Export Controls."

2. Debate the pros and cons of restricting U.S. firms from trading with countries designated as unfriendly to us or our allies or as harboring terrorists, while our competitors are not similarly restricted.

3. Think of an American product—one actually made in this country—and go through the export classification process, starting with the CCL, to determine the ECCN, and then consult the CCC to determine the controls, if any, on your selected case study country. Do you think those controls are reasonable and fair to the exporter? Are they consistent with our free-enterprise economy?

4. As other countries' economies gain experience and strength, how will the United States be able to compete in future global markets? Should it loosen export controls, subsidize exports, and provide other incentives to get the American entrepreneur, individual, or business to export more—even if such programs are not legal under the WTO trading rules?

Chapter 5 Case

Neiman Marcus Chooses Direct Distribution in China

Catering to the luxury Asian market, the specialty department store Neiman Marcus has long known that affluent customers in China have created a growing demand for its goods. For a number of years Chinese tourists to the United States have been avid customers at Neiman's Bergdorf Goodman store in New York City as well as the 41 Neiman Marcus stores across the country. Its legendary Christmas catalogs have featured "his and her" matching submarines, trips to exotic environs, and fabulous gems among other items. Customers throughout the world can view the company's website and order whatever they want—and can pay for.

Today fashion-minded consumers in China can visit Neiman's dedicated website with copy in Mandarin explaining the available merchandise. Neiman Marcus has continued to show its faith in the Chinese market, strengthening its investment there by acquiring an interest in Glamour Sales Holdings, an Asian website specializing in flash sales—short selling time periods adored by fashion-hounds when special designer items are on sale at deeply discounted prices. Neiman's recently added another $10 million to its initial $28 million investment in Glamour Sales. The two companies have a symbiotic relationship: Glamour Sales sends its customers to Neiman's website where they can watch fashion shows and videos and learn about luxury brands. Neiman's, in turn, provides a larger customer base for Glamour's flash sales.

Initially, Neiman Marcus stored its goods for China in its Shanghai warehouses. The company had believed that keeping inventory in China instead of the United States would provide faster delivery and better customer service. In a later effort to reduce costs and yet maintain customer service, Neiman Marcus decided to downsize its Shanghai warehouses, leaving basic web-based goods and customer service there, but shipping in all other customer orders. The company's reasoning, according to Ginger Reeder, vice president of corporate communications, was that working from the United States, "We can offer a wider breadth of assortment and orders are more timely. . . . We are committed to China. We believe we can serve the Chinese luxury customers and there is a future for that."

Source: David Moin, "Neiman's Alters China Plan," *Women's Wear Daily*, May 21, 2013, pp. 1, 4.

Questions

1. Aside from the reasons stated in the case, why do you think Neiman Marcus decided to ship directly to customers in China instead of from a warehouse in Shanghai?
2. From your chapter reading, were there any unusual documents that Neiman's has to fill out in maintaining a substantial inventory in China?

References

1. "Don't Let This Happen to You: An Introduction to U.S. Export Control Law: Actual Investigations of Export Control and Anti-Boycott Violations," September 2010 ed., p. 13, Export Enforcement, Bureau of Industry and Security, U.S. Department of Commerce. Retrieved September 20, 2013, from http://www.bis.doc.gov/index.php/forms-documents/doc_view/535-don-t-let-this-happen-to-you-2010.

2. "Bureau of Industry and Security Announces $2.8 Million Civil Settlement with Computer Links FZCO for Charges Related to Unlawful Exporting of Technology to Syria," Bureau of Industry and Security, U.S. Department of Commerce. Retrieved September 21, 2013, from http://www.bis.doc.gov/index.php/about-bis/newsroom/press-releases/102-about-bis/newsroom/press-releases/press-releases-2013/524.

3. Op. cit., "Don't Let This Happen to You," p. 27.

4. "New Foreign Trade Regulations (FTR) Export Requirements," Global Reach: The Official Blog of the U.S. Census Bureau's Foreign Trade Division, Export Administration Regulations, March 14, 2013. Retrieved September 20, 2013, from http://globalreach.blogs.census.gov/2013/03/14/the-new-ftr.

5. "EAA Penalties," Office of Export Enforcement, Bureau of Industry and Security, U.S. Department of Commerce. Retrieved September 21, 2013, from http://www.bis.doc.gov/index.php/enforcement/oee/penalties.

6. Op. cit., "Don't Let This Happen to You."

7. "Principle Parties in Interest," and "Voluntary Self-Disclosure," Office of Export Enforcement, Bureau of Industry and Security, U.S. Department of Commerce. Retrieved September 21, 2013, from http://www.bis.doc.gov/index.php/enforcement/oee/voluntary-self-disclosure.

8. "Introduction to Commerce Department Export Controls," Bureau of Industry and Security, U.S. Department of

Commerce. Retrieved September 21, 2013, from http://www.bis.doc.gov/index.php/forms-documents/doc_view/142-eccn-pdf.

9. "Export Basics," Bureau of Industry and Security, U.S. Department of Commerce. Retrieved September 21, 2013, from http://export.gov/exportbasics/index.asp.

10. Ibid.

11. Ibid.

12. Ibid.

13. "U.S. Export Controls," U.S. Department of State. Retrieved September 21, 2013, from http://www.state.gov/strategictrade/resources/c43182.htm.

14. "Dual Use Exports," Electronic Code of Federal Regulations: Commerce and Foreign Trade. Retrieved September 20, 2013, from http://www.ecfr.gov/cgi-bin/retrieveECFR.

15. "Export Basics," Export.gov. Retrieved September 20, 2013, from http://export.gov/exportbasics/index.asp.

16. "New to Export," Export.gov. Retrieved September 22, 2013, from http://export.gov/newhampshire/newtoexport/index.asp.

17. "Export Control Reform: Update 2013," July 23–25, 2013, Washington, DC, Bureau of Industry and Security, U.S. Department of Commerce. Retrieved September 25, 2013, from http://www.bis.doc.gov/index.php/component/content/article/81-compliance-a-training/export-administration-regulations-training/seminar-details/558-update-2013-presentations.

18. Ibid.

19. Commerce Secretary Penny Pritzker, "Remarks at 2013 Update Conference." Retrieved September 24, 2014, from http://www.commerce.gov/news/secretary-speeches/2013/07/23/remarks-2013-update-conference-export-controls-and-policy.

20. "Export Regulations," Export.gov. Retrieved September 24, 2013, from http://export.gov/regulation/eg_main_018229.asp.

21. "Export Enforcement," Bureau of Industry and Security, U.S. Department of Commerce. Retrieved September 24, 2013, from http://www.bis.doc.gov/index.php/enforcement/oac.

22. "Export Classification," Export.gov. Retrieved September 25, 2013, from http://www.bis.doc.gov/index.php/licensing/commerce-control-list-classification/export-control-classification-number-eccn.

23. Ibid.

24. "Export Licensing," Electronic Code of Federal Regulations. Retrieved September 26, 2013, from http://www.ecfr.gov/cgi-bin/retrieveECFR.

25. Ibid.

26. "Commerce Control List," Bureau of Industry and Security, U.S. Department of Commerce. Retrieved September 26, 2013, from http://www.bis.doc.gov/index.php/licensing/commerce-control-list-classification.

27. "Commerce Country Chart," Bureau of Industry and Security, U.S. Department of Commerce. Retrieved

September 26, 2013, from http://www.bis.doc.gov /index.php/regulations commerce-country-chart -ccc.

28. "International Logistics: ECCN," Export .gov. Retrieved September 25, 2013, from http:// export.gov/logistics/eg _main_018803.asp.

29. "EAR99," Export.gov. Retrieved September 25, 2013, from https://www .export.gov/ . . . /eg_main _022617.asp7.

30. "Office of Foreign Assets Control," U.S. Department of the Treasury. Retrieved September 25, 2013, from http://www.treasury.gov /about/organizational -structure/offices/Pages /Office-of-Foreign-Assets -Control.aspx.

31. "Economic Sanctions Programs," U.S. Department of the Treasury. Retrieved January 17, 2014, from http://www.treasury.gov /resource-center/faqs /Sanctions/Pages/ques _index.aspx#gen_ques.

32. "Introduction to Commerce Department Export Controls." Retrieved September 25, 2014, from http://www

.bis.doc.gov/index.php /forms-documents/doc . . . /142-eccn-pdf?.

33. "FAQ-Regulations and Licensing," Export.gov. Retrieved September 25, 2013, from http://www .export.gov/%5C /regulation/index.asp

34. "Lists of Parties of Concern," Bureau of Industry and Security, U.S. Department of Commerce. Retrieved September 26, 2013, from http://www.bis.doc.gov /index.php/policy -guidance/lists-of-parties -of-concern.

35. "Entity List," Bureau of Industry and Security, U.S. Department of Commerce. Retrieved September 26, 2013, from http://www.bis.doc.gov /index.php/policy -guidance/lists-of-parties -of-concern.

36. "Red Flags," Bureau of Industry and Security, U.S. Department of Commerce. Retrieved September 26, 2013, from http://www.bis.doc.gov /index.php/component /content/article/23 -compliance-a-training /51-red-flag-indicators.

37. "Denied Persons List," Bureau of Industry and

Security, U.S. Department of Commerce. Retrieved September 26, 2013, from http://www.bis.doc.gov /index.php/policy -guidance/lists-of-parties -of-concern.

38. "U.S. Treasury Specially Designated Nationals," U.S. Department of the Treasury. Retrieved September 26, 2013, from http://www.treasury.gov /resource-center /sanctions/SDN-List /Pages/default.aspx.

39. "Unverified List," Bureau of Industry and Security, U.S. Department of the Treasury. Retrieved September 26, 2013, from http://www.bis.doc.gov /index.php/policy -guidance/lists-of-parties -of-concern.

40. "End-use," Bureau of Industry and Security, U.S. Department of the Treasury. Retrieved September 26, 2013, from http://www.bis.doc.gov /index.php/regulations /export-administration -regulations-ear.

41. "Authorization to Export," http://www.bis .doc.gov/index.php/forms -documents/doc_view /142-eccn-pdf, p. 8.

42. "Simplified Network Application Process-Redesign (SNAP-R)," Bureau of Industry and Security. Retrieved January 16, 2014, from http://www.bis.doc.gov/index.php/licensing/simplified-network-application-process-redesign-snap-r.

43. "Track Your Application: STELA," Bureau of Industry and Security, U.S. Department of Commerce. Retrieved September 26, 2013, from http://www.bis.doc.gov/index.php/licensing/track-your-application-stela.

44. "Electronic Export Information (EEI)." Retrieved April 25, 2014, from http://www.ups.com/content/us/en/resources/sri/gen7/html.

45. "Certificates of Origin," ezCertOrigin. Retrieved January 16, 2014, from https://www.ezcertorigin.com/.

46. "Temporary Imports, ATA Carnets," Retrieved January 16, 2014, from http://export.gov/logistics/eg_main_018129.asp.

47. "Revised U.S. Export Control System," White House, Fact Sheet of October 15, 2013. Retrieved January 14, 2013, from http://www.whitehouse.gov/the-press-office/2013/10/15/fact-sheet-announcing-revised-us-export-control-system.

48. "Anti-Boycott Laws under the Export Administration Act," Bureau of Industry and Security. Retrieved January 15, 2014, from http://beta-www.bis.doc.gov/index.php/enforcement/oac?tmpl=component&layout=default.

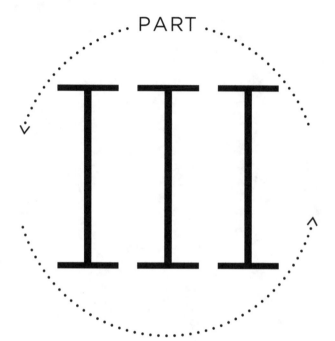

PART

III

Importing into
the United States

Figure 6.1 From 2008 to 2013, Ten Thousand Villages was named one of the "World's Most Ethical Companies" by the Ethisphere Institute and *Forbes Magazine*.

CHAPTER 6
BASICS OF IMPORTING INTO THE UNITED STATES

Ten Thousand Villages, Importers Putting Fair Trade into Action. Half the world is poor, desperately poor by U.S. standards. Many people survive with incomes of less than $2 dollars a day. What's more, many of the impoverished have little occasion to improve their state. What does this mean to the rest of the world and its industrialized nations? For one thing, people in poverty frequently are not equipped to participate in a larger world society. For another, the rest of the world cannot maximize its potential when half of its population cannot take part.

When people find an opportunity to better their lives, they can forge ahead and make a difference. Fortunately, a number of businesses, governments, and other organizations have been working to alleviate poverty by promoting fair trade. When fair trade organizations work in given locales, they make sure that the trade agreements reached with local inhabitants contain certain provisions, including decent working and living conditions and earnings that provide sufficient income to meet expenses with even some left over to set aside.

One of the early promoters of the fair trade idea was Edna Ruth Byler who, while traveling through Puerto Rico in 1946 and looking for ways to alleviate poverty there, saw one way the local people could engage in trade. She began collecting the work of local artisans, such as vases and bowls, sculpture, and textiles. Back in the United States, she started peddling those goods out of the trunk of her car. Soon she was building a network of markets at home and one of artisans in impoverished areas. Working with the Mennonite church, a Christian organization fostering world peace and service, together they formed Self Help. In 1996, the nonprofit organization became Ten Thousand Villages, the name originating from Mohandas Gandhi's saying that India's population could be found not in its cities but in its many villages.

Today, more than 120 stores in the United States and Canada plus the Ten Thousand Villages' website offer fair trade goods imported from 38 countries in Latin America, the Middle East, Africa, and Asia. The merchandise offered includes many handmade gifts, jewelry, home décor items, and paper goods. To assist the local producers, Ten Thousand Villages buyers pay half of the order's cost in advance. This payment enables artisans to purchase raw materials for the order; the remaining payment comes when the order is complete. Through its equitable pricing and long-term arrangements, fair trade agreements throughout the developing world have changed the lives of many artisans, their families, and community members for the better.[1]

The Internet has made it easy for anyone to find and purchase products or services from almost anywhere in the world. However, many individuals and businesses are discovering that getting a foreign-bought item successfully imported into the United States is much more complicated, time-consuming, and expensive than they ever imagined.

WHY IMPORT?

If imports are time-consuming and possibly costly to bring into the country, why bother? A check of your closet is like a walk through a global marketplace. One of your jackets may have come from Italy; your shoes may be from Spain, and your denim jeans from Indonesia. Your living room sofa may be French-inspired while the floor it sits on is made from Brazilian cherry wood. Our clothes, homes, and daily lives are surrounded by imports.

As the world's largest consumer market, we are the target of producers of goods and services from virtually every country around the globe. Americans are acquisitive, and we seem to have an insatiable appetite for imports as well as domestic merchandise.

The United States imported $2.38 billion worth of goods in 2012, the highest amount on record, from more than 150 countries. Primary imports were food, feeds, and beverages ($110 billion); capital goods ($548 billion); automotive vehicles ($297 billion); and consumer goods ($516 billion); all the highest levels on record.[2]

Why is the United States the largest importing nation in the world? There are many reasons, but the primary one is the need to satisfy consumer demand; a second reason is that consumers believe they have the capability to pay for all of these purchases. Consumers seek out the most unique—or the cheapest—product and find it often in imported goods. And the demand for these goods appears in all price ranges, from the designer level using fine fabrics and complex construction to the moderate and budget price ranges using less expensive materials and fabrication. Without imports—at the high or low end—the fashion industry, including manufacturers, wholesalers, and retailers, could not survive because it could not serve the needs and wants of its markets.

Although price is still an important consideration in deciding on an import, today's customer is also looking for quality, value, uniqueness, and sustainability. Of course, the status appeal of a Rolex watch, Ferrari automobile, or Chanel handbag cannot be ignored, but American-made brands have come to challenge imports in fashion areas such as wines (consider Napa Valley), home furnishings (Baker and Henredon), and apparel (Oscar de la Renta, Joseph Abboud, and Ralph Lauren).

Although major trading partners and sources for U.S. imports remain Canada, China, Mexico, Japan, and Germany (see Figure 6.3), shifts have also taken place in countries of origin for imports at both the high and low end. China, India, and Pakistan are replacing Japan as the source for high-tech electronics such as computers, while South Korea's Samsung is now one of the leading manufacturers of cell phones and television sets. Quality automobiles, stocked with many imported parts, now come from U.S.-based assembly plants owned by South Korean, German, Japanese, and—expected soon—Chinese and Indian companies. While much of the profit made selling foreign cars to Americans heads back to the foreign owners

Figure 6.2 Import buyers have to make a number of decisions even before choosing goods on their buying trips.

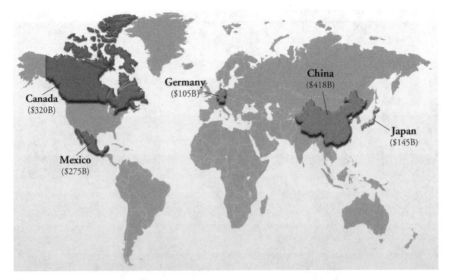

Figure 6.3 Top five countries by import value.

(creating wealth overseas), the foreign car companies are investing in their U.S. plants at a high rate, hiring American workers, and stimulating local economies.[3]

U.S. imports are concentrated among relatively few countries, even though the country purchases from 234 nations (see Table 6.1). Only 20 countries account for over $4 out of every $5 worth of goods imported in 2012. More than 70 percent of non-oil U.S. imports came from the top 10 sourcing nations, or $1 of every $5 imported value in 2012.[4]

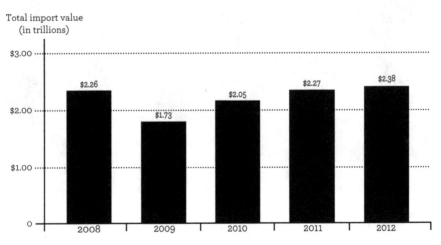

Figure 6.4 Total import value (in trillions).

Table 6.1. Top 20 Sources of U.S. Non-Oil Merchandise Imports, 2012

Value	Total	Share of imports
China	$424.7	22.2%
Canada	237.0	12.4
Mexico	236.9	12.4
Japan	144.1	7.5
Germany	104.8	5.5
Korea	55.7	2.9
United Kingdom	47.2	2.5
France	39.9	2.1
Taiwan	38.5	2.0
India	37.1	1.9
Italy	34.8	1.8
Ireland	33.2	1.7
Malaysia	25.7	1.3
Switzerland	25.5	1.3
Thailand	25.3	1.3
Brazil	24.5	1.3
Saudi Arabia	22.8	1.2
Israel	22.0	1.1
Singapore	20.0	1.0
Vietnam	19.8	1.0
Top 10	1,365.4	71.2
Top 20	1,693.6	84.5
All other	298.0	15.5
Total from world	1,917.0	100.0%

Note: Customs value in billions of dollars and percent.

Source: U.S. Department of Commerce/U.S. International Trade Commission. Retrieved January 30, 2014, from http://www.tradepartnership.com/pdf_files/Imports%20Study%20May%202013 .pdf, p. 9.

RISKS TO IMPORTING

As with any business venture, purchasing goods from factories and suppliers thousands of miles away involves certain risks. The language may be unfamiliar, as are the sets of laws, and the same forms of protection are not afforded foreign traders. Global sourcing may add several weeks to the **lead time**, the amount of

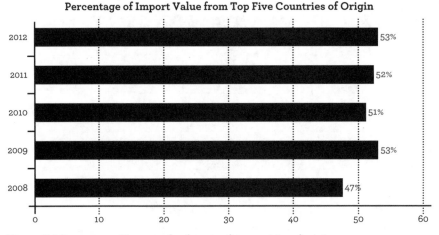

Figure 6.5 Percentage of import value from top five countries of origin.

Source: "Import Trade Trends, Fiscal 2012," U.S. Customs and Border Protection.

time between ordering goods and receiving the shipment. For fashion merchandise, importers must consider whether the goods will still be in demand when they reach the store. Slow or unpredictable delivery—often because of outdated transportation systems or infrastructure failures—can result in delivery delays. If goods cannot reach the retailer's shelves on time, retailers need to sever even long-standing relationships.

Strict U.S. import controls imposed after the 2001 terrorist attacks on the United States can hold up entry of a shipment for weeks or months, depending on the country of origin, as the government is determined to inspect a greater percentage of the more than 70,000 truck, rail, and sea containers that arrive in this country every day, at more than 300 seaports, land border crossings, postal facilities, and other ports-of-entry. Annually, more than 825,000 importers bring shipments into the United States. Approximately 80 percent of these shipments are by one-time or infrequent importers.[5]

New controls and procedures have affected all importers, such as the **Container Security Initiative (CSI)** focus on the threat to border security and global trade posed by the potential for terrorist use of a maritime container to deliver a weapon. The CSI plan stations multidisciplinary teams of U.S. officers from both the Customs and Border Protection (CBP) and Immigration and Customs Enforcement (ICE) agencies to work together with host foreign government counterparts.[6]

REASONS FOR IMPORTING

Nevertheless, as you can tell from this chapter's opening vignette, Ten Thousand Villages and other retailers have many reasons for searching out goods from other countries. These include customer demand (the market) and the opportunity to offer a variety of goods and prices.

The Market

The first and most important step in deciding whether to import goods is to determine an existing demand for those goods in the United States. That demand is called a **market**, or a particular group of people, companies, or other organizations that not only have the desire to buy goods but also have the means (money or credit) to pay for them. This chapter focuses on **import traders**, those who import goods for resale, as opposed to manufacturers who may import **components**, materials and parts that go into a finished good that is sold domestically.

Remember that the demand for any product or service depends on the marketer's ability to satisfy the needs or wants of the target market consumer or industrial user—at a price each is willing to pay. Even though a potential import may be attractive for a number of reasons—price, quality, uniqueness, or design—the actual size of the market cannot be assessed accurately until you know how much the item will cost delivered to the United States. In international trade, a company may quote a **first price**, the manufacturer's selling price in the factory showroom, but the importer must calculate the actual **landed cost**, which includes all shipping and entry costs and duty charges to the port of foreign entry.

The delivered-into-store cost plus delivery and insurance to reach the store and overhead expenses and profit margin determine the resale price of the imported goods. For this reason, the retail prices for fashion goods are often four or five times the price quoted in the foreign showroom. Figuring out the actual retail price should help to indicate the potential for sales and ultimate profit from your import.

Some Questions to Ask about the Market for an Imported Product

Before buying any foreign goods, here are some questions a potential importer needs to ask:

- Is there an existing domestic need and demand for the product?
- If yes, who are the major suppliers of these products, and what are their market shares?
- Are the suppliers domestic or foreign companies?
- Is the market dominated by one or two large companies, or is it divided among many small suppliers?
- What is the approximate size, in dollar amount, of the current market?
- Who are the current end-users, the final consumers or industrial users of a product, for this item?

- Where are they located?
- What is their average income?
- What is their disposable income?
- What are their spending habits?
- To what advertising media are they exposed?
- What kind of work do they do?
- To what kind of message will they respond?
- How much will they be prepared to buy?
- What will they be prepared to pay?
- How often will they buy?
- Which domestic or imported products compete with those you intend to import?
- How are these products distributed in the United States?
- What are their average manufactured, wholesale, and retail price points?
- As a category, how are they regarded in the marketplace—needed, wanted, or neutral?
- What competitive advantage (design, warranties, and after-sales service) do existing domestic or imported products have in the current market?
- What competitive advantages would the new imports have?

Keeping in mind that a main objective in business is to make a profit, the best way to do that is to identify a substantial, lucrative, long-term market for the products you plan to import. See Table 6.2 for an overview of leading U.S. non-oil imports from free trade agreement (FTA) trade partners in 2012.[7]

Table 6.2. Leading U.S. Non-Oil Imports from FTA Partners, 2012

Country	Product
Australia	Meat (including lamb); wine
Bahrain	Aluminum and aluminum products; fertilizer; apparel
Canada	Motor vehicles and parts; machinery; plastics
Chile	Copper and copper products; fish; grapes; wine
Colombia	Gold; coffee; flowers
Costa Rica	Semiconductors; medical equipment; fruit
Dominican Rep.	Medical equipment; cigars; electrical circuitry
El Salvador	Apparel; sugar; coffee
Guatemala	Bananas; gold; coffee
Honduras	Apparel; insulated wires/cable; coffee
Israel	Diamonds; pharmaceuticals
Jordan	Knit apparel; woven apparel; precious metal jewelry
Korea	Motor vehicles and parts; telephones; semiconductors
Mexico	Computers and monitors; motor vehicles; telephones
Morocco	Phosphates and fertilizers; semiconductors
Nicaragua	Apparel; coffee; gold
Oman	Fertilizers; plastics; precious jewelry
Panama	Fish; gold; sugar
Peru	Gold and silver; tin; coffee
Singapore	Organic chemicals; printers; semiconductors

Source: "Imports Work for America." Retrieved January 30, 2014, from http://www.trade partnership.com/pdf_files/Imports%20Study%20May%202013.pdf, p.11.

CONDUCTING A SWOT ANALYSIS

When a company considers importing, it should first review its own situation by conducting an assessment of corporate (and product) strengths, weaknesses, opportunities, and threats, known as a **SWOT analysis**. The purpose is for the organization to realize its major attributes (strengths); areas where it can improve (weaknesses); internal and external factors that can impede its progress (threats); and where it can capitalize on its strengths (opportunities). The goal of this exercise is for the company to maximize its opportunities while minimizing its risks. Take a look at the SWOT analysis shown in Figure 6.6, noting each element. Then, try your hand at preparing a SWOT analysis for a company you know.

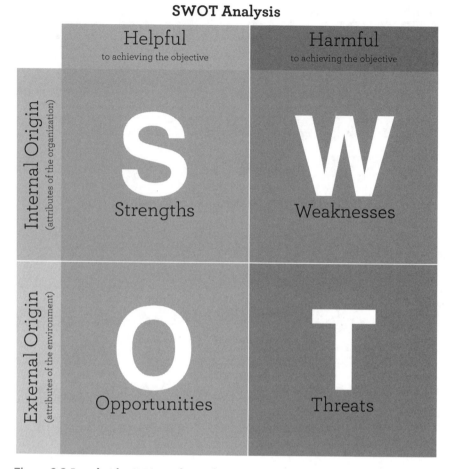

SWOT Analysis

	Helpful to achieving the objective	Harmful to achieving the objective
Internal Origin (attributes of the organization)	**S** Strengths	**W** Weaknesses
External Origin (attributes of the environment)	**O** Opportunities	**T** Threats

Figure 6.6 Armed with a SWOT analysis, a business can more accurately identify potentially successful import opportunities.

Armed with a SWOT analysis, an organization is then prepared to analyze its domestic and international competitors to identify potentially profitable marketing opportunities. Before trying to source goods from foreign countries, potential importers should first research suppliers in the United States to determine if the types of goods they are seeking are already being imported into this country and, if so, from which countries. The competitive research data provided by the SWOT analysis will reveal the strengths, weaknesses, opportunities, and threats—competitive or environmental—of those firms who may challenge your success.

Domestic suppliers can be identified by referring to trade association directories, manufacturers' indexes, or industry journals. Valuable research tools include the annual show issues of leading trade publications for specific industries. Usually available at industry trade association-sponsored annual trade shows and conventions, these special publications list all major manufacturers, wholesalers, distributors, manufacturer's representatives, and often leading retailers—a market researcher's dream come true.

The case for importing a certain product can be made much stronger if domestic suppliers can't match the quality, price, delivery, or unique features of your potential import.

LOCATING FOREIGN SUPPLIERS

Once opportunities are confirmed, the next step is to find a number of international supply sources. There are many ways to do this. First, identify a country or group of countries where the product may be available. In addition to the Internet, many organizations can help in the process of supplier identification. Some are located overseas but many are here. For example:

Overseas

- Government trade promotion agencies or departments of commerce
- Foreign chambers of commerce
- Industry associations' export programs
- City government export promotion agencies

In the United States

- Foreign embassies
- Foreign consulates
- Trade commissioners
- Bi-national chambers of commerce

Other sources of information about overseas suppliers include

- Industry trade journals
- Trade fairs and exhibitions
- Other importers
- Ethnic community organizations
- Foreign banks' U.S. branches
- Freight forwarders
- Customs brokers
- The Internet

The next step is to contact prospective suppliers and ask for their catalogs and price lists. You first need to introduce yourself and provide a brief description of your international trade qualifications. Most foreign manufacturers or

INTERNATIONAL FASHION FOCUS 6.1
American Fashion Imports Are Global Business

The glamorous fashion weeks held in New York City occur several times a year. One main purpose is to give retail store fashion buyers a preview of upcoming fashion looks that the buyers then must translate for their customers at home. It used to be that Americans would opt for their own sportswear look, which has become classic throughout the world. Thanks to the Internet, the casual apparel of Ralph Lauren, Liz Claiborne, or Tommy Hilfiger are clearly recognizable signs of American fashion everywhere. Perhaps too recognizable.

Current market weeks are showing more diverse looks, often ones that no longer can be identified with a single country. At a recent New York City Fashion Week, designers and their ideas hailed from across the globe, major European countries such as France and Italy, to be sure, but also the Asian nations of Thailand, Japan, and China, as well as Brazil and Turkey.

Vera Wang found inspiration from ancient Roman society, and Diane von Furstenberg located bright flowery prints in Bali, while Tia Cibani, who designs for a Chinese line, Ports 1961, gathered ideas from East African patterns and fabric treatments such as tie-dyeing. When asked about sources of global design inspiration, Lazaro Hernandez, who, with Jack McCullogh, creates the Proenza Schouler label, admits that although the team does not have the money to travel extensively, they can travel in their heads. Hernandez believes that, "with technology, you can go anywhere on the Internet."

In addition to the fact that the fashion industry requires a new season four or five times a year, each possessing its unique qualities, the designers of luxury fashion goods want to stay ahead of lower-price manufacturers who are quick to copy any new look that catches on. So top-level designers search continuously for special qualities that characterize their styles as luxe, whether it is the addition of couture embroidery for an evening gown, a hand-rolled hem on an Hermès scarf, or tiny gems hand-sewn on a blouse. Inspired by designers, affluent fashion consumers seek out what is new that sets them apart for a while from the rest of the world. Often that element is provided by an import, one that can soon be produced at a lower price.

Source: Adapted from Kate Betts, "Geography Lesson: The coolest designers redefine the idea for American style in an increasingly global business," *Time*, September 2007, p. 61.

distributors are eager to export to the United States or to sell their goods to U.S. importers because of the size of this market—the largest in the world. However, they may hesitate to do business with an entrepreneur or very small business—at least until a personal working relationship can be established. It is for that reason potential—and current—American importers who are able to should attend foreign trade shows where they can meet future suppliers face-to-face to start building a relationship. For example, the popular interest in Asian fashions in the United States may prompt U.S. importers to visit fashion shows in Asian countries.

Many industry trade associations, or their trade publications, foreign chambers of commerce, the U.S. Commercial Service of the U.S. International Trade Administration, and foreign embassies and consulates can provide information on profiles, dates, and locations of foreign trade shows for industries across the board.

While foreign travel may not be practical for the start-up company, some potential importers visit major trade shows in the United States, where the number of foreign country pavilions and individual foreign exhibits and booths increase dramatically each year. Many of these companies are seeking U.S. distributors or venture partners. The *National Trade and Professional Association Directory*, published by Columbia Books, features detailed contact and background information on more than 8,100 trade associations, professional societies, technical organizations, labor unions, and their more than 14,000 important executives in the United States. It lists U.S. trade shows and annual conventions for most of these organizations. Other trade publications frequently list trade shows and exhibitions by industry or by state and city (Figure 6.7).

Convention centers that typically host international trade shows offer enough floor area to accommodate several thousand attendees. The largest in the United States is McCormick Place in Chicago, Illinois, (Figure 6.8) with more than 2.7 million square feet of exhibit space.[8] More than three million people visit each year, many seeking foreign customers for their exports or looking for foreign-exhibited products they can import.

The major domestic trade shows for the fashion industry are held in New York City, such as those produced at Lincoln Center during Fashion Week. The MAGIC apparel trade shows for men, women, and children are held at the Las Vegas Convention Center in Las Vegas, Nevada, also one of the world's largest in terms of exhibit space. The Orange County Convention Center (OCCC) in Orlando, Florida, is also a significant trade show location. The OCCC currently ranks as the second-largest convention center in the United States, with 2.2 million square feet of exhibition space. Other trade shows are held in Dallas, Miami, and Seattle, among other U.S. cities.

Without U.S. and foreign trade shows, the business of exporting and importing would be much more difficult and costly. Where else could exhibitors—and attendees—research global markets for their export products or find new sources for their imports, in one location, over a concentrated time frame of several days? Since many manufacturers and marketers of consumer products are dispersed all over the world, often in remote locations, it would not be cost or time effective to

Personnel:

Executive Director: Elaine Strass

Membership Manager: Barbara Abbott

Meetings Manager: Suzy Brown
E-Mail: sbrown@genetics-gsa.org

Historical Note
Organized in 1931 in New Orleans as an outgrowth of the Genetics Section of the American Society of Zoologists and the Botanical Society of America. Incorporated in Maryland in 1984. Membership: $120/year (full member), $50/year (student).

Meetings/Conferences:
2008 – San Diego, CA(Town & Country Hotel)/Apr. 2-6
2009 – Chicago, IL(Sheraton Chicago Hotel & Towers)/March 4-8
2010 – Washington, DC(Marriott Wardman Park Hotel)/Apr. 7-10
2011 – San Diego, CA(Town & Country Hotel)/March 30-Apr. 3
Number of non-conference events/year: 3

Publications:
Genetics. monthly.
Membership Directory. biennially.
GSA Newsletter. quarterly.

Geochemical Society *(1955)*
Dept. of Earth and Planetary Sciences
Washington Univ., One Brookings Dr., CB 1169
St. Louis, MO 63130-4899
Tel: (314)935-4131   Fax: (314)935-4121
E-Mail: gsoffice@geochemsoc.org
Web Site: www.geochemsoc.org
Members: 2800 individuals
Staff: 2
Annual Budget: $100-250,000

Personnel:

Manager, Business: Seth Davis
E-Mail: seth.davis@geochemsoc.org

Administrative Assistant: Kathryn Hall
E-Mail: kathryn.hall@geochemsoc.org

Historical Note
Founded November 7, 1955 and incorporated in the District of Columbia in 1956. Encourages the application of chemistry to the solution of geological and cosmological problems. Membership: $30/year (Professional); $10/year (Student); $12/year (Senior-above 65 years of age).

Meetings/Conferences:
Annual: Fall/1,600
2008 – Houston, TX/Oct. 5-9

Publications:
G3 - Geochemistry, Geophysics, Geosystems.
Reviews in Mineralogy & Geochemistry. quarterly.
Geochemical News. quarterly. adv.
Geochimica et Cosmochimica Acta. semi-monthly.
Elements magazine. irregular. adv.

Geological Society of America *(1888)*
P.O. Box 9140
Boulder, CO 80301-9140
Tel: (303)357-1000   Fax: (303)357-1074
Toll Free: (800)472 - 1988
E-Mail: gsa@geosociety.org
Web Site: www.geosociety.org
Members: 20000 individuals
Staff: 50
Annual Budget: $5-10,000,000

Executive Director: John W. Hess
E-Mail: jhess@geosociety.org

Senior Director, Information Technology: Todd Berggren
E-Mail: tberggren@geosociety.org

Director, Communications and Marketing: Ann Cairns

Director, Meetings: Melissa Cummiskey

Controller: Kay Dragon
E-Mail: kdragon@geosociety.org

Director, Membership: Pat Kilmer

Director, Education and Outreach: Gary Lewis
E-Mail: glewis@geosociety.org

Director, Strategic Initiatives: Deborah Nelson

Director, Publications: Jon Olsen
E-Mail: jolsen@geosociety.org

Historical Note
Founded in 1888 and incorporated in New York in 1929. GSA includes topical divisions, specializing in Archaeological Geology, Coal Geology, Engineering Geology, Geobiology/Geomicrobiology, Geology and Society, Geophysics, Geoscience Education, History of Geology, Hydrogeology, International Division, Limnology, Planetary Geology, Quaternary Geology and Geomorphology, Sedimentary Geology, and Structural Geology and Tectonics. GSA has six regional sections, each of which holds its own annual meeting in the spring. Also has 35 member, associated and allied societies. GSA is a member society of the American Geological Institute. Membership: $65/year (members/fellows).

Meetings/Conferences:
Annual Meetings: Fall
2008 – Chicago, IL/Oct. 26-30
2009 – Portland, OR/Oct. 18-21
2010 – Denver, CO/Oct. 31-Nov. 3
2011 – Minneapolis,
          MN(Minneapolis)/Oct. 9-12

Publications:
Geological Society of America Bulletin. irregular.
Environmental & Engineering Geoscience. quarterly.
GSA Today. monthly. adv.
Geology. monthly. adv.

Geoscience and Remote Sensing Society *(1962)*
445 Hoes Ln.
Piscataway, NJ 08854
Tel: (732)981-0060   Fax: (732)981-1721
Web Site: www.grss-ieee.org
Members: 2100 individuals
Tax Exempt Status: 501(c)(3)

Personnel:

President: Dr. Leung Tsang
E-Mail: tsang@ee.washington.edu

Communications and Informatin Policy Representative: Dr. David B. Kunkee
E-Mail: David.Kunkee@aero.org

Historical Note
A technical society of the Institute of Electrical and Electronics Engineers (IEEE). Membership in the Society, open only to IEEE members, includes a subscription to a technical periodical in the field published by IEEE. Has no paid officers or full-time staff.

Publications:
GRSS Newsletter. quarterly.
Transactions on Geoscience and Remote Sensing Journal. monthly.
JSTARS. quarterly.

Geoscience Information Society *(1965)*
3026 Shapiro Science Library, University of Michigan,
Ann Arbor, MI 48109-1185
Tel: (734)936-3079   Fax: (734)763-9813
E-Mail: pyocum@umich.edu
Web Site: www.geoinfo.org
Members: 200 individuals
Annual Budget: $10-25,000
Tax Exempt Status: 501(c)(3)

Personnel:

President: Patricia B. Yocum
E-Mail: pyocum@umich.edu

Chair, Membership: Miriam Kennard

Secretary: Andrea Twiss-Brooks
E-Mail: atbrooks@uchicago.edu

Historical Note
Founded in Kansas City, GIS was incorporated in the District of Columbia in 1966. Affiliated with the Geological Society of America and the American Geological Institute. GIS membership includes national and international representation from colleges and universities, business and industry, publishing, geological surveys, geological societies

and other aspects of the field. Membership: $45/year (individual), $100/year (institution), $20/year (student or retired), $135/year (sustaining).

Meetings/Conferences:
Annual Meetings: Fall
2008 – Houston, TX/Oct. 5-9
2009 – Portland, OR/Oct. 18-21
2010 – Denver, CO/Oct. 31-Nov. 3
2011 – Minneapolis, MN/Oct. 9-12
Number of non-conference events/year: 5

Publications:
GIS Newsletter. bi-monthly.
Proceedings. annually.
Membership Directory. annually.
Membership List Available to Non-members

Geospatial Information Technology Association
          (1982)
14456 E. Evans Ave.
Aurora, CO 80014
Tel: (303)337-0513   Fax: (303)337-1001
E-Mail: info@gita.org
Web Site: www.gita.org
Members: 244 organizations ;
          2200 individuals
Staff: 11
Annual Budget: $2-5,000,000

Personnel:

Executive Director: Robert M. Samborski
E-Mail: bsamborski@gita.org

Membership Services Manager: Lisa Connor
E-Mail: lconnor@gita.org

Education and Exhibits Coordinator: Julie Eckhart
E-Mail: jeckhart@gita.org

Manager, Marketing and Communications: Kathryn Henton
E-Mail: khenton@gita.org

Deputy Executive Director: Henry Rosales
E-Mail: hrosales@gita.org

Education Coordinator: James Sakamoto
E-Mail: jsakamoto@gita.org

Historical Note
GITA is a non-profit, educational association which fosters information exchange and educational opportunities and scientific research and development in the field of geospatial information technology. Membership: $125/year (Individual).

Meetings/Conferences:
Conference Chair: Julie Eckhart
Annual Meetings: Spring/3,200
2008 – Seattle, WA/March 1-1
2008 – Houston, TX(Marriott Westchase Hotel)/Sept. 21-24
2009 – Tampa, FL(Tampa Convention Center)/Apr. 19-22
2009 – Houston, TX(Marriott Westchase Hotel)/Sept. 14-16
2010 – Phoenix, AZ(Phoenix Convention Center)/Apr. 25-28

Publications:
Geospatial Technology Report. annually.
GIS for Oil & Gas Conference Proceedings. annually.
GITA Networks. irregular. adv.
Conference Proceedings. annually.

Geosynthetic Materials Association
1801 County Rd. B.W
Roseville, MN 55113-4061
Tel: (651)225-6907   Fax: (651)631-9334
Toll Free: (800)636 - 5042
E-Mail: amaho@ifai.com
Web Site: www.gmanow.com

Personnel:

Managing Director: Andrew Aho

Historical Note
Promotes the technical and economic benefits of geosynthetics to the user community and, in turn, assists in building stronger civil infrastructures in a cost-efficient manner. GMA represents the entire geosynthetics industry, including manufacturers as well as companies that test or supply materials and offer services to the industry. Membership fee ranges from $500 to $16000.

Figure 6.7 The *NTPA Directory* is a comprehensive source of trade associations that sponsor national and international trade shows.

visit them individually. The trade show brings all the key characters of an industry together—to meet, greet, and compete.

IMPORT PENETRATION

Since the flood of imports began in the 1970s, they have become an integral part of American life. Japanese electronics and later their automobile manufacturers were pioneers in giving American consumers new choices of quality products at lower prices than those available domestically. Manufacturers from other countries, notably South Korea, Taiwan, and Hong Kong, quickly followed Japan into the lucrative U.S. market. Government attempts at **protectionism**, or restraining trade between nations through methods such as tariffs, quotas, and **antidumping** laws, or selling products in foreign countries at prices less than wholesale in their originating country, did not diminish the American consumer's demand for imported goods. Even when **currency revaluation**—the government-initiated, official changes in the value of a country's currency relative to other currencies—increased the cost of Japanese and European imports, the better quality and distinctive styles seemed to justify the higher prices.

Figure 6.8 Located only minutes away from downtown Chicago, McCormick Place attracts more than three million visitors annually.

During the past two decades, the rate of world trade has grown much faster than world output. According to the Organization for Economic Cooperation and Development (OECD), world gross domestic product (GDP) growth in 2011 was about 3.7 percent, while world real trade growth was nearly double, at 6.1 percent. After a poor performance in 2012, with recessions in Europe and slow growth in the United States, the global economic recovery during recent years has been modest, but uneven. GDP growth was forecast to be higher in the United States than in the Eurozone; Japan experienced a strong recovery in 2013, but there was considerable uncertainty as to whether it can be sustained. In top emerging market economies, China has been seen to have the strongest growth potential, with India and Brazil struggling to overcome structural flaws in their economies.[9]

A major contributor to that growth has been the explosion of **e-commerce**, the buying and selling of products or services over electronic systems such as the Internet and other computer networks. Companies can now offer their products to markets anywhere in the world, and consumers can now import products from suppliers in virtually any country (as permitted by their import laws).

IMPORTING BY E-TAILERS AND RETAILERS

Retailers have been a major force in fashion importing since the introduction of **global sourcing**, the process of purchasing imported goods from markets around the world. Now, with Internet shopping malls and retailers' websites supplementing their bricks-and-mortar stores, consumers are exposed to more imports than ever before.

The E-tailing Explosion

Total U.S. retail sales for the November through December 2013 holiday sales period increased by 4.0 percent above 2012, according to MasterCard Advisors Spending Pulse.[10] In recent years, websites have registered a dramatic increase in holiday shopping. Online sales were expected to hit a new sales record, at $57 billion, while mobile purchases expected to surpass $8 billion for the first time.

Most e-tailers have made it easier for consumers to buy clothes online by adding extra incentives, such as free shipping on returns and exchanges. **E-tailers**—retailers offering consumers the convenience of shopping online, from their home or office computers, without visiting traditional store locations—are integrating new technologies onto their websites where customers can zoom and rotate merchandise or see the item in different colors before buying.[11]

Sourcing Options for Retailers

Fashion retailers have the option of buying imported garments ready-made, for direct sale to the final end-user, or buying all or part of their raw materials abroad and importing them into the United States for domestic production. With global sourcing, a single apparel item may even include components from as many as five countries. Retailers who produce their own private labels (to be discussed in the next section) have been using **off-shore production**, with their garments being entirely made outside the United States. This trend is starting to change, however, and many firms are bringing production back home as "Made in America" regains popularity.

A majority of U.S. offshore apparel manufacturing is in China. In 2013, U.S. direct investment there totaled a record $300 billion market for all American companies. However, persistent market barriers, a slower economic growth rate, and increasing costs and competition have led to a shift in U.S. executives' expectations for China's prospects, according to a report by the U.S.-China Business Council (USCBC). But China is still a top priority for U.S. firms—and would be much larger without the market access barriers, according to USCBC President John Frisbie.[12]

Ninety-six percent of survey respondents—the highest percentage reported since the question has been asked over the past five years—said China was among their top five priorities. But fewer respondents labeled it as their number one strategic investment priority. Illinois-based Caterpillar, Inc., the world's largest maker of earth-moving equipment, opened a plant in the southern Jiangsu province. China's ballooning trade surplus is primarily because of the nation's role as a final assembly point for manufacturers. About 80 percent of the assembly factories are foreign-owned.

According to the American Apparel & Footwear Association's Apparel Stats 2013 report,[13] more than 97 percent of all apparel sold in the United States is made globally. So retail buyers are continuously reviewing their sourcing options, including the following:

Figure 6.9 **Southern China apparel factory.**

- Foreign fashion markets and trade shows. Perhaps the two best-known trade shows are the French prêt-à-porter held in March and October and featuring the ready-to-wear designs of high-end designers such as Karl Lagerfeld, Sonia Rykiel, and Jean-Paul Gaultier. Lower-priced ready-to-wear fashion is shown at another venue around the same time. Showings in Italy and Britain also draw buyers for those goods.
- Direct assistance from importers. There are independent American companies who import goods for retail buyers and often show these at domestic markets in New York and Las Vegas.
- Store-owned buying offices. Large chain retailers such as Macy's and Neiman Marcus have access to company-owned buying offices located in fashion centers such as Paris, Milan, London, and Tokyo. Local store buyers may visit these offices during market weeks, and the buying office buyers may purchase goods for the stores in between markets.
- Independent agents, known in the fashion industry as commissionaires and found in the major fashion cities, assist retail buyers not affiliated with an overseas buying office. They assist with buying and expediting delivery and are usually paid a fee.

IMPORTING BY MANUFACTURERS

Manufacturers who import raw materials as well as finished products are another major segment of the American import industry. This group also includes chain retailers such as the Gap, Walmart, and Forever 21 that produce private labels. Their objective is to offer good value and quality—but in the least expensive way, which usually requires foreign sourcing. Using the apparel industry as an example, domestic production with domestic materials is still the standard against which all other production methods are compared, but newer options have emerged with the growth of global sourcing.

The cost of producing clothing is largely determined by two components—the costs of labor and, to a lesser extent, materials. Clothing production is therefore likely to relocate to countries where labor costs are lower—but working conditions and child labor laws are more often violated.

The U.S. Department of Labor, Bureau of International Labor Affairs, has engaged China to work together on strengthening bilateral cooperation in labor law enforcement, worker rights, and workplace safety and health. The two nations signed two memorandums of understanding on this sensitive subject in 2011 and continue to work on the components of the decade-long cooperation.[14]

Significant changes have occurred in the apparel industry in recent decades. Once concentrated in the United States and other industrialized countries, this industry has gradually spread to countries with lower production costs, becoming a globalized industry whose geographical distribution is constantly changing.

A number of factors have contributed to this globalization. Many developing countries have based or are basing their industrialization on labor-intensive export sectors, particularly the apparel sector. Developing countries have almost doubled their share of world clothing exports since the early 1970s to account for more than half of all exports today. At the same time, companies in the United States and other industrialized countries have adopted strategies to relocate certain labor-intensive activities, such as clothing assembly, to low-wage countries through direct investment or outsourcing. Thus, as the International Labour Organization (ILO) states on its website, the industrialized countries have "promoted the expansion of the clothing industry in the developing countries and participated actively in the growing globalization of the sector."

Intense competition in the U.S. retail sector has resulted in significant restructuring of the apparel industry in recent years. Contributing to this trend has been the rise of mass marketing stores and discount retailers with low overhead costs and low prices. These nontraditional retailers have displaced a significant share of the sales of traditional apparel retailers such as department and specialty stores. There have been a growing number of bankruptcies and consolidations, resulting in an increased concentration of large firms at the retail level.

Many experts point to changes in consumer attitudes as a driving force behind the restructuring that is occurring in the retailing industry. Not only have consumers become more cautious in their buying habits, but they have been reducing the portion of their disposable income that they spend on non-electronic merchandise, or soft goods, such as apparel. Consumers are increasingly demanding quality goods at low prices. Retailers have often been forced to sell merchandise permanently at sale prices, with promotions occurring throughout the year.

Economists and sociologists have attributed the increasingly volatile consumer demand to growing numbers of new products, the rise of fashion-consciousness for even the lowest-cost apparel, and selling seasons, and more recently to the state of the economy. In response, retailers are increasingly utilizing new technology to facilitate communication with suppliers and speed the distribution of goods. Apparel manufacturers who wish to remain competitive must reduce cycle times for apparel design, manufacture, and delivery. Many manufacturers have adopted **quick response** replenishment systems that allow retailers to trim inventory, respond more quickly to changes in consumer preferences, restock almost instantly, and offer a wider choice of clothing styles.

The uneven recovery in the U.S. economy in recent years has resulted in weakened consumer demand and, when combined with higher raw-material costs, has placed increased pressures on apparel manufacturers. Unable to pass higher costs onto consumers in a market with excess supply, both apparel manufacturers and retailers have been squeezed by lower margins. Since retailers have gained growing bargaining power through consolidations, apparel manufacturers have had to absorb higher costs and cope with lower profit margins to maintain production.

In this increasingly competitive environment, the lines between apparel retailers and manufacturers are being blurred as each takes on new roles and enters new aspects of the garment industry. Many retailers, for example, have entered product development and manufacturing as they develop their own private labels. In some cases, department stores and other retailers are directly contracting goods from the same foreign factories used by the brand-name producers from which they buy.

Apparel and other merchandise manufacturers and retailers increasingly turn to imports from lower-cost producers to retain their competitive edge in the U.S. market. Retailers are developing global sourcing alliances with suppliers and directly sourcing brand-name and private-label merchandise domestically and internationally. Many of the largest retailers, such as Walmart, also have become the largest importers of general merchandise and apparel.

Domestic Production—Foreign Materials

Many products, including fashion and home furnishings, can be produced in the United States with foreign raw materials or components. This method is popular with American firms who specialize in using unique or unusual materials. Manufacturers can offer a wider range of products than they would if they were buying all materials and components domestically. Design organizations such as Donna Karan, Oscar de la Renta, and Calvin Klein make great use of fine imported fabrics.

Foreign Production—Foreign Materials

Sometimes a private-label fashion buyer cannot find exactly what customers want, such as a certain style of Scottish cashmere sweater to coordinate with an Italian woolen skirt. In this case, the buyer may go to a factory in Scotland and one in Italy with the croquis (sketches) of the designs to be made. This is called **specification buying**; the domestic private label company (e.g., J. Crew or Talbot's) has designed the product, even the entire product line, and the foreign manufacturer creates it using local materials at the buyer's directions.

Complete foreign production can mean smaller, more specialized runs that are an advantage to smaller and mid-sized manufacturers, but large manufacturers, such as the Ford Motor Co., also are producing goods overseas that eventually may show up as imports in the United States.

The elimination of all textile and apparel quotas, limits on the amount of specific goods from certain countries, in January 2005 opened the door to this option, especially apparel goods from China and India. The Agreement on Textiles and Clothing provided for the gradual dismantling of the quotas that existed under the Multi-Fiber Arrangement (MFA).

Foreign Production—Domestic Materials

A third option gives U.S. manufacturers control over their raw materials while saving production costs by going offshore to Mexico or Canada under the North American Free Trade Agreement (NAFTA) or the Caribbean Basin Initiative (CBI).

Initially launched in 1983 through the Caribbean Basin Economic Recovery Act (CBERA), and substantially expanded in 2000 through the U.S.-Caribbean Basin Trade Partnership Act (CBTPA), the CBI currently provides 19 beneficiary countries with duty-free access to the U.S. market for most goods. Referred to as *9802 production*, this program permits some phase of production, usually assembly, to be done outside the United States, then brought into the country with the tariff, or import tax, paid only on the value-added portion of the item.

A disadvantage of these programs is the extra time it takes for sending domestic raw materials to the foreign production site. Nevertheless, because of favorable regulations, some domestic jeans producers have the denim manufactured here and the garments cut and sewn in Mexico or Caribbean countries.

Manufacturer-Owned Foreign Production

American apparel manufacturers and retailers are also increasingly turning to low-cost suppliers abroad to supplement their U.S. production. In some cases, manufacturers contract out apparel assembly operations to overseas contractors. In other cases, U.S. apparel manufacturers have shifted production abroad to take advantage of lower costs and, in some cases, preferential trade programs.

U.S. manufacturers have recently increased their foreign direct investment (FDI) with mergers and acquisitions in such countries as China, India, Pakistan, and Russia. The United States is the largest investor in foreign markets and the largest recipient of FDI in the world. U.S. economic gains as the result of foreign investment policies have been tempered by such perceived losses as the displacement of U.S. workers and lower wages. While some analysts believe U.S. firms invest abroad to avoid labor unions or high wages at home, 70 percent of U.S. FDI is concentrated in high-income developed countries. Even more notable, according to an October 2012 report on U.S. FDI abroad by the Congressional Research Service, is the fact that the share of investment going to developing countries has actually fallen in recent years. Most economists conclude that FDI abroad does not lead to fewer jobs or lower incomes overall for Americans and that the majority of jobs lost among U.S. manufacturing firms during the past decade reflect a broad restructuring of U.S. manufacturing industries.[15]

New spending by U.S. firms on businesses and real estate abroad, or U.S. FDI abroad, rose by 27 percent in nominal terms in 2011 over the amount invested in 2010, reflecting improvements in the rate of economic growth in Europe and elsewhere. Net investments rose from $328 billion in 2010 to $419 billion in 2011 according to the Department of Commerce.[16]

Competing manufacturers and labor unions are critical of this option, as it leads to the outsourcing of American jobs and the delegation of noncore operations from internal production to an external entity specializing in the management of that operation. Some manufacturers are starting to bring the jobs back home, as rising foreign wages and materials costs have made outsourcing less competitive.

SPOTLIGHT ON GLOBAL TRADE 6.1
U.S.-China Trade Relations: Partners or Protagonists?

U.S.-China economic ties have expanded dramatically during the past three decades. Total U.S.-China trade rose from $5 billion in 1981 to $536 billion in 2012. During this period, the economies of the United States and China have become increasingly integrated. Perhaps as the result of growing globalization or maybe China's economic reforms and rapid economic growth, the nation has emerged as a major economic power. China is currently the United States' second-largest trading partner (only neighbor and NAFTA partner Canada is larger), its third-largest export market (estimated at $250 billion annually), and its biggest source of imports.

Many U.S. firms regard international trade with China's market as critical to staying competitive in the global marketplace. For example, General Motors has invested heavily in China and, as a result, sold more cars in China than in the United States from 2010 to 2012. U.S. imports of low-cost goods from China greatly benefit U.S. consumers seeking lower-cost items and more selection, while U.S. firms can lower production costs when using China as the final point of assembly for their products, or use Chinese-made materials or components for production in the United States.

Some U.S. trade policymakers contend that the large annual U.S. trade deficit with China—more than $300 billion in 2013—is evidence of an unbalanced, unfair trade relationship that is hurting the U.S. economy. But others respond that China's ranking as the largest foreign holder of U.S. Treasury securities ($1.3 trillion as of May 2013) is critical to the health of the U.S. economy, as its purchases of U.S. government debt help keep U.S. interest rates low.

According to the U.S. Special Trade Representative report, "2012 USTR Report to Congress on China's WTO Compliance, December 2012," current Chinese leadership has growing confidence in its economic model. U.S. trade policy toward China is based on responding to their confidence with several key challenges to Chinese government leadership:

- First, China must accept its responsibility to maintain the international trading system. The nation should take a more active leadership role in maintaining that system, because it was the prime factor in the country's economic success.

- Second, progressive economic and trade reforms are the pathway for China to expand and modernize its economy. For example, the United States, and other trade partners, have been pressing China to stimulate domestic spending and allow its currency to appreciate. (The artificially low value of their currency has given China a competitive edge in prices over other exporting nations and little incentive to pay more for imports.) Those moves, currency revaluation, and programs to spend on their own economy, if initiated, would cause China's imports to increase, benefiting the economies of other countries eager to export more to China. More stable and balanced economic growth in China also would diminish calls for trade protectionism from around the world.
- Third, by improving intellectual property rights protection in China and providing nondiscriminatory treatment to foreign intellectual property (IP) firms, the country would attract more FDI in high technology than has occurred under recent government policies.
- Finally, by lowering trade barriers on imports, competition would increase in China, with the result of lower costs for consumers, and greater economic efficiency. This suggested policy change has been met with resistance from one leadership faction that insists on the status quo, as greater free-market reforms threaten the future of state-owned enterprises and successful export-oriented firms. However, reform-minded officials in China will hopefully continue to push for free—and fair—trade policies. Since change does not occur quickly in central-government command economies, the most effective way for the United States to deal with China on major economic issues is the subject of much debate.

Some U.S. trade policymakers support an aggressive program of high-level meetings with Chinese officials, to try to resolve complex and long-term issues, which would also prevent either side from imposing new protectionist measures. Still others, who see China's economic policies as damaging to U.S. economic interests, advocate a more aggressive U.S. trade policy toward China. These critics would use all tools available to U.S. policies, including such multilateral institutions as the World Trade Organization (WTO) and International Monetary Fund (IMF), as well as U.S. trade remedy laws, such as antidumping and countervailing measures (import surtaxes), to counter China's "unfair trade practices." Frequent news analyses and trade association studies have encouraged Congress and the current administration to insist on trade and investment reciprocity with China to ensure a more "balanced" economic relationship and to avoid an economically debilitating global trade war.

Source: Wayne M. Morrison, "China-U.S. Trade Issues," Congressional Research Services, July 17, 2013. Retrieved October 19, 2013, from http://www.fas.org/sgp/crs/row/RL33536.pdf; "U.S.-China Business Council, China and the U.S. Economy, Advancing a Winning Trade Agenda." Retrieved October 20, 2013, from http://www.uschina.org/ . . . /uscbc-report -china-and-us-economy-advancing-win; "Crafting Asia Economic Strategy in 2013," January 28, 2013, China-U.S. Trade Issues: Congressional Research Service, retrieved October 20, 2013, from http://csis.org/publication/crafting-asiaeconomic-strategy-2013.

THE IMPORT DEBATE

During fiscal year 2011, about 24 million shipments of FDA-regulated products were imported into the United States from 228 foreign jurisdictions. This represents a fourfold increase over the past decade. The growing volume of imports has made it more important than ever for the FDA to build relationships with regulators and industry abroad, according to senior FDA officials in their report, "FDA's China Offices Focus on Product Safety."[17]

Foreign outposts have been established to give the FDA a way to address safety issues before products leave the country of origin. By helping other nations develop stronger regulatory systems and helping industry to understand our expectations and realize they will benefit from them, we're also helping ourselves and keeping U.S. consumers safe, the FDA reports.

In addition to China, the FDA now has staff stationed permanently in New Delhi and Mumbai, India; Brussels, Belgium; London, England; Parma, Italy; San Jose, Costa Rica; Santiago, Chile; Mexico City, Mexico; Pretoria, South Africa; and Amman, Jordan.

The FDA's foreign offices have been a critical part of its new global strategy, which has focused on building coalitions with regulators in other countries. These partnerships have allowed the FDA to develop information networks through which regulators worldwide can share knowledge about criminal enterprises, as well as cutting-edge investigative tools.

In the modern era of global supply chains, international trade, and the foreign sourcing and manufacture of regulated products, the FDA has encountered serious challenges to its monitoring of the safety and quality of U.S. food and medical products. This sea-change in how FDA regulates foreign food and products will improve the quality and safety of FDA-regulated products and benefit consumers and industry through streamlined regulation and additional assurance of quality and safety, the FDA cautions.

The safety issue of imported products is just one facet of the political debate between protectionists and free trade proponents—on both sides of Congress. The advocates of **isolationism** or limiting international trade—frequently labor union officials or legislators from strong union-influential states—call for import restrictions, such as quotas or tariffs, to be imposed, in an effort to protect domestic manufacturers from unfair competition caused by cheaper labor or government subsidiaries in many foreign countries.

Those who believe in free trade advocate international trade with no or few limitations. They stress that U.S. manufacturers should learn to compete with foreign businesses or concentrate on other industries in which they may have a competitive or technological edge. They also point out that any protectionist action by the United States may be matched by its trade partners, with the possibility of a trade war, to the detriment of all societies involved.

In recent years, discussions have centered on the issues of free trade versus fair trade. Adherents to fair trade believe in forms of international trade that provide for human rights including fair wages for workers; safe, clean places to work and live; and protection for the environment. An increasing number of trade agreements incorporate fair trade provisions.

Proponents of free trade argue that voluntary exchange meets the demands of justice because each party to the trade leaves the trade richer than he or she was before. Johan Norberg writes in his book *In Defense of Global Capitalism* that, "it may seem odd that the world's prosperity can be augmented by swapping things with each other, but every time you go shopping you realize, subconsciously, how exchange augments wealth. You pay a dollar for a bottle of milk because you would rather have the milk than your dollar. The shop sells it at that price because they would rather have your dollar than keep the milk. Both parties are satisfied with the deal, otherwise it would never have taken place. Both emerge from the transaction feeling that you have made a good exchange, your needs have been provided for."[18]

In any case, the impact of global trade, whether importing or exporting, means more markets for businesses and more choices for consumers, as globalization has created an interdependent, linked global market.

KEY TERMS

Summary

Although most Americans use imported clothing, autos, food, or appliances, few people stop to think about how imported items arrive in this country. Nevertheless, today's consumer is the best informed, most technologically savvy, and best equipped to find the widest variety of products, with the lowest price tags, thanks to importing and e-commerce.

The number one reason for importing is to satisfy customer demand at a profit. Therefore, the first and most important step in deciding whether to import goods or services is to determine the size of the potential market. Some importers resell their goods to wholesalers or retailers; others import components, or materials and parts that go into finished goods that are ultimately sold to consumers in the domestic marketplace. Most consumers don't realize the complexities involved in sourcing goods in distant countries: negotiating in a language or with business customs that are unfamiliar; transporting the purchases thousands of miles; clearing U.S. customs entry; and finally distributing products in the United States.

Potential importers need to assess their company's strengths, weaknesses, opportunities, and threats by conducting a SWOT analysis. This competitive analysis then will aid in evaluating sourcing costs, domestic suppliers, and other competitors as well as the size and value of the current market. Information on current end-users' demographics and psychographics must preclude any import buying. The main business objective is to make a profit, and the best way to do that is to identify a substantial, long-term need for the product you plan to import.

Once marketing opportunities are confirmed, the next step is to find a number of qualified international supply sources. The commerce agencies or chambers of commerce of foreign governments, located here or abroad, as well as industry-specific trade magazines, exhibit shows, and associations are good sources for suppliers' names and email addresses, if no Internet home page is available.

If foreign travel is not economically feasible, potential importers should visit major trade shows in the United States—but marketing plans should include foreign show visits as soon as possible.

With imports of more than $2.7 trillion worth of goods and services, in 2012, the rationale for importing is obvious: more choices at better prices will result in more sales and profits, with the added advantage of diversified sourcing or manufacturing.

Those businesses new to importing should also consider the risks. Foreign sourcing can add weeks to lead times; slow or unpredictable delivery, quality control issues, and infrastructure failures can be costly or even terminal for long-term domestic relationships.

Strict U.S. government import controls, in the wake of the 2001 terrorist attacks, can be challenging to the smaller firm or individual importer. Import tariffs or duties—taxes on goods or services coming into the United States—as well as nontariff barriers to trade, such as quality standards, can be strong disincentives for those wishing to import.

Both manufacturers and retailers engage in importing into the United States. The safety of imports, especially from China, continues to make headlines and sparks debate from both Republican and Democratic members of Congress, as well as the administration, calling for stricter U.S. customs' controls, quality and safety checks, and even the prospect of more tariffs to protect American consumers from unsafe imports.

Review Questions

1. Why are imported goods appealing to American consumers, and what are some of the risks of importing?

2. What are the delivered-into-store merchandise costs an importer incurs?

3. State three or four questions a potential importer needs to pose before buying foreign goods.

4. Identify four ways fashion retailers can buy goods overseas.

5. Describe the major issues in the import debate: fair trade versus free trade.

Discussion Questions and Activities

1. How do the U.S. government's tariffs, quotas, or other restrictions on imported products that may compete with domestically produced items violate the rights of U.S. importers, individuals or businesses, in the pursuit of free enterprise?

2. In what ways do imports create the export of American jobs? How do imports contribute to American employment?

3. What measures can be taken to protect American jobs without becoming a protectionist, antitrade nation?

4. The Buy American Act, passed in 1933, mandates preferences for the purchase of domestically produced goods in direct procurements by the U.S. government. State your views on "Buy American" legislation that would require that state or federal government procurement be from U.S. suppliers—unless these items were not available from domestic companies. What could be the possible fallout from such policies, should they become a reality in our country?

Chapter 6 Case

Dealing with Import Glitches

Imports can attract customers in a way that much domestic merchandise cannot equal. Imports are often colorfully adorned and uniquely distinctive. Customers know they stand out from the crowd when wearing a decorative imported shirt or piece of jewelry. Hostesses are proud of their imported table settings, patterned ceramics, and hand-woven linens, all showing their origin in far-away parts of the world. For many, driving a foreign automobile imparts a panache unobtainable with a domestic car. And through satisfying these customer wants, imports can make businesses more profitable.

Buying goods from other countries, while enabling marketers to offer unique assortments at a profit, is not always easy. As this text points out, often orders for shipments must be made and paid for in advance, transportation arranged among several carriers, and customs regulations observed. In addition, returning faulty import shipments is often impossible. Under these circumstances it's easy to see that import glitches can happen. Consider three examples of foul-ups that have occurred and decide how you would deal with similar situations.

In the first situation, a chain of department stores was proud of their seasonal Christmas shops set up before Thanksgiving and closing the week after Christmas. Along with the Santa Clauses and snow-covered evergreens, among the most popular items were the shiny hand-decorated Christmas tree ornaments imported from China. One year the shipments were held up at the West Coast port of entry until just before Christmas day. The store buyers were frantic, wondering how to stock their Christmas shops until the ornaments arrived, or if they were to arrive at all.

In another instance an accessories wholesaler offering an assortment of scarves, along with handbags, small leather goods, and hats, ordered from her domestic vendor some fashionable light-weight printed scarves made in India. When they arrived, the odor they gave off was unbearable. Apparently the scarves had not dried thoroughly after dyeing and were exuding an unpleasant smell.

In a third situation, an online fashion shoe retailer had ordered a line of reptile-patterned heels among the shoes she regularly obtained from her supplier in Italy. Shortly after the shoes arrived in boxes marked "reptile," she was visited by an agent from the U.S. Department of Natural Resources (DNR). The agent wanted to know where the snakes were and if they had been imported legally. U.S. customs had spotted the boxes at the port of entry and wanted assurance its regulations were being followed and ordered DNR to check it out!

Source: Harvey R. Shoemack and Patricia Mink Rath, *Essentials of Exporting and Importing, U.S. Trade Policies, Practices, and Procedures*. New York: Fairchild Books, 2010.

Questions

1. If you were the buyer in each of these situations, how would you have handled them?

2. What, if anything, might you do in each of these situations to prevent similar occurrences in the future?

References

1. Ten Thousand Villages website. Retrieved July 9, 2013, from http://www.tenthousandvillages.com.

2. "Imports Work for America," May 2013, Trade Partnership Worldwide, sponsored by CEA, National Retail Federation, U.S. Chamber of Commerce and American Apparel & Footwear Association, p. 5. Retrieved October 4, 2013, from http://uschamber.com/report/imports-work-for-america.

3. "Import Trade Trends, Fiscal Year 2012, Year-End Report," U.S. Customs and Border Protection, January 2013, p. 6. Retrieved October 4, 2013,

from http://nemo.cbp.gov/ot/fy12_yearend.pdf.

4. Ibid.

5. "Exports and Imports: The 2012 Statistical Abstract," U.S. Census Bureau. Retrieved October 21, 2013, from http://www.census.gov/compendia/statab/cats/foreign_commerce_aid/exports_and_imports.html.

6. "Container Security Initiative (CSI), "U.S. Department of Homeland Security. Retrieved October 22, 2013, from http://www.dhs.gov/container-security-initiative-ports.

7. Op. cit., "Imports Work for America."

8. McCormick Place Facilities. Retrieved October 20, 2013, from http://www.mccormickplace.com/facilities/facilities_01.html.

9. "General Assessment of the Macroeconomic Situation," OECD Economic Outlook, vol. 2013/1. Retrieved October 21, 2013, from http://www.oecd-ilibrary.org/economics/oecd-economic-outlook-volume-2013-issue-1_eco_outlook-v2013-1-en.

10. Lindsey Rupp and Cotten Timberlake, "U.S. Holiday Sales Rose 3.5% (in 2013)," MasterCard Advisors Spending Pulse, December 26, 2013.

Retrieved June 23, 2013, from http://www .bloomberg.com/news /2013-12-26/u-s-holiday -sales-rise-3-5-spending pulse-says.html.

11. Ibid.

12. "U.S.-China Business Council 2013 China Business Environment Survey," August 20, 2013. Retrieved October 23, 2013, from http://markets .financialcontent.com /stocks/news/read /25335989/USCBC_2013 _China_Business _Environment_Survey _Results_.

13. "AAFA Releases ApparelStats 2013 and ShoeStats 2013 Reports," American Apparel & Footwear Association, January 5, 2014. Retrieved June 23, 2014, from https://www.wewear.org /aafa-releases-apparel stats-2013-and-shoestats -2013-reports.

14. "U.S.-China Labor Cooperation," U.S. Department of Labor, Bureau of International Labor Affairs. Retrieved October 23, 2013, from http://www.dol.gov/ilab /diplomacy/sed.htm.

15. James K. Jackson, "U.S. Direct Investment Abroad: Trends and Current Issues,"

Congressional Research Service, October 26, 2012. Retrieved October 24, 2013, from http://www.fas .org/sgp/crs/misc/RS21 118.pdf.

16. Ibid.

17. "FDA's China Offices Focus on Product Safety," U.S. Food and Drug Administration, updated August 22, 2013. Retrieved October 25, 2013, from http://www.fda.gov /ForConsumers /ConsumerUpdates /ucm284461.htm.

18. Johan Norberg, *In Defense of Global Capitalism,* 2003. Cato Institute.

Figure 7.1 Every import shipment is subject to detention and examination by U.S. Customs officers to insure compliance with all U.S. import laws and regulations.

CHAPTER 7
ENTERING THE
IMPORT BUSINESS

uess what? Individuals or companies of any size don't need to invest millions of dollars to enter the import business. Using eBay, Yahoo, Amazon, or other websites, importers are bringing goods into the United States from throughout the world, without a major investment or even an importer's license.

Although the **U.S. Customs and Border Protection (CBP)**, known as **Customs**, the primary agency controlling all imports into the United States, does not demand that importers have a license or permit; other government agencies may require a permit, license, or other certification, depending on the specific import. Customs entry forms do require an importer's number, which is either an Internal Revenue Service (IRS) business registration number, Federal Employer Identification Number (FEIN), or personal Social Security number.

Businesses interested in importing foreign goods (as well as individuals importing for personal use) need to understand and comply with the basic U.S. import requirements of the Customs Territory of the United States, the District of Columbia, and Puerto Rico. They must follow certain procedures governed by the CBP, whose primary mandate is to help expedite **entry**, the presentation of required documents declaring the import shipment's origin and value. Every import shipment is subject to detention and examination by Customs officers, to ensure compliance with all U.S. import laws and regulations.

FIVE STEPS TO IMPORTING

Before deciding to allocate any time and money resources to a transaction, first-time importers will find it useful to proceed through a series of steps that may yield the answers as to whether or not their venture might be profitable. Their first call should be to the nearest CBP office. The number can be found online or in the local telephone directory. Ask for a *commodity control specialist* in charge of the basic product or category description of the intended import. Then follow these steps.

Step One: Determine Customs Classification

Determine the WCO/HTS Classification Number(s). All intended imports must be classified according to this schedule. The **World Customs Organization (WCO)** represents 179 Customs administrations that operate on all continents and represent all stages of economic development. Today, WCO members are responsible for processing more than 98 percent of all international trade.

The **Harmonized Tariff Schedule of the United States (HTSUS)**, issued by the United States International Trade Commission, has been combined with the WCO to create the WCO HTS schedule that numerically classifies merchandise by type of product, such as textile fibers and textile products and animal and vegetable products.[1]

These steps need to be taken before any price quoting to management or offers of sale to prospective customers, as duty changes can alter purchase costs and profit projections, as well as your selling price.

Customs Automated Commercial System

To speed Customs clearance, the import community and Customs has created the **Customs Automated Commercial System (ACS)**, which electronically receives and processes entry documentation and provides cargo disposition information. Cargo carriers, customs brokers, and individual importers may use the system, which reduces clearance time from days to hours or even minutes. Importers, who file their own entry documentation with Customs, find this method to be very efficient.[2]

Automated Broker Interface

Those individuals or companies importing merchandise either for their own use or for commercial transactions may decide to use a **customs broker**, an independent business, licensed by the U.S. Treasury Department, engaged in clearing goods through U.S. Customs. Brokers commonly use the **Automated Broker Interface (ABI)**, an integral part of ACS that permits qualified participants to file import data electronically with Customs. ABI is a voluntary program available to brokers, importers, carriers, port authorities, and independent service centers.

INTERNATIONAL FASHION FOCUS 7.1

Loomstate, Rogan, and Edun: Import Duties and Quotas Negotiated in Many Countries While Fair Trade Prevails

Just about every fashion organization around—huge companies such as J.C. Penney, Walmart, and Target, and smaller ones such as Loomstate, Rogan, and Edun—imports apparel, accessories, home furnishings, and other goods to offer American consumers wider selections. The last three companies are a bit different from the rest, however. They offer high fashion, and in the case of Edun, high-priced merchandise carried by stores such as Barneys and Nordstrom and manufactured under fair trade standards.

Loomstate, Rogan, and Edun were started by designer Rogan Gregory with his partner Scott Hahn. Like the managers at Patagonia, Gap, Nike, and a few others with a social conscience, Rogan and Scott wanted to be certain that their goods were manufactured according to fair trade rules, meaning that the factory workers receive fair pay, suitable working conditions, and are not otherwise exploited. One day, Ali Hewson saw the Edun line, and she thought her husband might be interested. Hewson's husband happened to be U2's Bono, and indeed he was interested. Through Bono's efforts in Africa, Edun was able to expand and develop more factories where fair wages and working conditions result in superior products.

While some of the apparel for Loomstate, Rogan, and Edun is manufactured in the United States, other sources include Peru, Turkey, India, and the African nations of Lesotho and Tunisia. Negotiating international customs regulations in a number of countries is mind-boggling. For example, to make the garments, Turkey levies a duty but Africa does not unless the fabric originates in another country. For entry into the United States, a shirt in a Chinese factory may carry a "Made in Bangladesh" label if the garment was sewn there but sent to China for finishing (including collars and cuffs).

Since duties and quotas are the laws of each government, they must be strictly followed for goods to flow smoothly to customers. To do this and to be sure that goods are made under fair trade standards takes even more effort, but the owners sleep well at night.

Sources: Rachel Louise Snyder, *Fugitive Denim, A Moving Story of People and Pants in the Borderless World of Global Trade*, New York: Norton, 2008; *Wallpaper**, April 18, 2004. Retrieved on February 13, 2008 from http://www.wallpaper.com.

Currently, more than 96 percent of all U.S. import entries are filed through the ABI. Additional information on ACS and ABI can be found on the CBP website at http://www.cbp.gov.[3]

The WCO HTS updates apply to the ACI and ABI.[4] An importer who is unsure of the proper way to classify an item may submit a request, in writing, for a binding classification ruling to the National Commodity Specialist Division, U.S. Customs, Attn: Classification Ruling Requests, New York, NY 10048. The rulings will be binding at all ports of entry unless revoked by the Headquarters' Office of Regulations and Rulings.

Importers who are not satisfied with the binding ruling received from New York can appeal it to the Headquarters' Office of Regulations and Rulings, Washington, DC 20229. Import specialists can give advisory rulings orally, but the classification-related opinions or advice of Customs personnel at one port are not binding for other Customs ports. Oral inquiries may be made to Customs offices regarding existing binding rulings that might cover a specific importation. Binding rulings may also be researched on the Customs website at http://www.cbp.gov.

Figure 7.2 **A CBP officer checks for specific chemicals arriving in cargo from another country.**

Step Two: Calculate Customs Quotas and Duties

The WCO HTS number also indicates the amount of Customs duties and/or quotas that may be applicable upon entry into the United States. In some instances Customs quotas and duties can be complex, difficult, and onerous. As worldwide trade increases, steps to lower or eliminate these requirements have become more favorable to exporters and importers. For example, the North American Free Trade Agreement (NAFTA) has worked to eliminate most duties and quotas between the United States, Canada, and Mexico. Here's how quotas and duties work in today's economy.

Import Quotas

An **import quota** is a quantity limit on imported merchandise for a specific period of time. Quotas are established by legislation, by directives, and by proclamations issued under the authority contained in specific legislation. The majority of import quotas are administered by CBP. The commissioner of CBP controls the importation of quota merchandise but has no authority to change or modify any quota.

U.S. import quotas may be divided into two types: **absolute quotas**, specific quantities of certain products that may be permitted entry during a quota period, and **tariff-rate quotas**, which provide for the entry of a specified quantity of the quota product at a reduced rate of duty during a given period. Under NAFTA, there are **tariff preference levels (TPLs)**, which are administered as tariff-rate quotas.[5]

For tariff-rate quotas, there is no limitation on the amount of the product that may be entered during the quota period, but quantities entered in excess of the quota for the period are subject to higher duty rates. In most cases, products of Communist-controlled countries or areas are not entitled to the benefits of tariff-rate quotas.

Some absolute quotas are global, while others are allocated to specified foreign countries. Imports in excess of a specified quota may be held for the opening of the next quota period by placing it in a foreign trade zone or by entering it for warehouse, or it may be exported or destroyed under CBP supervision.

The import of textiles and apparel has special quota requirements. CBP administers import controls on certain cotton, wool, man-made fiber, silk blends, and other vegetable-fiber articles manufactured or produced in designated countries. CBP administers the Special Access Program and the Andean Trade Preference Act on certain products that are made of U.S.-formed-and-cut fabric. These controls are imposed on the basis of directives issued to the commissioner of CBP by the chairman of the Committee for the Implementation of Textile Agreements.[6]

For example, a **textile visa**, an endorsement in the form of a stamp on an invoice or export control license that is executed by a foreign government, is used to control the exportation of textiles and textile products to the United States and to prohibit the unauthorized entry of the merchandise into this country.[7]

Figure 7.3 CBP laboratory personnel check textiles imported into the United States.

The visa system is the most effective way to prevent illegal *trans-shipments* (goods produced in one country such as China, but labeled as originating in another, such as Thailand) and quota fraud. It also ensures that both the foreign government and the United States count merchandise and charge quotas in the same way so that overshipments, incorrect quota charges, and embargo infractions can be avoided. If a visa cites an incorrect category or quantity, or contains other incorrect or missing data, or a shipment arrives without a visa, the entry is rejected and the merchandise is not released until the importer reports the discrepancy to the foreign government and receives a new visa or visa waiver from the government.

However, a visa does not guarantee entry of the merchandise into the United States. If the quota closes between the time the visa is issued in the foreign country and the shipment's arrival in the United States, the goods will not be released to the importer until the quota opens again. To avoid expensive warehousing costs, or even the loss of a perishable shipment, importers must advise their foreign source of the status of any applicable quotas or other restrictions that might delay entry. In other words, exporters shouldn't ship goods to another country unless they are certain entry will take place without extensive delays.

When a shipment arrives at a port in the United States, the Customs import specialist reviews the visa documents for accuracy and completeness before release of the merchandise. The review ensures that the category number, quantity, signature, date, and visa number are correct and match the shipment. Only after this action is completed and the merchandise is charged to the quota (if required) is the shipment released to the importer.

Goods brought in for the importer's personal use and not for resale, regardless of value, whether or not accompanying the traveler (except for custom-made suits from Hong Kong), are exempt from quota, visa, and exempt certification requirements.[8]

Quotas are product- and country-specific and are usually for a one-year period. Information concerning current and specific import controls may be obtained from the CBP commissioner. Information concerning the textile program may be obtained from the Committee for the Implementation of Textile Agreements, U.S. Department of Commerce, in Washington, DC.

Import Duties

Another possible challenge to profitable import trade is **customs duties**, also known as tariffs, or taxes on certain goods brought into the country. Most industry professionals use the terms *duty* and *tariff* interchangeably—both refer to the tax placed on imports, according to duty rates established by Congress.[9]

Using the example of an import of women's wool carcoats, let's examine the HTS classification number procedure to determine this item's duty rate:

1. On the Internet, go to the homepage of the U.S. International Trade Commission at http://www.usitc.gov.

2. On the left-side menu, click the link *Tariff Information Center (TIC)*. If you are new to the import business, read the HTS background information to better understand the U.S. classification system.

3. From the home page of the ITC, click on the left-side menu link *Official Harmonized Schedule*.

4. After reading the HTS coding explanation, click (at the bottom of the page) the link for the current year *HTSA Basic—by Chapter*.

5. Scroll down through the chapter-by-chapter listings until you find a description of your import category; in our example, we find women's coats in Chapter 62, titled "Articles of apparel and clothing accessories, not knitted or crocheted." Click on the chapter listing (in blue type.)

6. Enlarge the page and scroll past the Chapter 62 notes (which may apply to your imports, in some cases, but not our example) until you find the listing for women's coats, which is on page 10. So the heading for our example is Chapter **62** ("women's or girls' overcoats, carcoats, capes, cloaks, anoraks. . . ."), with a subheading of **11**, for "of wool or fine animal hair." The HTS number is **6202.11.00**.[10]

Heading/ Subheading	Stat. Suffix	Article Description	Unit of Quantity	Rates of Duty		
				1		2
				General	Special	
6202		Women's or girls' overcoats, carcoats, capes, cloaks, anoraks (including ski-jackets), windbreakers and similar articles (including padded, sleeveless jackets), other than those of heading 6204:				
		Overcoats, carcoats, capes, cloaks and similar coats:				
6202.11.00		Of wool or fine animal hair	. . . .	41¢/kg + 16.3%	Free (BH,CA, CL,CO,IL,JO,KR, MA,MX,P,PA, PE,SG) 8% (AU) 20.5¢/kg + 8.1% (OM)	46.3¢/kg + 58.5%
	10	Women's (435).	doz. kg			
	20	Girls' (435).	doz. kg			
6202.12		Of cotton:				
6202.12.10	00	Containing 15 percent or more by weight of down and waterfowl plumage and of which down comprises 35 percent or more by weight; containing 10 percent or more by weight of down (354).	doz. . . . . . kg	4.4%	Free (BH,CA, CL,CO,IL,JO,KR, MA,MX,OM,P, PA,PE,SG) 3.9% (AU)	60%
6202.12.20		Other.	. . . .	8.9%	Free (BH,CA, CL,CO,IL,JO,KR, MA,MX,OM,P, PA,PE,SG) 8% (AU)	90%
		Raincoats:				
	10	Women's (335).	doz. kg			
	20	Girls' (335).	doz. kg			
		Other:				
		Corduroy:				
	25	Women's (335).	doz. kg			
	35	Girls' (335).	doz. kg			
		Other:				
	50	Women's (335).	doz. kg			
	60	Girls' (335).	doz. kg			

Figure 7.4 U.S. duty rates on imports are listed in the Harmonized Tariff Schedule of the United States.

7. Note the two columns under the title "rates of duty." The first column is subdivided into "General" and "Special." The general duty rate is for imports of countries that have general or normal trade relations (NTR), the most common and lowest duty rate (except for "special"), with the United States at the time of the import transaction. Rates in the "special" column are for countries with active U.S. free trade agreements or other special tariff treatment.

The second column rates apply to products, whether imported directly or indirectly, of certain countries that are controlled by trade laws, or by action taken by the president of the United States. As of this writing, products from Cuba and North Korea were listed, but import restrictions will be applied to any country in accordance with U.S. international trade policies and the embargoes and sanctions in place at the time of import entry.

8. In the case of our wool carcoats, HTS number 6202.11.00, the duty rate is $.41/kg + 16.3 percent, assessed on the Customs value, if imported from a country under a column one "general" classification.[11]

Using the eight steps above, import duty rates can be calculated by individuals or businesses contemplating goods from certain foreign countries. However, since tariff rates and country restrictions change frequently, it is always wise to confirm duty rates with a U.S. Customs Commodity Specialist at a local CBP office or with national offices accessed via the Internet. Professional customs brokers can also assist but may give you a sales pitch for your import transportation business.

Duties are generally assessed at **ad valorem rates**, a percentage of the value of the goods when clearing Customs that is added as a tax to the import price. Thus, an ad valorem duty-assessed imported designer raincoat would be the same percentage, say 9 percent (but obviously far higher in terms of the dollar amount), as that of a lower-priced imported raincoat. Some articles, however, are dutiable at a **specific rate**, for example, per piece, liter, or kilo; leather boots might be levied a specific rate of $3 per pair. Other products are assessed at a **compound rate** of duty, which is a combination of both ad valorem and specific rates. Women's woolen cardigans might be assigned an ad valorem rate of 15 percent plus a specific rate of $.35 per kilogram.

It is the responsibility of the importer—not Customs—to declare the **dutiable value**, the value of a shipment that will be subject to import duties. The final appraisal, however, is fixed by Customs at the time of entry. Several methods are used to arrive at the official Customs value. The **transaction value**, the price actually paid or payable by the buyer to the seller for the goods when sold for exportation to the United States, is the primary basis of appraisal. The European Union (EU) employs the term **CIF (cost, insurance, and freight) values** to sum up the elements in the transaction value.

Other factors may also add to the dutiable value of merchandise, such as packing costs; any selling commission incurred by the buyer; any royalty or license fee that the buyer is required to pay, directly or indirectly, as a condition of the sale; and the proceeds of any subsequent resale and disposal or use of the imported merchandise that accrue, directly or indirectly, to the seller.

When the transaction value cannot be determined, then the value of the imported goods being appraised is the transaction value of identical merchandise. If merchandise identical to the imported goods cannot be found or an acceptable transaction value for such merchandise does not exist, then the value is the transaction value of similar merchandise. Merchandise that is produced in the same country and by the same organization as the merchandise being appraised would qualify as similar merchandise. It must be commercially interchangeable with that merchandise. Also, identical or similar merchandise must have been exported to the United States at or about the same time the merchandise being appraised.

Figure 7.5 Importers of fashion follow trends from all over the world.

In addition to duties, processing fees may also be applicable, according to Customs' final determination of the correct tariff rate. Tariffs are intended to level the playing field, or protect domestic producers from imports made with foreign government subsidies or with very low wages in underdeveloped countries. The duty rate of an item is tied to its classification number.

The WCO HTS applies several rates of duty for each item: general rates for **normal trade relations (NTR)** countries where the United States maintains the lowest possible duty rates; *special rates* for certain programs (free, or lower than the rates currently accorded NTR countries); and *column two rates* for imports not eligible for either general or special rates.

The United States is one of the most open countries in the world with regard to import duties and regulations. More than 95 percent of the import categories have zero duty rates and no quotas. However, the collection of duties is the second-highest revenue source for the U.S. Treasury; only the IRS's collection of income taxes contributes more.

Where imported items are placed on the Tariff System determines their value. In accordance with the **Customs Modernization Act (Mod Act)**, the 1996 legislation declared it is the responsibility of the importer of record to use "reasonable care to enter, classify and value the goods and provide any other information necessary to enable Customs to properly assess duties, collect accurate statistics, and determine if all other applicable legal requirements have been met."[12]

Step Three: Find Out Special Customs Regulations
Another type of import restriction, **Non-Tariff Barriers to Trade (NTBs)**, can also be imposed, but it does not involve the payment of taxes or penalties. NTBs can be in the form of manufacturing standards or safety requirements, or even how an animal is caught or the use of endangered species in the production process. If the imports don't meet NTB requirements, they will be denied access. Some are applied only in special circumstances, which can spark controversy, as they border on protectionism, which is the government's protection of domestic business by restricting or regulating foreign trade. An example would be import quotas, introduced in earlier Step Two, that technically qualify as NTBs, since they are government-sponsored import restrictions on amounts of specific items from certain countries, but do not involve the assessment of taxes.[13]

If the NTBs are too costly or difficult to comply with, importers may decide to cancel efforts to bring the items into this country. For a more in-depth discussion of NTBs, go to the Office of the U.S. Trade Representative website: http://www.ustr .gov/trade-topics/industry-manufacturing/non-tariff-barriers.

New importers should ask their local Customs commodity control specialist for tips on the most common problems or mistakes related to labeling, packaging, or marking experienced by other importers for the same types of goods. Clarification of specific NTBs, such as industry standards or safety certifications, can

Figure 7.6 A CBP officer at the Port of Long Beach inspects a child's toy to see that it meets the requirements for lawful entry into the United States.

usually be obtained by contacting the U.S. trade association for the industry in which the imported products would be included.

Textiles and Apparel Import Regulations

The Federal Trade Commission (FTC) website, http://www.ftc.gov, offers a guide to compliance with federal labeling requirements for textile, wool, and fur products. The law requires that textile and wool products have a label listing the fiber content, the country of origin, and the identity of the manufacturer or another business responsible for marketing or handling the item. Labels for fur products are required under a separate statute and rule.[14]

Care labels for wearing apparel also are required by FTC rule, and information about preparing labels can be found in the FTC publication *Writing a Care Label: How to Comply with the Care Labeling Rule,* which can also be found on the following website: http://www.ftc.gov/os/statutes/textilejump.shtm. Another example of textile import restriction covered in that publication applies to the fabric itself. "Any article of wearing apparel, fabric, or interior furnishing cannot be imported into the United States if it fails to conform to an applicable flammability standard issued under the Flammable Fabrics Act." These flammability standards cover the following:

- General wearing apparel
- Children's sleepwear
- Mattresses
- Mattress pads, including futons
- Carpets and rugs

Certain products can be imported into the United States, as provided in Section 11(c) of the act, in order to finish or process them to render these products less highly flammable and thus less dangerous when worn by individuals. In such cases, the exporter must state on the invoice or other paper relating to the shipment that the shipment is being made for that purpose.[15]

Who's Covered and Who's Not
Businesses that manufacture, import, sell, offer to sell, distribute, or advertise products covered by the Textile and Wool Acts must comply with the labeling requirements. The requirements do not apply until the products are ready for sale to consumers. Items shipped or delivered in an intermediate stage of production, and not labeled with the required information, must include an invoice disclosing the fiber, country of origin, manufacturer or dealer identity, and the name and address of the person or company issuing the invoice. If the manufacturing or processing of the goods is substantially complete, they are considered to be ready for sale to consumers. Even if small details have not been finished—such as hemming, cuffing, or attaching buttons to garments—the products must be labeled.[16]

Step Four: Obtain Outside Agency Approvals
Importers must determine—before issuing a purchase order—what outside agency approvals or certificates might be necessary and how much they could add to the import price of each item. For example, the U.S. Department of Agriculture is responsible for overseeing the importation of certain food products. Once applicable agencies are identified, direct contact should be made to determine whether or not specific imports are subject to testing, specific modifications, or certificates—and how much they may cost. Ask agency officials what were the most common problems or mistakes made by other firms importing the same category or type of product, including documentation errors, standards, or prototype requirements. If certification is too costly or time-consuming, it may not be practical to import the intended products.

Step Five: Follow Sampling Procedures
Check with Customs to determine how they define a *sample* of the intended import. An apparel item, for example, imported as a sample—not for sale—may require a 4-inch-diameter hole in the center of the garment, to prevent its sale without paying any duties. Check for an explanation of the proper documentation required from Customs for this type of sample.

Figure 7.7 The Federal Trade Commission (FTC) website, http://www.ftc.gov, offers a guide to compliance with federal labeling requirements for textile and wool products.

Since one country's import is another country's export, the laws governing a single international trade transaction may differ considerably. Firms exporting to the United States will have to conform to laws of their country, as well as to U.S. import laws. Therefore, potential importers should obtain specific import information from a Customs officer at the port nearest their business or home and then share that information with foreign trading partners. A list of U.S. ports of entry is available at http://www.cbp.gov.

Summary

Going into the importing business does not necessarily mean investing a great deal of money. It does mean, however, that in bringing goods into the country successfully, a business needs to operate within the government's Customs system, which is run by the CBP office. To assist in determining the eventual profitability of bringing in goods from foreign sources, potential importers will want to consider these five steps:

1. Determine the Customs classification of the intended imports according to the Harmonized Tariff Schedule of the United States (HTSUS). All goods are classified in this schedule that also includes applicable duties and quotas.

2. Ascertain Customs quotas and duties when applicable. Some goods may be brought in under a quota system. There are two types: absolute quotas, meaning no additional goods may be imported during that time period; and tariff rate quotas, meaning that additional goods may be brought in at a higher tariff rate. Duties or tariffs are classified as ad valorem, a percentage of the value of an item; specific, per a measured amount such as a kilo; or compound, a combination of ad valorem or specific duties.

KEY TERMS

- ABSOLUTE QUOTAS
- AD VALOREM RATES
- AUTOMATED BROKER INTERFACE (ABI)
- COMPOUND RATE
- COST, INSURANCE, AND FREIGHT (CIF) VALUES
- CUSTOMS (see U.S. CUSTOMS AND BORDER PROTECTION)
- CUSTOMS AUTOMATED COMMERCIAL SYSTEM (ACS)
- CUSTOMS BROKER
- CUSTOMS DUTIES
- CUSTOMS MODERNIZATION ACT (MOD ACT)
- DUTIABLE VALUE
- ENTRY
- HARMONIZED TARIFF SCHEDULE OF THE UNITED STATES (HTSUS)
- IMPORT QUOTA
- NON-TARIFF BARRIERS TO TRADE (NTBs)
- NORMAL TRADE RELATIONS (NTR)
- SPECIFIC RATE
- TARIFF PREFERENCE LEVELS (TPLs)
- TARIFF-RATE QUOTA
- TEXTILE VISA
- TRANSACTION VALUE
- U.S. CUSTOMS AND BORDER PROTECTION (CBP)
- WORLD CUSTOMS ORGANIZATION (WCO)

3. Find out special Customs requirements. Some goods such as textiles have special requirements that importers need to meet to secure their importation.

4. Obtain outside agency approval. Some goods must be cleared with other agencies, such as certain food items, which need the approval of the Agriculture Department.

5. Follow sampling procedures. If a garment is brought in as a sample, in order not to be liable for duties, it must have a four-inch hole in the center.

A list of specific Customs information is available from all Customs offices.

Review Questions

1. Describe the five steps that are necessary for first-time importers to follow before bringing in goods from other countries.

2. Why is it important for potential importers to understand the requirements of the five steps before deciding whether or not to enter the business?

3. What factors contribute to the *dutiable value* of a shipment that will be subject to import duties?

4. Barriers to importing into the United States are either tariff or non-tariff; explain how they differ.

5. For many industries, including apparel, the use of samples is routine for showing a new line before taking future production orders. Should these samples be imported duty free? What steps need to be taken to ensure they are not sold without proper duties being paid?

Discussion Questions and Activities

1. Identify class members who think the United States should limit imports (to save American jobs as one reason) and members who think all trade should be liberalized, and debate the following questions: Why does this nation need to import foreign goods? Does it produce everything needed here? If not, why can't it? Do import restrictions deprive the American consumer of foreign goods or services?

2. Discuss whether or not you think American consumers will be willing to spend more—maybe 10 percent or more on each purchase—to inspect all imports and ensure to their best ability that our imports are safe.

3. Using the WCO HTS classification system, found on the USITC.gov website, determine the tariff rate for several common import items that may be found in your closet or dresser drawers.

Chapter 7 Case

Entering the Import Business

Entering the import business is one thing. Staying in it is another. Granted, defining target markets, sourcing desirable products, and arranging for shipments to pass customs and enter the country are all hurdles to overcome. But figuring out how best to market goods profitably over time is the key to staying in business.

Consider Gerald Shvartsman, an entrepreneur in his mid-30s, who several years ago started Source Outdoor, an import wholesaling business offering patio and deck furniture from China. At first he sold his furniture himself, but by 2012 his business had grown to annual sales of $7 million and he employed more than 50 people. Shvartsman was no newcomer to business. At age seven he could be found working with his family selling jewelry at flea markets. He skipped college and went into other family ventures. He became interested in patio furniture, but when shopping for his family's Miami condo he was astounded at the prices. "A sectional to seat four or five? Fifteen thousand dollars? . . . I was flabbergasted. I looked in store after store but couldn't afford to buy what I liked."

As successful as his business has become, Shvartsman has been worried about future growth and an emerging conflict in his channels of distribution. He marketed his furniture in a number of ways. While most of his wholesale customers have been located in south Florida, some include hotels and resorts outside of the state. In his nearby area, many furniture retailers carry Source Outdoor catalogs; he negotiated with designers and condo groups, offering appropriate trade discounts to all three groups. He also maintained a website offering Source Outdoor goods. A while back, he decided to participate in periodic Florida Home Shows, providing direct retail access to consumers. In six or seven shows a year, he very profitably sold current styles at full markup and earlier season's goods at lower prices.

One day a major retail store customer called him and said that while he realized the Home Show sales must be lucrative for Source Outdoors, those sales created a conflict of interest for the company. Shvartsman knew that the Home Shows were a most profitable part of his business, averaging 20 percent of sales in a recent year. Also, they gave him a chance to unload old stock at a reasonable markup. Plus, he had never run into any of his retailer customers at any Home Show. Nevertheless, he knew that operating at both the wholesale and retail levels could risk losing the retail stores as customers. In the furniture field, everyone knew what everyone else was doing, and Shvartsman knew his reputation could be at stake.

Source: John Grossmann, Small Business Case Study, "A Wholesaler Finds Himself in Competition with Retail Clients," *New York Times,* April 26, 2013, p. B6, and May 2, 2013, p. B6.

Question

What should Gerald Shvartsman do? Stay with the Home Shows? Maintain his status as a wholesaler and drop the Home Shows? Perhaps create a way of selling both through the Home Shows and to retailers? Plan other strategies? Which would be best? What do you think?

References

1. "World Customs Organization: History," World Customs Organization. Retrieved December 12, 2013, from http://www.wcoomd.org /en/about-us/what-is-the -wco/au_history.aspx.

2. "Automated Commercial System (ACS)," U.S. Customs and Border Protection. Retrieved December 13, 2013, from http://cbp.gov /xp/cgov/trade/automated /automated_systems/acs /addtl_capabilities.xml.

3. "Automated Broker Interface," U.S. Customs and Border Protection. Retrieved December 13, 2013, from http://cbp .dhs.gov/xp/cgov/trade /automated/automated _systems/abi.

4. Op. cit., "World Customs Organization: History."

5. "Tips for new exporters and importers," U.S. Customs and Border Protection, May 31, 2011. Retrieved December 13, 2013, from http://www .cbp.gov/xp/cgov/trade /trade_outreach/didu know.xml.

6. "Committee for the Implementation of Textile Agreements," International Trade Administration, Office of Textiles and Apparel (OTEXA). Retrieved December 13, 2013, from http://otexa.ita.doc.gov /cita.htm.

7. "Textile Visas," U.S. Customs and Border Protection. Retrieved December 12, 2013, from http://www .cbp.gov/xp/cgov/trade /trade_programs/textiles _and_quotas/quota_frq /gen_text/text_visa.xml.

8. Ibid.

9. "Determination of Duties," U.S. Customs and Border Protection. Retrieved December 14, 2013, from https://help .cbp.gov/app/answers /detail/a_id/400/kw/duty %20rate.

10. Harmonized Tariff Schedule of the United States (2013), Chapter 62, p. 10. U.S. International Trade Commission. Retrieved on December 14, 2013, from http://www.usitc.gov/tata/hts/bychapter/index.htm.

11. Ibid.

12. "Customs Modernization Act (Mod Act)." Retrieved December 14, 2013, from https://www.govtrack.us/congress/bills/103/hr700.

13. "Non-Tariff Barriers to Trade," Office of the United States Trade Representative. Retrieved December 14, 2013, from http://www.ustr.gov/trade-topics/industry-manufacturing/non-tariff-barriers.

14. "Overview of Textiles: A Priority Trade Issue," U.S. Customs and Border Protection. Retrieved January 21, 2014, from http://www.cbp.gov/xp/cgov/trade/priority_trade/textiles/textiles_pti.xml.

15. Ibid.

16. Ibid.

Figure 8.1 **During the night of December 16, 1773, in Boston Harbor, three ships carrying tea were boarded by Massachusetts colonists who tossed 45 tons of tea overboard in retaliation to oppressive British taxes.**

CHAPTER 8
NAVIGATING THE MAZE OF IMPORT CONTROLS

The early settlers in colonies such as Virginia and Massachusetts began importing goods since they first arrived nearly 400 years ago. But the import taxes that the colonies were forced to pay the British government (for their goods ranging from sugar to newspapers and playing cards, and later paint and paper) became the fuel for the revolution to come. By 1773, in reaction to excessive taxation plus an attempted British monopoly on the sale of tea, Bostonians dressed as indigenous Americans and dumped hundreds of chests of it into Boston Harbor in what became known as the Boston Tea Party. That action ignited the flames that would burn in the War of Independence three years later.

Facing a chaotic treasury burdened by the heavy debt of the Revolutionary War, a major interest of Alexander Hamilton, the first Secretary of the Treasury, when he took office was the repayment of the war debt in full.

"The debt of the United States . . . was the price of liberty," Hamilton affirmed, and the idea of regulating imports as a source of income seemed a natural. He devised a revenue system based on *customs duties* and *excise taxes*. Hamilton's attack on the debt helped secure the confidence and respect of foreign nations.[1]

Shortly after the United States Constitution was ratified in 1788, President George Washington signed into law the **Hamilton Tariff Act**. Enacted on July 4, 1789, it was the first substantive legislation passed by the first Congress and often called "the second Declaration of Independence" by commentators of that era. Set up as a way to both protect trade and raise money for the federal government, the act authorized the collection of **customs duties**, or taxes, on imported goods. Geographic entry points were determined shortly after, and everyone—citizens and visitors—coming into the country had to account to the new government for goods they shipped or carried into the United States.[2]

Most of the rates of the tariff (duties) were between 5 and 10 percent, depending on the value of the item. Hamilton was eager to establish the tariff as a regular source of revenue for the government and as a protection of domestic manufacturers. In economic terms, the government at that time embraced the principle of protectionism—the policy of restricting trade among nations through such barriers as tariffs, or taxes, on imported goods, quotas, and a limit on the amount of imports (by commodity and by country) within a given time period, as well as other government regulations designed to discourage imports. The Hamilton Act is closely aligned with today's antiglobalization sentiment that is in contrast with that of free trade (where no artificial barriers exist to the entry or exit of goods and services in international business) and opened a persistent political dispute that remains more than 200 years later.[3]

The act authorized the collection of taxes on imported goods, primarily from England. For more than a century, Customs' collections supported virtually the entire government and its **infrastructure**—bridges, communications, and transportation. Later, President Thomas Jefferson's purchase of the Louisiana Territory, the accession of Florida and Alaska, and the transcontinental railroad were financed by import duties. Customs revenues built the city of Washington, DC, many of the nation's lighthouses, and the U.S. military and naval academies, and had, by 1835, reduced the national debt to zero.[4]

Import duties were the number one income source for the U.S. government until the Internal Revenue Act was enacted in 1913, when the 16th Amendment to the Constitution made the income tax a permanent fixture in the U.S. tax system.

HISTORY OF U.S. CUSTOMS

The history of the United States Customs Service goes back to the same month and year as the Hamilton Tariff Act, which established duties on imports. The Fifth Act of the First Congress, signed by President Washington on July 31, 1789, created the first agency of the federal government: U.S. Customs, a field organization of collectors, which would "regulate the collection of duties imposed by law on the tonnage of ships or vessels and on goods, wares, and merchandises imported into the United States."[5]

As the nation developed into a world power, the role and importance of the U.S. Customs Service grew with it. It assumed a more extensive and complex role in responsibilities to protect and provide revenues for our country. For more than 125 years, the primary responsibility of the U.S. Customs Service was to administer the tariff acts, which were designed to protect our nation's revenue by assessing and collecting duties or taxes and fees related to our international trade. In more recent years, Customs' responsibilities grew, with the need to control narcotics trafficking and imports of counterfeit goods, and even more recently to protect the United States from terrorists and other security threats.

Import Controls

Today, import controls still exist—in every sovereign nation—because governments want to have the option of protecting their domestic industries by imposing import duties or nontariff barriers to trade. Governments also have the right to know *what* is coming into their countries. They want a count of products coming in, to measure imports against exports, and to help determine the economic health, strength, and competitiveness of their economies versus those of other countries. In addition, each government wants to ensure that imported goods are in compliance with its laws, such as those concerning consumer protection, safety, and health. Today, the U.S. Customs and Border Protection (CBP) agency is responsible for the legal movement of imported goods into the country.[6]

U.S. Customs and Border Protection

In March 2003, the U.S. Customs Service became the CBP as a result of the merger of the functions of Customs, Immigration and Naturalization Service, Border Patrol, and the Animal and Plant Health Inspection Service. Now an agency of the **Department of Homeland Security (DHS)**, CBP's priority mission is to secure the nation's boundaries by detecting, deterring, and preventing terrorists and their weapons from entering the United States.

SPOTLIGHT ON GLOBAL TRADE 8.1

A Day in the Life of the US Customs and Border Protection Agency (CBP)

On a typical day in 2012, the CBP accomplished the following:

Admitted
- 963,121 passengers and pedestrians, including
  - 269,428 incoming international air passengers and crew
  - 53,234 passengers/crew arriving by sea
  - 640,459 incoming land travelers
  - 66,615 truck, rail, and sea containers
  - 1,260,143 incoming privately owned vehicles

Conducted
- 999 apprehensions at and between U.S. ports of entry
- 54 arrests of wanted criminals at U.S. ports of entry

Refused
- 931 inadmissible aliens at U.S. ports of entry

Discovered
- 476 pests at U.S. ports of entry (nearly 50 percent of which are harmful to agricultural and natural resources)
- 4,437 materials for quarantine (plant, meat, animal byproduct, and soil)

Seized
- 11,660 pounds of drugs
- $274,065 in undeclared or illicit currency
- $3.5 million dollars' worth of products with intellectual property rights violations

Identified
- 66 fraudulent documents
- 115 individuals with suspected national security concerns

Protected more than
- 5,000 miles of border with Canada
- 1,900 miles of border with Mexico
- 95,000 miles of tidal shoreline

Employed
- 60,668 CBP people including
  - 21,790 CBP officers
  - 2,366 CBP Agriculture specialists
  - 21,394 Border Patrol agents
  - 1,215 Air and Marine personnel
  - 1,580 canine teams

Flew
- 15 hours of drug interdiction missions in P3 airplanes
- 14 hours of unmanned aircraft systems over the United States

Conducted operations at
- 329 ports of entry within 20 field offices
- 139 Border Patrol stations within 20 sectors, with 31 permanent checkpoints

Source: U.S. Customs and Border Protection. Retrieved December 8, 2013, from http://www .cbp.gov/linkhandler/cgov/about/accomplish/typical_day_fy12.ctt/typical_day_fy12.pdf.

It is a big job and a daunting responsibility. The United States shares a 5,252-mile border with Canada and a 1,989-mile border with Mexico, with a combined total of more than 300 international land-based ports of entry. Intertwined with the U.S. borders is a maritime system that includes 95,000 miles of coastline and navigable waterways and a global transportation network—more than 300 seaports, 429 commercial airports, and several hundred thousand miles of highways and railroads—that offers access to almost every community in the nation. The CBP includes more than 60,000 employees including officers, canine enforcement officers, Border Patrol agents, aircraft pilots, trade specialists, and mission support staff. The challenges to homeland security are immense.[7]

Seizing Counterfeit Trademarked Goods
In addition to the border control responsibilities, the DHS agencies must meet the challenges of imported fakes (counterfeits) and pirated goods. These imports violate the **Intellectual Property Rights (IPRs)** of American and foreign companies. It is U.S. trade policy to stop these commodities from entering the country, to protect the patents, trademarks, and copyrights of legitimate commodity producers.[8] The U.S. government, along with partner governments, private-sector groups, and international organizations, sponsor the website **StopFakes.gov** to help consumers and businesses spot fakes and provide information for reporting counterfeit and pirated goods.[9]

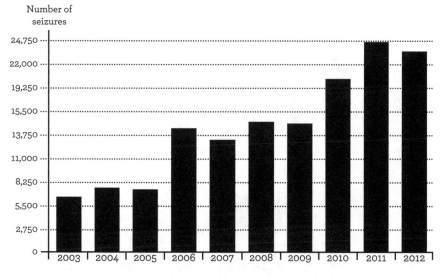

Number of Seizures by CBP, 2003–2012

Figure 8.2 **Number of seizures by CBP, 2003–2012.**

Source: U.S. Customs and Border Protection, Office of International Trade, U.S. Department of Homeland Security. Retrieved on January 30, 2014, from http://www.cbp.gov/linkhandler/cgov /trade/priority_trade/ipr/seizure/fy2012_final_stats.ctt/fy2012_final_stats.pdf, p. 5.

During fiscal year 2012, the DHS, CBP, and **Immigration and Customs Enforcement (ICE)** seized $1.262 billion worth of infringing goods, as measured by **MSRP**, the **manufacturer's suggested retail price** for merchandise offered to the consumer—if the goods had been properly sourced—with an average seizure value of more than $10,450. This vigilance led to 691 arrests, 423 indictments, and 334 prosecutions for the year.[10]

These illegal imports are a serious threat to the American economy as well as to the health and safety of consumers. They cause not only financial damages to the firms whose rights have been violated, but also possible harm to the American infrastructure and national security, should substandard or dangerous products gain access to the country.

The rapid growth of Internet purchases in recent years has resulted in larger numbers of small packages being shipped via express carriers and the mail. DHS found many of the new websites were involved in the trafficking of illicit goods. In 2012, 697 such sites were shut down by ICE, with the CBP handling the forfeitures.[11]

An example of the Customs' IPR mandate is the action by U.S. Customs and Border Protection officers at the Long Beach, California, seaport when they seized more than $1 million worth of counterfeit handbags and footwear in 2012. If legitimate, the items would have been valued at more than $24 million. The CBP officers and import specialists first intercepted a **shipment manifest**—official papers filed

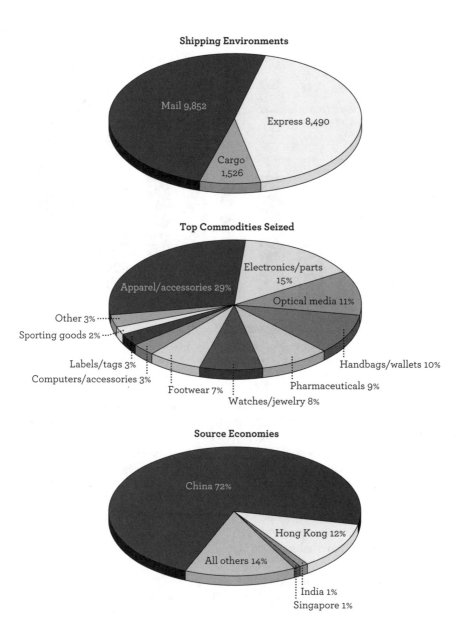

Figure 8.3 The shipping environments, top commodities seized, and the source economies are illustrated for U.S. IPR seizures in FY2012.

Source: U.S. Customs and Border Protection, Office of International Trade, U.S. Department of Homeland Security. Retrieved on January 30, 2014, from http://www.cbp.gov/linkhandler/cgov /trade/priority_trade/ipr/seizure/fy2012_final_stats.ctt/fy2012_final_stats.pdf, pp. 14–15.

and sworn to as being accurate—for electronic appliances arriving from China. The CBP officers examined the container and discovered 59,198 counterfeit Coach and Chanel handbags and 17,400 pairs of fake Coach footwear. The items had counterfeit trademarks, a U.S. federal violation. The merchandise was not claimed by the importer; violations of these laws may subject the importers to civil penalties and/or criminal prosecution. See the "Spotlight on Global Trade 8.2" for an example of serious health risks connected to the seizure of 200,000 dolls arriving from China.[12]

In July 2013, the United States and China announced the first joint IPR operation. The month-long program resulted in the seizure of more than 243,000 counterfeit consumer electronics products. It also resulted in the arrest of a U.S. citizen who repeatedly imported counterfeit specialty headphones that he then sold on Craigslist. The CBP and its Chinese counterpart, the General Administration of Customs, have committed to further cooperation on IPR enforcement, including additional joint operations.[13]

The CBP provides a new urgency to assisting the import community, which enhances and increases compliance with domestic and international customs laws and regulations. These activities are aimed at keeping U.S. imports free from terrorist or other malicious interference, tampering, or corruption of containers or

Figure 8.4 Counterfeit children's toys are seized as violations of intellectual property rights.

Figure 8.5 The U.S. Customs and Border Protection agency seized what would have amounted legitimately to $24 million worth of fake Coach and Chanel handbags and Coach footwear at Long Angeles–Long Beach seaport.

commodities. The challenge for DHS and its affiliated agencies, such as the CBP, is to enforce IPR while, at the same time, facilitate the secure and timely flow of legal trade and travel.

Container Security Initiative

The CBP is also responsible for the **Container Security Initiative (CSI)**, a joint program that addresses the threat to border security and global trade posed by the potential terrorist use of a maritime container. CSI deploys multidisciplinary teams to foreign seaports to target and examine high-risk cargo—*before* it is loaded on a vessel bound for the United States.[14]

CSI is now operating in 58 ports worldwide—in North America, Europe, Asia, Africa, the Middle East, and Latin and Central America. The CBP now prescreens approximately 90 percent of all transatlantic and transpacific cargo imported into the United States. The CBP has stationed multidisciplinary teams of U.S. officers from both the CBP and ICE to work together with our host foreign government counterparts. Their mission is not only to target and prescreen containers but also to develop additional investigative leads related to any terrorist threat to cargo destined for the United States.[15]

Figure 8.6 U.S. Customs confiscates and destroys fake imports, such as these counterfeit watches about to be steamrolled.

Figure 8.7 CBP officers use mobile technology to scan incoming cargo in Seattle, Washington.

Customs Trade Partnership Against Terrorism

While the CSI is a U.S. government-imposed program, the **Customs Trade Partnership Against Terrorism (C-TPAT)** is another layer of secure handling for processing cargo entering the United States. It is a partnership of private and government participants in international trade transactions. The goal of the partnership programs is to create a system with all participants in trade approved in advance of specific standards in the secure handling of goods and relevant security information. The partnership develops and adopts measures that add security but do not impede a smooth flow of U.S. international trade. As of this writing, more than 10,000 certified partners have been accepted into the program. Members include the following:

- U.S. importers
- U.S. customs brokers
- Mexican manufacturers
- U.S., Canadian, and Mexican cross-border highway carriers
- Third-party logistics (3PL) providers
- Marine port authorities and terminal operators
- Mexican long-haul highway carriers
- Air carriers
- Rail carriers
- Sea carriers
- Air freight consolidators
- Ocean transportation intermediaries
- Nonvessel operating common carriers (NVOCCs)

When they join the C-TPAT anti-terrorism partnership, companies sign an agreement to work with the CBP to protect the supply chain, identify security gaps, and implement specific security measures and "best-practices."[16]

U.S. import trade and tariff laws are enforced by the CBP import and entry specialists and other trade compliance personnel. This helps to ensure that industry operates in a fair and competitive trade environment. Trade-related activities include the following:

- Protecting U.S. businesses from theft of intellectual property and unfair trade practices
- Collecting import duties, taxes, and fees
- Enforcing trade laws related to admissibility
- Regulating trade practices to collect the appropriate revenue
- Maintaining export controls
- Protecting U.S. agricultural resources via inspection activities at the ports of entry

Import Safety

In the United States, import safety is a public-private responsibility, and some agencies and private individuals (brokers and importers) are working to develop a more preventative system here. Government agencies, including the departments of Commerce, Transportation, Defense, and Agriculture among others, frequently produce interagency reports to the President that update the strategic framework for improving the safety of imported products while facilitating trade.

With more than $2.275 trillion in imports entering the U.S. economy in 2012, it would be unreasonable to expect the federal government to physically inspect every imported product. Doing so would not only bring international trade to a standstill but would also divert limited resources away from those imported goods (and importers) posing the greatest risk.[17]

Textiles Designated a Priority Trade Issue

The CBP maintains a priority trade enforcement program to ensure compliance with laws and regulations governing all imports. Because of the high-risk nature of imports of textile and apparel products, the CBP has designated the industry a priority trade issue. CBP reports that the textile industry represents more than $94 billion in annual imports and consists of about 47 percent of all duties collected by that agency. The textile industry is a key component of the U.S. manufacturing base, with more than 600,000 workers employed at a total of 68,000 importers of textile products.[18]

The CBP facilitates the legitimate importation of textiles and apparel, while combating the rising number of textile imports that are undervalued, misclassified, or illegally transshipped or entered into the U.S. economy.

There are numerous requirements placed on textile products entering the United States under various free trade agreements and legislative preference programs. In addition, the United States maintains quantitative limits—or quotas—on the amount of textile products that may enter the United States from China. Many different schemes are used to evade duty or quotas on imported goods being brought into the country. Some importers try to avoid quotas by transshipping goods through another country that they falsely claim as the official country of origin of their goods. Others use false documents or labels or provide incorrect descriptions of the merchandise.

CBP uses a multifaceted but complementary approach consisting of trade pattern analysis, on-site verification, review of production records, audits, and laboratory analysis to enforce U.S. trade laws and to ensure that appropriate fees are collected. Import specialists at the CBP with specialized commodity knowledge analyze and review textile imports for possible violations. Focusing on textile violations has paid off with seizures of major illegal shipments.

Figure 8.8 Dogs, trained by canine officers to sniff out bombs, regularly inspect the contents of imports held in a warehouse.

One of the enforcement tools being used is on-site verification of manufacturers. The CBP's **Textile Production Verification Teams (TPVTs)** travel to foreign factories to review and verify that wearing apparel that is shipped to the United States is produced at those facilities. As a result of these site visits, CBP import specialists will target shipments that are in violation. Sites are selected after extensive trade analysis. In 2011, the CBP's TPVTs visited 165 factories in nine countries. Twenty-seven percent of the reviews showed a violation of the trade preference program claimed on the entry, and 22 percent showed a discrepancy related to illegal transshipment.[19]

The CBP has initiated operations to address the intentional false descriptions of merchandise to achieve much lower import duty rates. The CBP's import specialists have identified many of these cases and have seized millions in misdescribed goods. In 2011, goods worth more than $14 million were seized by CBP for violating IPR laws involving just textile products.

Another area of risk is the misclassification of wearing apparel, often to circumvent high rates of duty. In 2011, 48 percent of textiles sampled by the laboratories were found to be misclassified. An example would be classifying imported scarves as being 100 percent polyester, rather than the actual silk or silk blend. The latter would have a much higher tariff rate the importer would have to pay for entry into the United States. The CBP is also reviewing the illegal transshipment of goods through the United States into Mexico. These goods, falsely claiming U.S. origin but actually coming from an Asian factory, are exported to Mexico under fraudulent North American Free Trade Agreement (NAFTA) claims, to avoid Mexican import taxes on goods made in Asia. The exports can range from completed apparel that is using a U.S. origin claim to circumvent Mexico's dumping duties against China to just the fabric. Ultimately, the fabric exports are used in production of apparel imported back to the United States, under false NAFTA claims.[20]

If CBP determines that the goods are different from the entered descriptions in quantity or value, that the classification of the goods is incorrect, or that a different rate of duty than the one indicated by the importer applies, the agency may assess an increase in duties. Should the CBP determine that the importer has deliberately failed to properly classify and value the goods, a court may assess a fine or even criminal penalties.

Import Procedures

The CBP does *not* require an importer to have a license or permit. Other agencies may require a permit, license, or other certification, depending on what is being imported. However, Customs must authorize entry and delivery of the merchandise before any goods can legally enter the United States. An individual may make

Figure 8.9 Border patrol agents regularly search trains entering the United States from Canada or Mexico.

his or her own Customs clearance of goods imported for personal use or business. This is normally accomplished by filing the appropriate documents, either by the importer or by the importer's agent. To expedite this process, Customs entry papers may be presented before the merchandise arrives, but official entry will not take place until the merchandise arrives within the port limits.

The Customs Service does *not* notify the importer of the arrival of the shipment. However, the carrier of the goods or sometimes the entry port authority will notify the importer that the goods have arrived. Importers or their customs brokers should be aware of estimated arrival dates, so entry papers can be filed in advance and delays in obtaining the goods avoided.[21]

SPOTLIGHT ON GLOBAL TRADE 8.2
U.S. Agencies Partner to Detect Dangerous Imports

CBP officers and Consumer Product Safety Commission (CPSC) investigators recently seized more than 200,000 potentially dangerous toy dolls arriving from China. These toys contain high levels of *phthalates*, a group of banned chemical compounds. A total of ten shipments valued at nearly $500,000 were seized at the ports of Chicago, Dallas, Los Angles, Norfolk, Memphis, Newark, Portland, and Savannah.

The Commercial Targeting and Analysis Center (CTAC) targeted the shipments because they presented a potential safety threat to the American public, particularly children, and contained items prohibited for import into the United States. Although dispersed across the country, officials flagged the shipments as high risk after CTAC identified key commonalities in the hazardous products.

CPSC compliance investigators are assigned to several major ports across the country and work side-by-side with CBP officers to examine shipments of potentially unsafe imported consumer products to help prevent them from reaching the hands of America's consumers. In fiscal year 2012, CTAC targeting efforts resulted in the seizure of more than 1.1 million unsafe products.

Use of advanced technology, to track suspect shipments before they reach U.S. shores, is helping the CPSC and CBP partnership to detect and detain dangerous imports, while also allowing for faster processing of compliant products.

Customs Entry

The Customs Service defines "**entry**" not merely as the arrival of goods at a port, but also as the process of presenting documentation for clearing goods through Customs. Imported merchandise not entered through Customs in a timely manner (within 15 calendar days of arrival) is sent by Customs to a general order warehouse to be held as unclaimed. The importer is responsible for paying storage charges while unclaimed merchandise is held at the warehouse. If it remains unclaimed at the end of six months, the merchandise is sold at auction.[22]

Customs Examination of Goods

In simple cases involving small shipments or certain classes of goods such as bulk shipments, such as boxes of socks or underwear, examination may be made on the docks or at container stations, cargo terminals, or the importer's premises. The goods are then released to the importer.[23]

U.S. Customs and Border Protection Declarations

All shipments of foreign goods into the United States require accompanying official U.S. documentation, including the **U.S. Customs and Border Protection Declaration Form**. This form, which is a full and accurate description of the merchandise, should be securely attached to the outside of each shipment. Declaration forms vary from country to country, and they don't all ask for the information required by the CBP.[24]

Entry Requirements

When imported merchandise enters the Customs territory of the United States, it is under the control of the CBP. The importer assumes control of the goods only after complying with certain entry regulations. As a general rule, the entry process has six requirements:[25]

- Evidence of right to make entry
- Filing of entry
- Filing of entry summary
- Evidence of surety (bond)
- Formal versus informal entry
- Other types of entry

Many importers are not aware that an entry form is required for every import, whether the merchandise is duty free or dutiable, regardless of value, unless exempted specifically by law. Some types of Customs entry declarations must be made at the first port of arrival.[26]

Ordinarily, entry is made for one of the following reasons: consumption for entry into a bonded warehouse, or transportation in bond to another port where a consumption or warehouse entry will be made.

Importers, particularly small businesses, may find the effort needed to gain delivery clearance too time-consuming. Their alternative is to hire a customs broker who, for a fee, acts as the importer's agent in shepherding shipments through Customs. A list of customs brokers may be obtained from the local CBP office or found on the Internet or in the local telephone directory.

In the case of a single noncommercial shipment, a relative or other designated individual may act as the importer's agent for customs purposes. This person must know the facts pertaining to the shipment and must be authorized in writing to act for the importer. The law prohibits Customs employees from performing entry tasks for importers; however, they will advise and give information about Customs requirements.

Formal versus Informal Entry

Formal entries are generally commercial shipments supported by a surety bond to ensure payment of duties and compliance with Customs requirements. A port director can require a formal entry for any import deemed necessary for the payment of the tax revenue or for the protection of the general public.[27]

Informal entries cover personal shipments, commercial shipments, and mail shipments that are being entered for consumption, that is, for use or sale. In most cases, informal entry will work if the merchandise is valued at $2,500 or less (revised from the former $2,000 limit on January 7, 2013). There are some exceptions such as textiles, certain types of footwear, and other goods subject to quota/visa restrictions. Personal shipments valued more than $2,500 also require a formal entry.

Goods admitted as informal entries do not require the posting of a bond, and goods are liquidated on the spot. The difference between an informal entry and a formal entry is the bond requirement and the liquidation process. **Liquidation** is the final computation of duties or *duty drawback* (refund) and is the final step in the entry process.

After the importer receives notification of the arrival of merchandise from the carrier and it is determined that all shipping charges are satisfied, an invoice is presented to Customs. When clearing an informal entry, the inspector, not the importer, is responsible for determining the classification number of the goods being imported. The inspector also completes the Customs forms used for informal entry.

Other Types of Entry

Imported goods may be sent in-bond from the first port of arrival to another Customs port. **In-bond entries**, the duties have not yet been paid, postpone final Customs formalities, including payment of duty and processing fees, until the goods arrive at the final port. Arrangements for in-bond shipments need to be made before the goods leave the country of export.

When all the information has been acquired, including the report of the Customs import specialist as to the customs value of the goods and the laboratory report, if required, a final determination of duty is made, the entry is liquidated, and the goods are turned over to the importer. At this time, any overpayment of duty is returned or underpayment billed.[28]

Documents for Entry of Goods

To make or file a consumption entry (for imported goods going directly into the commerce of the United States without any time or use restrictions placed on them), the following documents are generally required:

- Bill of lading
- Air waybill
- Commercial invoice
- Entry manifest
- Packing lists

When a **consumption entry**, such as for perishable goods, is filed, the importer indicates the tariff classification and pays any estimated duty and processing fee. A surety bond may also be required.

PROTEST

Within 90 days after the date of liquidation or other decision, an importer or consignee may **protest** the decision and receive an administrative review. The protest is filed with the port director whose decision is being protested. At the time the initial protest is filed, the importer or consignee must make a request for further review if one is desired. Review of the port director's decision by the Customs Service Center or headquarters is then automatic. Notice of the denial of all or part of the protest will be mailed to the person filing the protest or to his or her agent. Any person whose protest is denied may contest the denial by filing a civil action in the **United States Court of International Trade**, established under Article III of the Constitution, with nationwide jurisdiction over civil actions arising out of the customs and international trade laws of the United States.[29]

MAIL SHIPMENTS

Shipments by mail that do not exceed $2,500 in value, whether commercial or noncommercial importations (except for commercial shipments of textiles from all countries and made-to-measure suits from Hong Kong, regardless of value), are entered under a mail entry prepared by a Customs officer after the Postal Service submits the package for Customs examination.[30]

The parcel is delivered (to the addressee) by the U.S. Postal Service and is released upon the payment of duty, which is shown on the mail entry accompanying the package. A postal handling fee is also due at the time the package is delivered. This handling fee is not charged on packages sent through military mail channels.

A formal entry is required for any mail shipment exceeding $2,500 in value. A formal entry is also required, regardless of value, for commercial shipments of textiles from all countries and made-to-measure suits from Hong Kong. Certain other articles valued above $250 require a formal entry (billfolds, footwear, fur, gloves, handbags, leather, luggage, plastics, rubber, textiles, toys, games, sports equipment, and so on).

If formal entry is required on a package, it is held at the Customs international mail branch, and notice is sent to the addressee of the package's arrival. The addressee can then go to the nearest Customs office to file the formal entry on the package. An entry must be filed in the same manner as for shipments arriving by vessel or airfreight. Once the mail branch has been notified that entry has been filed, the package will be released to the Postal Service and forwarded to its final destination.

FOREIGN ASSETS CONTROL

U.S. trade sanctions administered by the Office of Foreign Assets Control (OFAC) generally prohibit the importation into the United States (including U.S. territories), either directly or indirectly, of most goods, technology, or services (except information and informational materials) from, or which originated from, Cuba, Iran, North Korea, Syria, Somalia, and Sudan; from foreign persons designated by the Secretary of State as having promoted the proliferation of highly destructive weapons; named Foreign Terrorist Organizations; designated terrorists and narcotics traffickers; the Taliban; and areas of Afghanistan controlled by the Taliban. Vessels and aircraft under the registry, ownership, or control of sanctions targets may not import merchandise into the United States. The importation of Cuban cigars or Iranian carpets is subject to certain restrictions. Contact your local Customs office. Diamonds may not be imported from Angola without a certificate of origin or other documentation that demonstrates to Customs authorities that they were legally imported with the approval of the Angola Government of Unity and National Reconciliation.

Import restrictions imposed against sanctions targets vary by program. Contact the Office of Foreign Assets Control at (202) 622–2490 with specific questions or concerns or visit OFAC's website at http://www.treasury.gov/about/organizational -structure/offices/Pages/Office-of-Foreign-Assets-Control.aspx.[31]

COMPLIANCE ASSESSMENT AND MEASUREMENT

The international trade community actively promotes **compliance assessment**, the systematic evaluation of importers' systems supporting their CBP-related activities. The assessment includes testing import and financial transactions, reviewing the adequacy of an importer's internal controls, and determining their compliance levels in key areas. Companies whose systems are noncompliant will be asked to formulate, in cooperation with CBP advisors, a compliance improvement plan or corrective actions. Serious violations of law or regulations may result in CBP referring the company for a formal investigation or other enforcement actions.

Compliance measurement is the primary tool CBP uses to assess the accuracy of port-of-entry transactions and to determine the compliance rate for all commercial importations. Compliance not only ensures the collection of import revenues legally owed the U.S. government, but also helps CBP protect our country from illegal shipments by terrorist organizations, including nuclear, chemical, or biological weapons.

The CBP further facilitates trade through partnership programs, such as the **Importer Self-Assessment (ISA)** as well as account management, which helps frontline personnel facilitate the movement of legitimate, compliant trade and allows them to focus on those shipments that may present a risk to the United States.

CBP provides a detailed explanation of the Importer Self-Assessment program in a handbook available on its website at http://www.cbp.gov/sites/default/files/documents/isa_hb_3.pdf.[32]

Summary

U.S. taxes and controls on imports are older than the country itself. Early colonists were forced to pay the British government for a range of goods sent to the new settlers, necessities such as sugar, paper, and paint. When the new nation came into being, the Hamilton Tariff Act, the second act passed under Washington's presidency, established duties for goods brought into the country. The act authorized the collecting of customs duties to raise revenue for the government. In fact, duties remained the government's number one source of revenue until the Internal Revenue Act (income taxes) became law in the early twentieth century. Customs' duties today, however, remain a major revenue stream for the federal government.

Controlling imports is important not only as a continuing source of revenue, but also as a measure of protection, ensuring safe products for U.S. consumers. A number of government departments including State, Commerce, Agriculture, Treasury, and Homeland Security cooperate in incentives to strengthen our import system and its security.

In March 2003, the U.S. Customs Service (along with employees from other organizations such as the U.S. Border Patrol) became the U.S. Customs and Border Protection, an agency of the Department of Homeland Security. Today the CBP is responsible for ensuring that all imports and exports are legal and comply with U.S. laws and regulations, and for collecting revenues associated with the enforcement of those laws. The agency also performs the following functions:

- Seizes contraband, including illegal drugs and narcotics, and arrests people engaged in smuggling or other fraudulent behavior with the intent to get around customs laws.
- Processes people, luggage, cargo, and mail.
- Protects U.S. business and intellectual property rights by enforcing laws aimed at preventing illegal trade practices.

- Protects the general welfare and security of the United States by enforcing import and export prohibitions and restrictions, including money laundering and the export of data essential to the production of mass weapons of warfare.
- Gathers import and export data for the purpose of compiling international trade statistics.
- Enforces more than 400 provisions of law—many related to quality of life issues, such as pollution and health—for approximately 40 other agencies.
- Provides public information concerning the trade community's rights and responsibilities under customs regulations and related laws. Both the importers and CBP share responsibility for carrying out these requirements.

KEY TERMS, CONT'D

> U.S. CUSTOMS AND BORDER PROTECTION DECLARATION FORM

Review Questions

1. What did the Hamilton Tariff Act of 1789 authorize, and for what purpose? How is the act related to ideas on international trade today?

2. Why do governments establish controls on imports?

3. Why doesn't the U.S. government physically inspect every shipment coming into the country?

4. Under which major government department does the CBP belong, and what are the main duties of this agency?

5. As part of the importing process, according to what documented criteria are goods classified, and who is responsible for classifying them and determining their dutiable value?

6. What are the two kinds of the *entry process*, and when may the goods be released?

Discussion Questions and Activities

1. When a batch of Chinese-made ingredients for the popular drug Heparin was found to be tainted, causing hundreds of people to have allergic reactions and the deaths of at least four people, it was revealed that the U.S. Food and Drug Administration (FDA) was inspecting only 7 percent of the foreign factories producing pharmaceutical components. Discuss who should bear the blame for this unfortunate incident and who should be responsible for future safeguarding of our imports of drugs? The foreign factory? The U.S. pharmaceutical company that imports the drug compounds? Or the FDA?

2. Why should quality "fakes" be prohibited from entering the United States? If they service the consumers who are looking for the prestige brand while paying much less for the counterfeit goods, why should they be confiscated at the points of entry?

3. Discuss the role of American unions in fighting liberalization of imports and the answers to their positions, by free-trade advocates.

Chapter 8 Case

Rodarte: Dealing with Import Controls

Sisters Kate and Lauran Mulleavy spent the first year after college viewing horror films eight to ten hours a day. Not a typical way of capitalizing on college degrees in art history and literature, but then they never followed other peoples' paths. Growing up in Aptos, California, they graduated from that state's university at Berkeley. Their post-college film-viewing venture centered on the actors' costumes that they found intriguing, leading them to create their own dramatic, often gothic interpretations. To give reality to their inspirations, their mother taught them how to sew.

Kate and Laura soon realized they needed to follow their instincts and show their work seriously. They invested all of their savings in a collection of ten garments that they took to New York City, where the editors of the fashion trade paper *Women's Wear Daily* (WWD) found their designs original enough to appear in the paper. The line, called Rodarte (the maiden name of the girls' mother), caught the attention of Anna Wintour, editor of *Vogue*. She recognized the sisters' talent and began to feature their garments in the magazine. Rodarte styles caught on. Exclusive stores in the United States such as Bergdorf Goodman, Barneys, and Neiman Marcus began to order the line.

Although the Rodarte brand is considered high end, the sisters ventured into other price lines, creating sweatshirts and T-shirts, as well as a promotional line exclusively for Target. Their work also encompasses the arts; for example, they created the ballet costumes for the film *Black Swan*, and operas, notably a Los Angeles production of Mozart's *Don Giovanni*. Their accomplishments inspired museum exhibits in their home state, and awards such as the Council of Fashion Designers' Women Designers of the Year award in 2009, and Fashion Group, International Star Honoree award in 2011. Celebrities who have worn Rodarte apparel include actresses Keira Knightley and Kirsten Dunst, among others.

Today the Rodarte brand is found in places throughout the world, such as exclusive stores and boutiques in London, Paris, Belgium, Moscow, Hong Kong, and Saudi Arabia. The secret to Rodarte's success? As Kate said, "Follow your own path. . . . It's not the path that other people take, because the people that follow their own are going to be the ones that lead us into the future."

Source: Rodarte website. Retrieved July 15, 2013, from http://www.rodarte.net/; Michelle Persad, "The Rodarte Sisters Give Advice on Fashion Design, Following Your Own Path and More" (video), *Huffington Post,* March 2, 2013, retrieved July 13, 2013.

Question

Assume you are the owner of a group of high-end specialty stores in the United States that feature garments and accessories from lines similar to Rodarte, the Row by sisters Mary-Kate and Ashley Olsen, and other young designers from Europe and Asia. Sometimes you buy goods from import fairs here, but periodically you travel to fashion markets in Paris and Tokyo.

From what you learned about imports in this text, explain three or four import concerns that you would want to put to rest as you deal in goods from overseas. Which of these concerns also apply to buying merchandise made in the United States?

References

1. "Boston Tea Party," United States History. Retrieved November 27, 2013, from http://www.u-s-history.com/pages/h646.html; "U.S. Customs and Border Protection Timeline." Retrieved November 27, 2013, from http://nemo.cbp.gov/opa/timeLine_04212011.swf.

2. "Hamilton Tariff Act of 1789," United States History. Retrieved November 27, 2013, from http://www.u-s-history.com/pages/h393.html; "Biography of Secretary Alexander Hamilton," U.S. Treasury. Retrieved November 27, 2013, from http://www.treasury.gov/about/history/Pages/ahamilton.aspx.

3. Ibid.

4. Ibid.

5. Op. cit., "U.S. Customs and Border Protection Timeline."

6. "Importing into the United States: A Guide for Commercial Importers," U.S. Customs and Border Protection. Retrieved December 8, 2013, from http://cbp.gov/linkhandler/cgov/newsroom/publications/trade/iius.ctt/iius.pdf.

7. "CBP at Ten Years Old," U.S. Customs and Border Protection. Retrieved December 1, 2013, from http://www.cbp.gov/xp/cgov/about/history/ten_years/ten_years.xml.

8. "Intellectual Property Rights: Fiscal Year 2012 Seizure Statistics," U.S. Customs and Border Protection, Office of International Trade/Homeland Security. Retrieved December 7, 2013, from http://www.cbp.gov/.

9. "Stop Fakes.gov." Retrieved December 7, 2013, from http://origin.www.stopfakes.gov/global-partners.

10. "About Border Security," U.S. Customs and Border Protection. Retrieved December 6, 2013, from http://www.cbp.gov/xp/cgov/border_security/bs/.

11. "Tips for New Importers and Exporters," U.S. Customs and Border Protection. Retrieved December 6, 2013, from http://www.cbp.gov/xp/cgov/trade/trade_outreach/diduknow.xml.

12. Ibid.

13. "U.S., China Announce Results of First Joint Intellectual Property Operation," U.S. Customs and Border Protection, July 31, 2013. Retrieved December 7, 2013, from http://www.iprcenter.gov/news-releases/u.s.-china-announce-results-of-first-joint-intellectual-property-operation.

14. "Container Security Initiative: In Summary," U.S. Customs and Border Protection, May, 2011. Retrieved December 6, 2013, from http://www.cbp.gov/linkhandler/cgov/trade/cargo_security/csi/csi_brochure_2011.ctt/csi_brochure_2011.pdf.

15. Ibid.

16. "C-TPAT: Program Overview," U.S. Customs and Border Protection. Retrieved December 7, 2013, from http://cbp.gov/linkhandler/cgov/trade/cargo_security/ctpat/ctpat_program_information/what is_ctpat/ctpat_overview.ctt/ctpat_overview.pdf.

17. Op. cit., "Importing into the United States."

18. "Overview of Textiles: A Priority Trade Issue

(PTI)," U.S. Customs and Border Protection. Retrieved December 4, 2013, from http://www .cbp.gov/xp/cgov/trade /priority_trade/textiles /textiles_pti.xml.

19. "CBP's Textile Production Verification Teams," U.S. Customs and Border Protection, Retrieved December 7, 2013, from http://cbp .dhs.gov/xp/cgov/trade /priority_trade/textiles /textiles_pti.xml.

20. Op. cit., "Overview of Textiles."

21. Op. cit., "Importing into the United States."

22. Ibid.

23. Ibid.

24. Ibid.

25. Ibid.

26. Ibid.

27. "CBP Increases Value for the Informal Entry Limit," U.S. Customs and Border Protection," press release December 6, 2012. Retrieved December 5, 2013, from http://www .cbp.gov/xp/cgov /newsroom/news _releases/national/2012 _nr/dec_2012/12062012 .xml.

28. Op. cit., "Importing into the United States."

29. Ibid.

30. Ibid.

31. "Sanctions Programs and Country Information," U.S. Department of the Treasury, Office of Foreign Assets Control. Retrieved December 10, 2013, from http://www .treas.gov/resourcecenter /sanctions/Programs /Pages/Programs.aspx.

32. "Importer Self- Assessment Handbook," U.S. Customs and Border Protection, June 2011. Retrieved December 8, 2013, from http://www .cbp.gov/linkhandler /cgov/trade/trade _programs/importer _self_assessment/isa _hb.ctt/isa_hb.pdf.

PART

IV

Rewards and Challenges of Export-Import Trade

Figure 9.1 Negotiating purchase terms suitable to both the exporter and the client is an essential part of building successful international trade.

CHAPTER 9
GETTING PAID OR PAYING FOR EXPORTS OR IMPORTS

I n order to turn international marketing opportunities into actual sales, exporters and importers need to learn the fundamentals of international trade finance. Thus equipped, their sales transactions will lead to the ultimate goal of getting paid in full and on time. This chapter presents the basics of getting paid for export sales and how to pay for imports that ultimately will be sold domestically to businesses and consumers. For a detailed presentation of this topic, see the Trade Finance Guide, which is available online at Export.gov, the U.S. government's export portal.[1]

Success in the global marketplace often depends on negotiating sales terms and credit as well as appropriate payment methods. Whether exporting or importing goods or services, this information is useful in selecting the method of payment most appropriate to the transaction.

Even an experienced exporting firm extends credit cautiously. You need to evaluate new customers with care and continuously monitor ongoing accounts. An exporter may decline a customer's request for open account credit if the risk level is too great. Instead, the exporter may propose payment in a number of ways: through a cash payment in advance of delivery; a letter of credit, documentary collections, or an open account; or even consignment sale. During—or before—contract negotiations, the seller (exporter) should consider which payment option affords the needed level of security while also minimizing the cost and inconvenience to the buyer (foreign importer). Long-term international trade relationships are built on mutually beneficial payment methods and terms. These primary delivery terms will be detailed in this chapter.

For a fully creditworthy international customer, exporters should consider **extended terms**, meaning they can pay invoices later than the traditional 30 days, which domestically is considered the same as cash. In this situation, the exporter needs to remember that, according to law, any export is a gift until payment is received. From the importer's perspective, any payment is a donation until the goods are received. In some countries, cash terms are the business custom, and extending credit on open account for 90 or even 120 days, without interest penalties, is frequently the case in Asian countries, such as Japan. Some exporters will be unable to manage their cash flow and inventory control profitably within this arrangement and therefore may have to arrange special financing or just walk away from long-term credit sales.

Credit terms usually depend on the quality of the business relationship, the economic strength of each party, and the payment terms competitors are offering. Getting paid in full and on time is the ultimate goal for every export transaction.

One way to reduce credit risks is to collect up-to-date credit information for potential or current business partners. This can be difficult when dealing with customers in countries where private financial information is only available from the business itself—for example, underdeveloped nations—which means having to rely on their honesty and integrity, and the solidity of the relationship.

If customers are established firms, or located in more advanced countries, private credit companies—such as Dun & Bradstreet (D&B), which offers both its International Comprehensive Report and the International Business Information Report, and Graydon International—provide, for a fee, useful credit information. Some of the reports may cite U.S. companies that conduct business with the firm

Figure 9.2 Dun & Bradstreet (D&B) and Graydon International are two companies offering international credit reports that may help determine the importer's ability to pay for goods or services.

the exporter is checking out. By contacting these U.S firms, an exporter may be able to find out the payment practices of a foreign prospect.

Companies new to export may first wish to check out what the U.S. Department of Commerce offers. It features the International Company Profile (ICP), a customized report that can be used in evaluating potential affiliates as well as clients.[2] Developed by the U.S. government's overseas posts, the profile includes a company's background information and standing in the local business community, plus bank references and overall reliability and suitability. This government program charges fees, but at a much lower rate than private companies.

With the recent volatility in global trade, good credit practices include being aware of any unfavorable changes in a customer's payment patterns, refraining from going beyond normal commercial terms, and consulting with Commerce Department trade specialist.

INTERNATIONAL COMPANY PROFILE REPORT
Report prepared on: XXX

Country:	**Australia**
Date:	**January 31, 2014**

REPORT GENERATED BY:

Contact:	John Kanawati, Commercial Specialist
Organization:	U.S. Commercial Service, Sydney
Telephone:	61-2-9373 9207
Fax:	61-2-9221 0573
Email:	John.Kanawati@mail.doc.gov

REQUESTING COMPANY INFORMATION:

Contact:	Mr XXX, Government Legal Counsel
Organization:	XXX
Address:	XXX
Phone:	XXX
Fax:	XXX
Email:	XXX

REPORT PREPARED ON THE FOLLOWING COMPANY:

Contact:	Ms XXX
Organization:	XXX
Address:	XXX
Telephone:	XXX
Fax:	XXX
End of report.	

Figure 9.3 The U.S Commercial Service's International Company Profile (ICP) provides exporters with credit checks and financial reports on companies in more than 80 countries.

SPOTLIGHT ON GLOBAL TRADE 9.1
The SWIFT Operating Center

An international wire transfer is commonly used and is almost immediate payment for goods—often before they are shipped. The exporter needs to provide bank routing instructions to the importer's bank, including the receiving bank's name and address, SWIFT (Society for Worldwide Interbank Financial Telecommunication) address, and ABA (American Banking Association) number, as well as the seller's name and address, bank account title, and account number. Wire transfers are more costly to the importer than other cash-in-advance options, since the banks charge a fee for the transfer that is usually paid for by the sender.

SWIFT is solely a carrier of messages. It does not hold funds nor does it manage accounts on behalf of customers, nor does it store financial information on an ongoing basis. As a data carrier, SWIFT transports messages between two financial institutions. This activity involves the secure exchange of proprietary data while ensuring its confidentiality and integrity.

METHODS OF PAYMENT

There are several ways in which exporters can receive payment when selling their products abroad. Typically with domestic sales, if the buyer has good credit, sales are made on **open account**, whereby goods are shipped first and paid for within a specific amount of time, usually 30 days, or with finance charges assessed for balances due beyond the terms. A typical example would be a bill bearing the terms 2/10, net 30, which is a 2 percent discount for paying within 10 days of receipt of an invoice, with the balance due within 30 days. If the buyer's ability to pay is in question, **cash-in-advance** or payment before shipment is required.

For export sales or import purchases, however, these are not the most common methods. From the exporter's perspective, the basic international payment terms, listed in descending order from the most secure to the most risky, are the following:

- Cash-in-advance
- Letter of credit
- Documentary collections (draft at sight or time)
- Open account
- Other payment mechanisms, such as consignment sales[3]

Figure 9.4 The Trade Finance Guide helps both exporters and importers get paid or pay for international exchanges.

Cash-in-Advance

Receiving cash-in-advance of a shipment might seem ideal, but you may insult your customer if you insist on this method. Although you may be relieved of collection problems and you get immediate use of the money, it could be the least attractive option for the buyer, and it doesn't help to build a long-term, trusting relationship. Not as common internationally as in the United States, this method seems to be acceptable only when the exporter's product is unique, is not available from other suppliers, or is in strong demand, such as a designer original wedding gown or formal wear.[4]

Exporters just getting started in the export-import business may explain to customers that they need the advance payment to get them the best pricing, as in an **early-pay program**—full payment to a manufacturer before shipment, or sometimes even prior to production—is an incentive for manufacturers to charge lower prices. A possible barrier to this method is the buyer's concern that the goods may not be sent if payment is made in advance. From an importer's perspective, advance payments also could create cash flow problems as well as increased risk. Buyers, however, expect payment terms as soon as the trade relationship is established.

Electronic Transfer of Funds

Cash-in-advance payments should be processed through the **electronic transfer of funds (ETF)**, when money is transferred from one bank to another, electronically, whether domestically or internationally. Also referred to as a **wire transfer**, it has the advantage of almost immediate, bank-to-bank payment.

Credit Cards

Many traders involved in exporting or importing directly with foreign buyers or sellers accept credit cards in payment for consumer and other products, generally of a low dollar value, purchased by end-users, especially on the Internet and in other e-commerce exchanges. Since domestic and international rules governing international credit card transactions can differ, exporters and importers should contact their processor or bank for current procedures. These transactions are typically done by telephone, fax, or email, so sellers, as well as buyers, should be aware of possible fraud and take steps to protect their business. Even though exporters have to pay fees to the credit card companies and assume the risk of disputed charges, the convenience credit cards offer customers on a global basis will help this type of payment method—and exports—grow.[5]

Payment by Check

Advance payment by check can result in a collection delay of several weeks, which defeats the original intention of the seller receiving payment before shipment. If the importer's check is in U.S. dollars and drawn on a U.S. bank, the collection process is the same as for any U.S. check. But funds deposited by nonlocal checks, especially those totaling more than $5,000 on any one day, may not become available for withdrawal for up to 10 business days, according to the Federal Reserve code.[6] The process becomes even more complicated if the check is in a foreign currency or drawn on a foreign bank.

SPOTLIGHT ON GLOBAL TRADE 9.2
List of 10 Most Popular U.S. Brands on the Internet

The most popular American fashion brand searched on the Internet, according to Digital Luxury Group, which creates market intelligence for luxury brands, was Michael Kors. DLG reported in 2012 that Michael Kors captured 19.6 percent of the more than 31 million Internet searches covering 35 U.S. fashion brands in 10 global markets (Brazil, China, France, Germany, India, Italy, Japan, Russia, UK, and United States), using insights from Google, Bing, Yandex, and Baidu.

Following Michael Kors, Marc Jacobs, Ralph Lauren, Calvin Klein, Vera Wang, Tory Burch, Kate Spade, Diane von Furstenberg, Betsey Johnson, and Tom Ford completed the top 10.

Most-Searched American Fashion Brands Worldwide

1	Michael Kors
2	Marc Jacobs
3	Ralph Lauren
4	Calvin Klein
5	Vera Wang
6	Tory Burch
7	Kate Spade
8	Diane von Furstenburg
9	Betsey Johnson
10	Tom Ford

Source: "Digital Luxury Group," Lisa Lockwood, *Women's Wear Daily*, 2013.

If shipment is made before the check is collected, the exporter is at risk that the check may be returned due to insufficient funds in the buyer's account or due to a stop-payment order.

Letters of Credit

Because cash-in-advance is the most secure payment method for exporters, but the least secure for importers, a compromise of sorts is the use of a **letter of credit (LC)**. An LC is a contractual agreement whereby an importer's bank, acting on behalf of its customer, authorizes the exporter's bank to make payment to the exporter upon the receipt of documents stipulated in the letter of credit. The issuing of a letter of credit alone is not a guarantee that the seller will be paid. The seller must comply with all the terms and conditions stated in the LC before funds will be transferred.[7]

Banks issue LCs, at the request of their customers (buyers) in an international trade transaction, based on their current account or line of credit. In this process, the bank—rather than the customer—assumes the promise to pay the seller. Payment must be for the exact amount of the credit. The buyers pays their bank a fee—a percent usually based on the value of the transaction—for this service.[8]

The involvement of established banks is important because it lowers risk levels and protects the interests of both the exporter and the importer in an international trade transaction. LCs require that banks process payment based on the presentation of documents verifying the transfer of title and that specific steps have been taken, primarily by the exporter. Exporters request LCs when reliable credit information about a foreign buyer is difficult to obtain, but they are satisfied with the creditworthiness of the buyer's foreign bank. Buyers are also protected in the sense that no payment obligation kicks in until the goods have been shipped or delivered as promised in the credit. In the LC, the importer or buyer is called the **applicant**, while the exporter or seller is called the **beneficiary** to the LC.[9]

The LC is a separate contract from the sales contract on which it is based, so the banks are not concerned whether each party fulfills the terms of the sales contract. For example, if a letter of credit is the agreed-upon payment method for an order for 10,000 100-percent silk scarves to be shipped from China to a Midwestern U.S. department store chain, payment will be made as soon as the stipulated documents, as described in the LC, have been received by the U.S. importer's bank. Even if the shipment contains 10,000 polyester (instead of silk) scarves, payment will still be made. When using an LC, the buyer's bank's obligation to pay is solely conditioned upon the seller's compliance with the terms and conditions of the LC. The banks deal only in documents—not goods—when using an LC. Shipping errors, as in the example above, whether accidental or intentional, must be resolved outside the arena of the letter of credit.

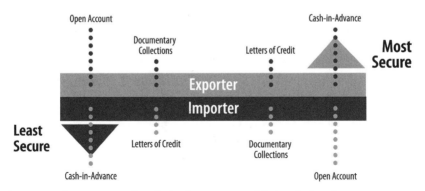

Figure 9.5 There are several methods of payments in global trade, from least to most secure, for exporters or importers.

Buyers paying for imported goods with a letter of credit want to remember always that an LC is never intended to be a substitute for the seller's honesty or competence. The working relationship and level of confidence in a seller's ability or willingness to ship exactly what the customer ordered is outside the function of the LC. For example, using D&B or Graydon International (cited earlier) will give an importer some idea of a supplier's reputation for paying its bills—but not on the delivery of the right goods and on time. Of course, most sellers interested in long-term, profitable relationships will not substitute lower-quality merchandise or the wrong orders—but the occasional crooked firm has been known to take the customer's money and run![10]

The buyers' recourses are few, as international lawsuits to recover the cost of mistakes or intentionally fraudulent transactions would most likely be much more costly than the actual value of the goods in dispute. Also, just shipping the wrong goods back is not the answer, as two-way transportation costs could be more than the value of the shipment.

The letter of credit specifies the required documents the exporter must present, such as an **ocean bill of lading** or **air waybill** (if shipped by air), consular invoice (if the importer's country requires one), and an insurance policy, if the terms of sale require one be purchased by the exporter. The LC states an expiration date that all parties to the credit must adhere to or the credit is considered void. Before payment is made, the issuing bank will verify that all documents received from the exporter's bank conform to the LC's requirements. If not, the discrepancy must be resolved before payment can be made and before the expiration date.[11]

Confirmed Letter of Credit

A higher degree of security is available to the exporter when a **confirmed letter of credit**, an LC issued by a foreign bank (the importer's issuing bank) that is confirmed by a U.S. bank, is required to comply with the terms of sale. The customer instructs the issuing bank to authorize a bank in the exporter's country to confirm the advising bank. The advising bank, which becomes the confirming bank, becomes obligated to pay the exporter, according to the terms of the credit—even if the buyer (or buyer's bank) defaults on the purchase. Remember, the banks are charging fees for their services, so they are happy to oblige.[12]

If a letter of credit is not confirmed, but still advised through a U.S. bank, it is referred to as an **advised letter of credit**, without the extra protection of confirmation. U.S. exporters should confirm letters of credit issued by foreign banks if they are unfamiliar with the foreign bank or concerned about the political or economic risk associated with the country in which the bank is located. Exporters

ORIGINAL

INTERNATIONAL BANKING GROUP

Megabank Corporation

P.O. BOX 1000, ATLANTA, GEORGIA 30302-1000
CABLE ADDRESS: MegaB
TELEX NO. 1234567
SWIFT NO. MBBABC 72

OUR ADVICE NUMBER: EA00000091
ADVICE DATE: 08MAR97   ****AMOUNT****
ISSUE BANK REF: 3312/HBI/22341   USD****25,000.00
EXPIRY DATE: 23JUN97

BENEFICIARY: APPLICANT:
THE WALTON SUPPLY CO.   HHB HONG KONG
2356 SOUTH N.W. STREET   34 INDUSTRIAL DRIVE
ATLANTA, GEORGIA 30345   CENTRAL, HONG KONG

WE HAVE BEEN REQUESTED TO ADVISE TO YOU THE FOLLOWING LETTER OF CREDIT AS
ISSUED BY:
THIRD HONG KONG BANK
1 CENTRAL TOWER
HONG KONG

PLEASE BE GUIDED BY ITS TERMS AND CONDITIONS AND BY THE FOLLOWING:
CREDIT IS AVAILABLE BY NEGOTIATION OF YOUR DRAFT(S) IN DUPLICATE AT
SIGHT FOR 100 PERCENT OF INVOICE VALUE DRAWN ON US ACCOMPANIED BY THE
FOLLOWING DOCUMENTS:

1. SIGNED COMMERCIAL INVOICE IN 1 ORIGINAL AND 3 COPIES.

2. FULL SET 3/3 OCEAN BILLS OF LADING CONSIGNED TO THE ORDER OF THIRD HONG KONG
   BANK, HONG KONG NOTIFY APPLICANT AND MARKED FREIGHT COLLECT.

3. PACKING LIST IN 2 COPIES.

EVIDENCING SHIPMENT OF: 5000 PINE LOGS – WHOLE – 8 TO 12 FEET
                        FOB SAVANNAH, GEORGIA

SHIPMENT FROM: SAVANNAH, GEORGIA   TO: HONG KONG
LATEST SHIPPING DATE: 02JUN97

PARTIAL SHIPMENTS NOT ALLOWED   TRANSHIPMENT NOT ALLOWED

ALL BANKING CHARGES OUTSIDE HONG KONG ARE FOR BENEFICIARYS ACCOUNT.
DOCUMENTS MUST BE PRESENTED WITHIN 21 DAYS FROM B/L DATE.

AT THE REQUEST OF OUR CORRESPONDENT, WE CONFIRM THIS CREDIT AND ALSO ENGAGE
WITH YOU THAT ALL DRAFTS DRAWN UNDER AND IN COMPLIANCE WITH THE TERMS OF THIS
CREDIT WILL BE DULY HONORED BY US.

PLEASE EXAMINE THIS INSTRUMENT CAREFULLY. IF YOU ARE UNABLE TO COMPLY WITH
THE TERMS OR CONDITIONS, PLEASE COMMUNICATE WITH YOUR BUYER TO ARRANGE FOR
AN AMENDMENT.

Figure 9.6 This sample international letter of credit indicates a bank's commitment to pay, on behalf of the importer, the exact amount of credit—provided the terms of credit are met by the exporter.

need to check with the U.S. Department of Commerce Export Assistance Center for notice of any current foreign bank fraud or warnings regarding fake, worthless LCs—not uncommon in Africa and parts of Asia. Warnings may also be listed on the websites of U.S. government offices involved in trade, such as the U.S. Department of State, the office of the Special Trade Representative (STR), and the Bureau of Industry and Security (BIS). Everyone, not just exporters, should be aware of the "Nigerian Letter" or "419" Fraud, explained in detail on the following FBI site: http://www.fbi.gov/scams-safety/fraud/fraud#419.[13]

Any change to a letter of credit after it has been issued is called an **amendment**. Banks charge fees for this service, even if just to extend the payment due date. It should be specified in the amendment if the exporter or the buyer will pay these fees. Every effort should be made to get the letter of credit right the first time, since these changes can be time-consuming as well as expensive.

Types of Letters of Credit

The following are the two basic types of LCs:

- Revocable
- Irrevocable

A **revocable letter of credit** can be withdrawn or modified at any time without notice to or consent from the seller. Employing a revocable letter of credit is inadvisable, as it carries too many risks for the exporter. Companies or individuals new to export should not use this payment form, unless they are doing an internal sale or transfer of goods between different branches of the same company. For example, General Motors U.S.A. may consign American-made autos to its subsidiary company in Spain. General Motors U.S.A. can feel pretty confident it will get paid through a revocable letter of credit, although payment may take place after the initial sales contract deadline and that of the letter of agreement.

An **irrevocable letter of credit** is a legally binding document that can't be changed by any of the parties to a credit (seller-exporter, buyer-importer, or issuing or applicant bank and the beneficiary bank), unless all parties agree to and sign off on an amendment.

A **confirmed irrevocable letter of credit** is opened by an issuing bank whose authenticity has been confirmed by the advising bank and where the advising bank has added its confirmation to the credit. The words "we confirm the credit and hereby undertake . . ." are usually included in the confirmed LC.[14]

An exporter whose terms of payment call for a confirmed, irrevocable LC can expect on-time payment—as long as the requirements of the LC are met. The confirmed, irrevocable LC is particularly important from buyers in countries that are economically or politically unstable. The exporter or importer will have to pay an extra charge, called the **confirmation fee**, which may vary from bank to bank. New or inexperienced exporters or those dealing with unfamiliar customers should use only confirmed, irrevocable letters of credit.

Lower Risks

One reason for the popularity of LCs is that they help reduce risk for both the buyer and the seller, when goods or payments are exchanged during exporting or importing, in the following ways:

- The seller's risk is reduced because a bank has promised to pay for the goods—providing the seller has met all the terms of the credit.
- The buyer/importer's risk is also reduced, knowing the seller won't get paid unless the importer's bank has received the proper documents— proving the terms as stated in the credit are met.

Key Points to Remember about the Letter of Credit

The following are important points in keep in mind when working with LCs:

- First, the LC does <u>not</u> guarantee payment to the seller. It only allows payment if the seller complies exactly with the terms of the credit.
- Second, the LC does not guarantee the buyer will receive goods that are the expected quality, color, style, or other specification described in the bill of sale.

Banks are concerned only with the financial aspects presented in the documents and not with the merchandise being exchanged. The LC is a separate contract from the export sales agreement and, therefore, the banks are not concerned with the commercial aspects of the sale. Banks make no guarantees that the merchandise ordered will be the same as that delivered—they are not concerned whether each party fulfills the terms of the sales contract.

Sellers make honest mistakes, however, and should immediately replace the wrong order—shipping by air, if necessary. To maintain an ongoing relationship, the seller may offer the buyer the option of purchasing the cheaper or erroneous goods at a very low price (to cover shipping costs) or at no cost if the buyer objects and the seller wants to rebuild trust and reliability—good customer relations.

Elements/Contents of Letters of Credit

- **Applicant:** The party applying for the letter of credit, usually the buyer/ importer in a transaction.
- **Issuing bank:** The bank that issues the letter of credit and assumes the obligation to make payment to the beneficiary, usually the seller/exporter.
- **Beneficiary**: The party in whose favor the letter of credit is issued, usually the exporter.
- **Advising or negotiating bank**: The bank that negotiates or approves the letter of credit and receives payment and documentation from the issuing bank, on behalf of the beneficiary.
- **Amount**: The sum of money, usually expressed as a maximum amount, of the credit defined in a specific currency.

- **Terms**: The requirements, including documents that must be met for the collection of the credit.
- **Expiration date:** The final date for the beneficiary to present against the credit.

A Typical Letter of Credit Transaction

Here are the basic steps of an irrevocable letter of credit transaction that has been confirmed by a U.S. bank:

1. After the exporter and buyer agree on an LC as the payment method for an international sales transaction, the buyer arranges for its bank to open a confirmed irrevocable letter of credit in favor of the exporter (seller). It specifies the documents needed for payment, including the commercial invoice and letter of credit. The exporter can request that a particular U.S. bank be the confirming bank, or the foreign bank may select a U.S. correspondent bank.
2. The buyer's bank electronically transmits the LC to the seller's bank, which forwards it to the exporter, usually a manufacturer or distributor. It includes all details relating to the purchase and payment with the LC.

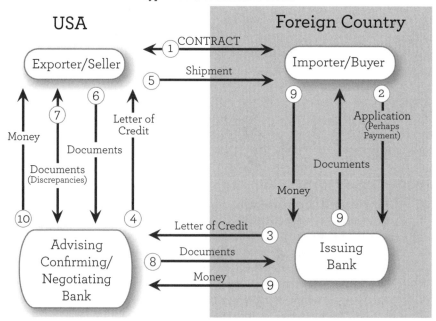

Typical Flow of a Letter of Credit

Figure 9.7 Typical flow of a letter of credit between the exporter/seller and the importer/buyer.

Source: Figure recreated from *The Global Entrepreneur,* Second Edition, by James Foley, Jamric Press International, 2004.

3. The exporter forwards the goods—and documents—to a **freight forwarder**, the service provider who prepares the goods for transit and who presents the export documentation necessary for exiting the United States and entering the buyer's country.
4. Once the forwarder receives the goods, it provides the exporter with a receipt from the shipper; **a bill of lading** (B/L) if by ship, train, or truck; or an air waybill if by air cargo. The B/L or air waybill is a contract between the exporter and the shipping company, not the buyer.
5. The exporter's freight forwarder ships the goods and submits the B/L or air waybill, along with any other required documents called for in the original terms of sale and the LC, to its bank. The U.S. bank checks the documents for compliance with the LC and presents them to the buyer's bank for payment.
6. The importer's bank then reviews the documents and, if compliant, pays the seller's bank; the importer's account is debited the amount of the credit, and the seller's bank credits that account for the sale.
7. The importer's bank releases the documents, enabling the importer to claim the goods from the carrier and to clear them at customs.

Documentary Drafts

A **documentary draft**, sometimes also called a bill of exchange, is analogous to a foreign buyer's check. Like checks used in domestic commerce, drafts carry the risk that they will be dishonored. However, in international commerce, title does not transfer to buyers until they pay the draft, or at least engage a legal undertaking that the draft will be paid when due.[15]

Sight Drafts

A **sight draft** is used when the exporter wishes to retain title to the shipment until it reaches its destination and payment is made. Before the shipment can be released to the buyer, the original ocean bill of lading (the document that evidences title) must be properly endorsed by the buyer and surrendered to the carrier. It is important to note that air waybills of lading do not need to be presented for the buyer to claim the goods. As such, risk increases when a sight draft is being used with an air shipment.

In actual practice, the ocean bill of lading is endorsed by the exporter and sent via the exporter's bank to the buyer's bank. It is accompanied by the sight draft, invoices, and other supporting documents that are specified by either the buyer or the buyer's country (e.g., packing lists, consular invoices, and insurance certificates). The foreign bank notifies the buyer when it has received these documents. As soon as the draft is paid, the foreign bank turns over the B/L, thereby enabling the buyer to obtain the shipment.

There is still some risk when a sight draft is used to control transferring the title of a shipment. The buyer's ability or willingness to pay might change from the time the goods are shipped until the time the drafts are presented for payment;

there is no bank promise to pay standing behind the buyer's obligation. Additionally, the policies of the importing country could also change. If the buyer cannot or will not pay for and claim the goods, returning or disposing of the products becomes a big problem for the exporter.[16]

Time Drafts and Date Drafts

A **time draft** is used when the exporter extends credit to the buyer. The draft states that payment is due by a specific time after the buyer accepts the time draft and receives the goods (e.g., 30 days after acceptance). By signing and writing "accepted" on the draft, the buyer is formally obligated to pay within the stated time. When this is done the time draft is then called a trade acceptance. It can be kept by the exporter until maturity or sold to a bank at a discount for immediate payment.

A **date draft** differs slightly from a time draft in that it specifies a date on which payment is due, rather than a time period after the draft is accepted. When either a sight draft or time draft is used, a buyer can delay payment by delaying acceptance of the draft. A date draft can prevent this delay in payment, though it still must be accepted.

When a bank accepts a draft, it becomes an obligation of the bank and, thus, a negotiable investment known as a **banker's acceptance**. A banker's acceptance may also be sold to a bank at a discount for immediate payment.[17]

Open Account

In foreign transaction, an open account means that when the exporter ships the goods and the bills, the customer is expected to pay by a certain date in the future, or else a finance charge will be assessed on the balance due. This can be a convenient method of payment—if the buyer is well established, has a long and favorable payment record, or has been thoroughly checked for creditworthiness.

Some of the largest firms abroad make purchases only on open account, but it's a risky method for those new to exporting. The fact that official documents are not used and a bank is not guaranteeing payment make it difficult to pursue the legal enforcement of claims. It is just too costly and time consuming for an exporter to collect overdue accounts abroad. There are several ways to reduce credit risk, through such means as export credit insurance.

Consignment

Although not recommended for international sales, **consignment**, or the transfer of possession of a seller's goods to a buyer without any formal commitment to pay for the goods if they are not sold, is sometimes used in specific industries, the diamond trade being one of them.[18]

The great risk is that the buyer is not really a buyer, just a repository for the exporter's goods until they are sold. At that time, the buyer is expected to pay the

Figure 9.8 Diamonds are among the fashion goods sold on consignment.

seller the agreed-on price. This is very risky for export trade, as the costs of recovering any unsold—or unpaid for goods—is usually prohibitive. This method is not recommended unless it's a standard practice in a given industry because the buyer is not getting credit until the goods are sold.

Exporters thinking about any open sales terms should be completely aware of current political, economic, and commercial risks. Although it is up to sellers to decide on the payment method, they will weigh the amount of protection they desire against the inconvenience caused the buyer. The following factors may influence the payment method required by the seller:

1. The value of the transaction
2. Type of merchandise exported
3. Market conditions—both the buyer's market and seller's market
4. Credit standing of the buyer

5. Political conditions, exchange controls, or currency fluctuations in the country of destination
6. Customs in the trade
7. Payment terms of competitors

Of course, buyers want a payment method that is most convenient for them, one that gives them the most advantage over the use of their money. So, if the buyer wants time payment delay, the exporter has the right to charge interest.

Payment terms, as well as prices, are important factors when marketing price-competitive products in global markets. Both exporters and importers should consult with their bankers if financing will be needed for the transaction before agreement on an international sales contract or issuing a pro forma invoice to a buyer.

SELECTING YOUR BANKER

Since banks make money on international trade finance, even your neighborhood banker will try to get your business. They may not be experienced in letters of credit or other financing options, but local bankers will use an international bank in larger cities as a correspondent bank to handle their transactions.

The practice should work out fine for the very small exporter who is only dealing with basic letters of credit. But if your business is on a larger scale, or you anticipate the need for more sophisticated international trade finance, you should consider going directly to banks experienced in this area. For exporters, the selection of an international bank can be crucial to their success. Banks can play a major role in expediting export sales transactions—or may be a major contributor to a failure. Consider a prospective bank's experience in the country where the majority of sales are expected. What are the legal lending limits? Is it full-service with respect to trade finance and letters of credit? Do bankers listen carefully to your needs and wants, not only concerning financial services, but also foreign market research and business contacts?

The larger international banks often have research departments and experts to give advice on more nontraditional financing methods. Their fees may be higher, but not as much as extra fees to a local bank that uses one of the bigger banks for its transactions. In times of global economic concerns, it is critical to seek out international bankers who have a better pulse on global financial risks, rewards, and methods for reducing risk.[19]

Figure 9.9 Large international banks can give advice on export financing methods.

KEY TERMS

Summary

Success in today's global marketplace depends on having a competitive edge over not only foreign firms but also other U.S. companies engaged in export-import trade. One strategy is to offer prospective customers attractive sales terms supported by appropriate payment methods. Although getting paid in full and on time for each sale is the ultimate goal for exporters, they do understand that a time payment delay will allow their importer customer the best use of their financial resources. Of course, the best payment method is one that minimizes risk for both the exporter and the importer.

Exporters, as sellers, must also accommodate the needs of their customers. For them, any sale is a gift until they are paid. Importers are often sellers as well, after importing goods or services for resale to the end-user. But for them, any payment is a donation until the goods are received in good condition and matching their specifications.

So agreement on payment terms takes the guesswork out of a transaction. The guidelines should be clearly spelled out in the original terms of sale of the contract. All parties to the exchange should take care to know when payment must be made and how the funds will be transferred.

Exporters want to get paid as soon as possible, preferably as soon as an order is placed or even before the goods are sent to the importer. Therefore, the most secure payment method for exporters is to receive cash-in-advance. In this method, the exporter can avoid credit risk because payment is received before the ownership of the goods is transferred. Wire transfers and credit cards are the most commonly used cash-in-advance options. However, insisting on cash-in-advance may lose business to competitors who offer more attractive payment terms. Foreign buyers may be concerned that the goods may not be sent if payment is made in advance and that also can create cash-flow problems.

Importers want to receive the goods shortly after an order is placed, but would like to delay payment as long as possible. They want the chance, if possible, to inspect the arrived shipments for both the right quantity and quality and the condition of the goods prior to making payment. Since they usually resell the goods, they would like to delay payment until they collect funds from their customers.

A compromise payment method, acceptable to both exporters and importers, is the letter of credit, which reduces risk levels for both parties. The other common payment methods are cash-in-advance, documentary collections, open account, and consignment. Both exporters and importers will negotiate a transaction's terms of sale to obtain the most advantageous payment method—in much the same way price is part of any sales transaction.

Although most of the basic payment methods can be initiated by most local banks, firms anticipating the need for more sophisticated international trade finance should consider going directly to banks experienced in this area.

KEY TERMS, CONT'D

> TERMS

> TIME DRAFT

> WIRE TRANSFER

Review Questions

1. How does use of the letter of credit reduce risk levels for the exporter? For the importer?
2. Which of the standard methods of payment are most risky for the exporter? Which are most risky for the importer?
3. Does the use of a letter of credit *guarantee* payment to the seller?
4. Is there any way to guarantee delivery of exactly what is ordered from a foreign source? What is your recourse if the wrong goods are received?
5. In what situations is a revocable letter of credit deemed acceptable?
6. Why should those firms new-to-export insist upon using a confirmed, irrevocable letter of credit in international transactions?

Discussion Questions and Activities

1. Interview a banker with a large international finance clientele. Ask for a checklist for use in evaluating a bank to handle a new-to-export account. Reproduce copies of the list for your class and prepare a short oral presentation on "selecting the right banker."

2. Identify local international freight forwarders and Customs brokers and plan a class visit to one of their facilities, if approved by your school. Ask them to provide an international order flow chart tracing an international sale from the sales contract to the delivery of the merchandise or service.

3. Contact an international trade lawyer and ask what recourse an importer may have if goods paid for with a letter of credit arrive damaged or are intentionally switched with lesser quality or other specs that were not according to the original sales agreement. Report to your class the lawyer's suggestions on how to protect your rights in an international sales transaction.

Chapter 9 Case

Patagonia's Support of Growth and Sustainability

Based in Ventura, California, Patagonia has long been a major supplier of outdoor apparel and gear for rock climbers, skiers, surfers, and other sports enthusiasts. Athletes, explorers, and workers in places as diverse as Yosemite, California, Greenland, Venezuela, Pakistan, Indonesia, and Panama depend on Patagonia products to sustain their activities and in many cases keep their lives safe.

Founded by Yvon Chouinard in 1988, the company has textile mills and factories throughout the world. Patagonia thrives as a retailer, but its goals have been loftier than just making a profit. Realizing that the world's resources are being consumed at a greater rate than they are being replaced, Chouinard's goal for the company has been to become totally sustainable, that is, to return to nature 100 percent of the resources it uses. Patagonia's products are made from environmentally conscious fabrics, often colored by nature and grown with a minimum of water. Fleece jackets are created from recycled plastic bottles. Yet all of the company's goods are renowned for their suitability and strength. The company's view prevails throughout the organization. Employees are paid fairly, have health insurance that includes maternity and paternity leave, and receive child care. Patagonia's philosophy has been to "reduce what you buy; reuse what you no longer need; reuse what's worn out; and reimagine a sustainable world."

A while back, Rose Marcario, with more than two decades in finance with private and publicly held companies, decided that she wanted to work in a situation where her personal values could have a larger part in her business decisions. She went to work for Patagonia in 2008 and began to develop an in-house venture fund that the company could use as a vehicle to give back. Patagonia could afford it. Over the years the company has grown substantially and profited. Sales in 2013 were $575 million, up from the previous two years, with forecasts for continuing steady global growth and profit. The fund's purpose was to invest in start-up businesses concerned with five areas: apparel, energy, water, food, and waste. Called $20 Million and Change, unlike most venture start-ups, the fund focused on social goals as well as growth and profits in the five areas.

Source: Patagonia website, May 11, 2013; "Patagonia's Latest Product: A Venture Fund," Apparel, *Bloomberg Businessweek*, May 13–18, 2013, pp. 23, 24.

Question

Think of an idea to start an export or import business in one of the five areas the venture fund supports. Your idea has both profit and social and environmental goals. To get your business up and running, you hope to obtain some financing and are beginning to develop your general views on your proposed company. In a paragraph, explain your business, describing its economic and social goals and stating why you need financing.

References

1. "Trade Finance Guide: A Quick Reference for U.S. Exporters," November 2012, International Trade Administration, U.S. Department of Commerce. Retrieved November 6, 2013, from http://export.gov/Trade FinanceGuide/2012.

2. "International Company Profile," Export .gov. Retrieved November 7, 2013, from http://export .gov/china/build/groups /public/@eg_cn /documents/webcontent /eg_cn025933.pdf.

3. "International Trade Payment Methods," Export.gov. Retrieved November 7, 2013, from http://export.gov/sb counselors/eg_main _038170.asp.

4. Op. cit., "Trade Finance Guide," p. 5.

5. Ibid., p. 6.

6. Board of Governors of the Federal Reserve, Regulation CC (12 CFR Part 229). Exception Hold Period § 229.13(h). Retrieved November 10, 2013, from http://www .federalreserve.gov/SECRS /2011/June/20110607/R -1409/R.

7. Op. cit., "Trade Finance Guide," p. 7.

8. Ibid., p. 8.

9. Ibid.

10. Ibid.

11. Op. cit., "International Trade Payment Methods."

12. Ibid.

13. "International Trade Scams," Export.gov. Retrieved November 11, 2013, from http://export

.gov/tradeproblems /eg_main_018586.asp; "Common Fraud Schemes," Federal Bureau of Investigation. Retrieved November 11, 2013, from http://www.fbi .gov/scams-safety/fraud /fraud#419.

14. Op. cit., "Trade Finance Guide," p. 8.

15. Ibid., p. 9.

16. Ibid.

17. Op. cit., "International Trade Payment Methods."

18. Ibid., p. 13

19. Peter Zipper, *Choosing An International Banking Center: Banking Laws and Beyond*, Hemispheres Publishing, March, 2011. Retrieved November 11, 2013, from http:// hemispherespublishing .com/Issues/2011/March.

Figure 10.1 **Hoodies are popular sportswear items exported and imported throughout the world.**

CHAPTER 10
CASES FOR ESSENTIALS OF EXPORTING AND IMPORTING

Thing here are many career paths to top management in business today. One of the shortest, and perhaps one of the most financially rewarding, is through a business's international division or department. Most companies in the United States are directly or indirectly involved in some aspect of international business, on the export marketing side or by importing materials, components, or finished goods into the country.

As the title of this textbook suggests, knowledge of U.S. trade policies and procedures, as well as corporate "best practices," is essential for successful exporting and importing. The following success stories or insights into the practices of a small sample of diverse companies are offered in this final chapter as incentives for both student and business readers.

The case history of Knights Apparel shows how an American manufacturer can employ a U.S. government offshore manufacturing program not only to make a profit, but also to give a foreign nation a "pathway out of poverty." Its story is a classic example of "fair trade," in addition to "free trade," when U.S. firms choose to source goods or components from foreign countries.

Le Fleur Imports, Ltd., offers a very personal insight into a sales executive's decision to become an entrepreneur importer, and owner of a company, rather than continue as a sales representative for those same imports. He offers several unique tips for success for future entrepreneurs in fashion importing.

One of the most basic operations of any business is the delivery of goods safely and on time. Chicago-based LR International, Inc., has faced many challenges in delivering client's exports or imports around the world. CEO Ric Frantz provides detailed descriptions of some of the firm's experiences, while also explaining the challenges of exporting and importing.

In the final case study, a veteran marketing executive discusses the key decisions involved in creating internal designs or outsourcing new product designs. The concepts and programs illustrated by this case study can be applied to both domestic and international businesses by answering the question: "Where do new product ideas come from?"

Case A

U.S. Apparel Importer Promotes "Fair Trade" Production

Knights Apparel, a South Carolina-based apparel manufacturer, sources its production from around the world, as do most of its competitors. The April 24, 2013, collapse of Rana Plaza Textile factory in Bangladesh that killed more than 1,100 workers has put a spotlight on importers of foreign-made apparel into the United States. The ethical, moral, and legal issues surrounding offshore production of apparel imports is central to the "fair trade" versus "free-trade" issues referenced in Chapter 6 of this text.

Knights Apparel became the first apparel company to have its social compliance program accredited under the Fair Labor Association's (FLA) New Principles of Fair Labor and Responsible Sourcing. According to the firm, it supplies licensed sports apparel and services retailers in all channels of distribution. Knights Apparel is a fully accredited participating member of the FLA.

The FLA is a nonprofit collaborative effort of U.S. universities, civil society organizations, and socially responsible companies. It describes its mission as "promoting adherence to international and national labor laws." The FLA was established in 1999 and evolved out of a task force created by President Bill Clinton following a series of child labor and other sweatshop scandals involving major apparel and footwear brands.

The name, Knights Apparel, may not be as recognizable as Nike or Adidas, but its new brand, Alta Gracia, supplies more than 400 college and university bookstores with, according to officials, "living wage/union made" T-shirts and sweatshirts. The firm reports that the Alta Gracia label offers students, their families, and alumni, for the first time, the opportunity to give the workers who sew their college logo T-shirts and hoodies a living wage, and as a result, a pathway out of poverty.

The offshore production of apparel imports—an estimated $4 billion market just for apparel branded with college and university logos—has become so large and so geographically dispersed that it is difficult for U.S. importers or retailers to monitor, let alone change any worker conditions. A single garment may combine components, such as fabric made in one or more countries, with labor provided in another and additional processes in multiple countries.

Student activism and actions by organizations such as the Worker Rights Consortium, a labor rights group whose members include large public universities as well as private schools, have already created changes in plants in Central America, Indonesia, and other countries where local laws did not protect factory workers. The consortium has created a database of factories that make apparel for colleges and universities. The University of Illinois at Urbana-Champaign, for example, listed thousands of foreign-based factories licensed to manufacture its hats, shirts, and other items with its logo.

In light of the collapse of the textile factory in Bangladesh, retailers and manufacturers around the world have been under intense pressure to take more responsibility for safety and other working conditions in plants they contract with in Asia and South America and in other world locations.

Knights Apparel has implemented a strict "Apparel Workplace Code of Conduct," available on its website (http://www.knightsapparel.com/compliance/english), that ensures employees' rights are respected and policies protecting those rights are implemented in its factories, including the Dominican Republic location where the Alta Gracia label is produced.

Thousands of American students have embraced Alta Gracia's new, socially responsible business/manufacturing model by seeking out and buying the brand. As a result of these students' loyalty, Knights Apparel's entire manufacturing community is thriving, with better health care, housing, education, and nutritious food. New jobs are being created, as new businesses open to serve the factories and their workers. According to Joseph Bozich, CEO at Knights Apparel, "Our firm pays our Dominican Republic factory workers more than three times the minimum wage. It is run with employee input and allows outside monitors to certify factory working conditions."

The higher wages and other costs initially lowered profit margins. But sales are picking up as more and more retailers (such as the Barnes & Noble book chain) and university bookstores (including Duke) are listening to student demands for only fair-trade manufactured imports.

Knights Apparel's imports from the Dominican Republic also enjoy tariff relief, as a result of the 2004 Central America-United States Free Trade Agreement (CAFTA-DR) with five Central American countries (Costa Rica, El Salvador, Guatemala, Honduras, and Nicaragua) as well as the Dominican Republic. CAFTA-DR was the first free trade agreement between the United States and a group of smaller developing economies. This agreement created new economic opportunities by eliminating tariffs, opening markets, reducing barriers to services, and promoting transparency. It moved beyond the one-way preferences of the former Caribbean Basin Initiative (CBI) and the

Caribbean Basin Trade Partnership Act (CBTPA) programs of 2000 to full partnership and reciprocal commitments, under which U.S. exports also benefit from duty-free access.

When Knights Apparel launched Alta Gracia, the *New York Times* called the new business model, "a high-minded experiment." Time will determine if the experiment ultimately is a corporate financial success. For the workers and their families, as well as the student buyers of its products, the answer is a resounding "yes."

Source: Howard Schneider, "College Group Wages 'Fair Trade' Fight," Chicago Tribune, retrieved June 7, 2013, sec. 2, p. 2; Knights Apparel website. Retrieved July 15, 2013, from http://www.knightsapparel.com; Fair Labor Association, "New Principles of Fair Labor and Responsible Sourcing," retrieved June 9, 2013, from http://www.fairlabor.org.

Questions

1. Why is Knights Apparel outsourcing manufacturing for its Alta Gracia line from the Dominican Republic? Wouldn't it be saving jobs if it produced the apparel imports at a U.S. facility? Why or why not?

2. What are the social or economic guidelines, such as health and safety, that U.S. manufacturers should be concerned about when sourcing product from foreign-based factories?

3. In tough economic times, how can marketers justify paying more for imported apparel sourced from "politically correct" foreign manufacturers?

4. What are the economic benefits of free trade agreements (FTAs)? What is an example of a disadvantage the United States might have with a Caribbean Basin free trade agreement?

Case B

From Sales Rep to Master Importer: A Personal Story

For more than ten years, Gerry Sky was on a successful career track as a young sales representative for one of the nation's leading distributors of home fashion décor. He sold a leading line of imported artificial floral products, Christmas items, baskets, ribbons, and other related accessories to wholesalers, retailers, manufacturers, and design centers in the United States. All goods were manufactured in China, under the direction of the American firm he represented exclusively.

Then without any advance warning, Sky's U.S.-based parent company ceased operations, declared bankruptcy, and informed Sky that none of his customer's orders (for two buying seasons) would be delivered! Stunned with a personal loss of his sales commissions, plus out-of-pocket expenses, Sky faced a life-changing decision: to seek a sales position at another floral import company, or to invest the time and money necessary for establishing his own import company. Sky took the riskier path and started his own company that eventually became Le Fleur Imports, Ltd.

Figure 10.2 These imported floral designs are manufactured in China and imported into the United States for distribution by LeFleur Imports, Ltd., an American company.

Photo courtesy of LaFleur Imports, Ltd.

A key factor in his decision to venture into entrepreneurship was a good personal relationship with the Hong Kong-based agent-of-record for his bankrupt U.S. manufacturer. This agent became a critical part of Sky's new company's import program, since the agent was familiar with Chinese factories that could provide merchandise that Sky's wholesale and retail accounts were already sourcing. This arrangement enabled Sky's established accounts to continue receiving floral products from him rather than finding other importers to fulfill their needs.

Although his agent in China continues to arrange factory production of floral items, Sky has become personally involved in many new facets of importing. He travels to showrooms and factories in China to select samples that he will offer to his U.S. accounts. Before he makes any presentations, he prices and tags each sample order, calculating all cost items. He admits that pricing is one of the most difficult aspects of importing, as companies are always trying to match a competitor's quality with cheaper prices. His price quotes are not just for the cost of goods—they also include freight charges, import duties, fees for forwarders or banks, and warehouse expenses, as well as U.S. and foreign travel and sales/marketing expenses. To that base, he adds a profit percentage, since he now is the owner of the firm as well as its top salesperson.

Sky imports multiple container loads, usually 40-foot containers, holding about 2,200 cubic feet of merchandise. The goods are sourced from multiple factories and consolidated in Shenzhen, China. Once the containers are full, they leave from the nearby port of Hong Kong for the U.S. port in Long Beach, California, arriving approximately 19 days later. Documents must be presented upon arrival for clearing his goods through U.S. Customs, known as "entry," before they can be released from Customs control. His customs broker, acting as his agent (for a fee), shepherds the goods through the entry process.

Entry documents include a bill of lading (B/L), commercial invoice, entry manifest, packing list, and Customs entry forms. Once all import duties have been paid by his customs broker, the merchandise is transferred by rail (a trip that takes about seven days) to the Joliet, Illinois, depot. Goods are then trucked to his warehouse in Carol Stream, Illinois, as inventory for order fulfillment.

Sky pays his customs broker for services, including applicable import duties (about 10 percent, except for Christmas items that come in duty-free), fees, and out-of-pocket expenses for the following:

- Ocean freight
- Entry fees

- Handling charges
- Cartage/inland services
- Miscellaneous logistics fees

Sky's warehouse company provides inventory storage and control, order fulfillment, and shipping services at cost plus fees for services. Sky is invoiced for the imported merchandise by his foreign agent, whom he pays via wire transfer, which is covered by an established bank line of credit. His wholesale and retail accounts are invoiced when the ordered goods arrive at the warehouse.

Initially having limited knowledge of U.S. import procedures and controls, Sky was concerned about his transformation from salesperson to "master importer." However, once he formed a strong working relationship with his reliable Chinese agent and through him accessed quality manufacturers, Sky was willing to "take the plunge" in the challenging—but lucrative—world of importing. He also credits the U.S. freight forwarders and customs brokers, as well as his local warehouse, for being supportive of his import plan.

His "tips for success" for entrepreneurs in fashion importing include the following:

- Provide outstanding customer service, including immediate—and honest—responses to any inquiries. For example, Sky immediately contacted his customers when his U.S. company went bankrupt, even though the news about the loss of their orders for two selling seasons was devastating. He knew that any delay would jeopardize any future relationships with them.
- Be organized. Sky sets up appointments several weeks in advance to be cost and time efficient.
- Keep low product inventories. Inventories are expensive to maintain and are a logistics and cash-flow problem when, by necessity, they become "closeouts," selling at deep discounts or even at a loss.
- Find new products. Home décor/fashion customers—as well as the wholesale and retail merchandisers/buyers—are fickle. According to Sky, the first question is usually, "What's new?" So his challenge is to find new and exciting offerings each season.
- Keep three words in mind as keys to success: relationships, relationships, and relationships.

Sky still travels to about 15 states, represents approximately 10 lines, and twice each year visits showrooms and factories in China. He's always searching for new and exciting designs for his home furnishings and floral design customers.

Source: Author interviews with Mr. Sky on February, 21, 2014 and March 3, 2014.

Questions

1. What other choices did Gerry Sky have when faced with his parent company's bankruptcy?

2. What would be the pros and cons of dropping the foreign agent and establishing his own relationships with factories in China?

3. How can Sky streamline his import procedures? Can you identify any time- and money-consuming steps that can be eliminated or reduced—while still providing service to his customers?

Case C

Delivering the Goods Worldwide: Meeting the Challenges of Exporting and Importing

Having goods or services available where and when the customer needs or wants them is one of the most basic principles of marketing. The process of delivery is complex for domestic marketing, but even more challenging when goods are exported or imported globally. That's why the majority of the world's exports and imports of manufactured goods depend on the services of international freight forwarders for exports and customs brokers for imports. These firms are part of the *global logistics industry*, transporting goods from manufacturers or distributors across national borders to suppliers or end-users that may be located in any port around the world.

One of the industry's most recognized experts in international logistics and world trade is Ric Frantz. As CEO of Chicago-based

Figure 10.3 Shipping containers at the Port of Miami hold a variety of imports into the United States from South and Central America.

Photo courtesy of Ric Frantz, LRI.

LR International, Inc. (LRI), he has faced some major challenges in delivering his merchandise. Some of his experiences are cited in this case study.

Exporting

There are basically two sides to the global logistics industry: integrated carriers or courier companies, such as FedEx and UPS, that handle small packages and documents; and international freight forwarders that typically service larger and heavier cargo shipments. The integrated carriers have their own trucks and planes, with systems established to handle their target cargo. Freight forwarders, however, do not own their transporters; they act as agents for all global carriers, creating systems as needed for their clients.

The kinds of export or import cargo handled by freight forwarders usually fit easily into trucks, train cars, cargo compartments of planes, and maritime shipping containers. Occasionally, forwarders handle projects with oversized, overweight, or hazardous cargoes.

One example of how LRI coordinated the export of an unusual item was when it was contacted by a U.S. company in the Midwest that needed a large motor delivered to a customer in Ruse, Romania, near Bucharest. The specialty engine at 130,000 pounds was far too large and heavy for the standard container holding a maximum of 44,000 pounds. LRI knew this project would require a special plan.

According to Frantz, "we arranged for the U.S. portion of the delivery in a special flat-bed truck to carry the export cargo to the Baltimore, Maryland, port of exit. We had to coordinate trucking permits and state police escorts to pass through each state from the Midwest to the east coast port." The forwarder also conducted bridge surveys to be sure the truck would not get stuck under a bridge along the way.

The planning did not end there, as LRI arranged for the crate to be unloaded and placed on an oversized loading platform used to cradle the export for placement onto a specially designed ship for oversized cargo. A booking was made for the cargo to be shipped to the port of Hamburg, Germany, where it was transferred to a barge to travel via the Rhine and Danube Rivers, through Germany and Slovakia. When it reached Ruse, Romania, the crate was put on a special truck for ultimate delivery to the customer.

"The actual procedure did not go as easy as it may sound, due to unexpected problems along the way," Frantz stated. "When the export shipment arrived at the Maryland state line, the highway to the port of exit was under repair, so the state police would not allow the truck through." The forwarder had to locate a secure cargo yard to store the shipment for a few days until the road construction was completed.

When the truck finally reached Baltimore, the port's heavy lift crane could not unload the shipment because of the excess weight. "Several days of meetings with engineers from the exporter's firm, the Baltimore Port Authority, and the manufacturer of the crate concluded that the crate design and construction was inadequate. It had been put together without taking into consideration the center of gravity and the load points of the actual machine enclosed in the crate," according to Frantz. "So the crate had to be reconstructed at the port." A similar problem occurred when the export was being off-loaded in Hamburg, Germany. Another specialty device was designed and built to fit the crane used for unloading.

The goods were finally delivered, via barge, to Romania and then by truck to the importer. Frantz cites this example as an illustration of the challenges an international freight forwarder may face and the creative planning exporters may need to employ and the adjustments needed along the way. "When proper planning is done and challenges are met, the customers can get their products where and when they need or want them," Frantz noted.

Importing into the United States

Whereas exporting usually involves the services of an international freight forwarder to move goods (or services) out of a country to markets in another country, importing often relies on customs brokers to bring in foreign products for use or resale to end-users in an importer's country.

Most imports fall into one of the following four categories:

- Imports by resellers who are seeking price, variety, or quality advantages when competing with domestically produced items
- Imported raw materials for use by domestic manufacturers

- Components that are combined with domestic-made parts to complete a whole unit
- Finished goods that complement or establish a new line for a domestic manufacturer or distributor

In each of the above categories, the cost savings, possible design or quality advantages, and worldwide selections of the imports contribute to the importer's success. Otherwise, they would source domestically and not need to go through the expense and risk of global sourcing.

Many international logistics companies, LRI included, offer clients not only two-way domestic and international transportation but also consulting services such as acting as a customs broker. Customs brokers' services include U.S. Customs and Border Protection (CBP) clearance of commercial goods imported into the United States. The end goal is the same—getting the goods transported to the customers where and when they want them.

One example of LRI's customs brokerage (import) services was a Dallas-based client who had regular weekly import shipments via sea container from Shanghai, China, through the port of Long Beach, California, to its national distribution facility in Chicago for the regular customs clearance. According to Frantz, this client urgently needed about one-half the contents of a sea container shipped immediately to Dallas. "At our suggestion, they stopped the full container in Long Beach for customs clearance rather than bringing it in-bond to Chicago for clearance, as was the usual procedure. The entire container was unloaded and divided into two shipments."

The process became more complicated when it was learned that the urgently needed goods were new items that had not yet been successfully customs-classified. LRI suggested obtaining a General Binding Ruling from the CBP, which is when the agency selects a classification based on recent rulings that are published on the U.S. government agency's website. Fortunately, one of the rulings fit the description of the new products and was used to successfully clear the goods for import. If a precedent was not set with a previous ruling, the importer would have had to petition U.S. Customs for a new ruling by supplying detailed product information for classification. LRI contracted with common carriers for trucks to take the diverted goods to Dallas and to send the remainder of the import shipment to the Chicago distribution center.

Source: Author interviews with Mr. Frantz on June 7, 2013, and July 10, 2013.

Questions

1. Do you think the services of a freight forwarder or customs broker adds significant costs to the final price of the export or import? If no U.S. government regulations require an exporter or importer to hire their transportation and global logistics services, why would they use them?

2. What resources are available for finding an experienced, reliable forwarder or customs broker?

3. What criteria should be used in selecting a forwarder or customs broker?

Case D

The Decision Process for New Product Design

Bob Rosenbaum has held key sales and marketing executive positions at Coleco Industries, Kenner Toys, Tyco, Revell-Monogram, and Digital Innovations. He has been instrumental in the marketing success of several well-known toy and electronic brands, including Cabbage Patch Kids, ColecoVision, Easy-Bake Oven, Spirograph, Skip Doctor, and Baby Alive.

Rosenbaum is currently the principal of Sales Source, a Chicago-based sales and marketing consulting firm. He notes that new product designs now originate in countries across the globe. Whether designed in China, France, or Brazil, they are either internally driven or the result of external creations or vendor offerings.

The following is a summary of an interview with him about how his clients approach new product designs.

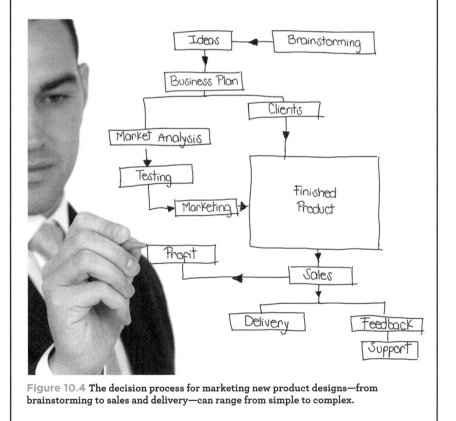

Figure 10.4 The decision process for marketing new product designs—from brainstorming to sales and delivery—can range from simple to complex.

Internal Designs

The reasons for an internally designed item can be any of the following:

- It is a form or extension of a similar item with a success record in the marketplace. This form provides new, more appealing styling or benefits. An example would be the smart phone. Global cell phone manufacturers and marketers engage in a constant battle of one-upmanship by offering the best features to attract the most customers.
- It is a unique, fresh idea that fits a need or a want.
- It is sufficiently appealing, so the consumer will buy it on an impulse. The impulse can be driven by the function or the appearance of the product.
- It is a departure from what a marketer has been offering and provides possible access to an enlarged customer base and new channels of distribution.

The challenges of creating new product designs include the following:

- Apparel and other sewn items require a sewing pattern with the sizing variations. With fabric items, the fabric must be chosen before the patterns are cut so that the geometric layout is coordinated.
- Manufactured items, such as toys or electronics, require much more preparation to develop. One costly step is the crafting of steel dies for all exterior and interior parts that will be formed by plastic injection. Some larger design studios have begun using the new computer 3D printing process to make the first sample. Steel die sets can cost $60,000 to $80,000 for a plastic toy or video game console.
- When designing an item that is a replica of an existing entity, such as a Jeep Cherokee toy model kit, the design specifications of the actual full-size vehicle are provided by the automaker to the model kit company. There they are designed and reduced to the appropriate scale.
- A plastic car that is not a replica of an actual full-size auto does not require the exactness of specifications and scale. In fact, this type of toy lends itself to the designer's whim as to how it should appear. An example is a vehicle designed for a preschool-age child. This toy is usually made with more rounded edges for safety, and sometimes it is given a humorous look.

External Sourcing Alternatives

There is the opportunity to also acquire nonproprietary items from either domestic or foreign vendors. The following are some external sourcing alternatives:

- As an alternative to internal designs, both designs and finished products can be sourced from domestic and foreign companies. These designs can be seen at domestic trade shows and their international pavilions or at foreign shows.
- In many cases, foreign producers or marketers do not have distribution in the U.S. market. Exclusive distribution can be negotiated, if that is part of the marketing strategy. Exclusivity is not always necessary with popular trend items, as they will create traffic to satisfy customer demands.

Marketing the Product

Designing a product is, of course, just the first step. It is up to the marketing department to get a product onto the store shelf, either through distributors or directly, and then off the shelf into the consumers' homes. A comprehensive marketing strategy is essential, but retailers are more likely to embrace and sell products that have some of the following attributes:

- The product is immediately appealing, and customers will act on impulse to buy it. If this is the reason for the retailer purchasing it, the product must be given prominent position in the store. The packaging and/or labeling is an important factor in presentation. In a mass market, self-service retail outlet, the consumer is drawn to the product, or not, with a single glance from approximately 10 feet away. Prime locations in the main traffic aisles and checkout lanes are used for this purpose.
- The product is a good candidate for online marketing. According to Nielsen research reports, online display advertising is the fastest-growing advertising media. Expenditures were up 32 percent in 2013, but that represents only 4.5 percent of the $243 billion dollar global advertising market.

- The product is presented to the retailer with a defined program of support advertising and/or publicity placement.
- The product is one that will generate word-of-mouth demand. This is particularly true of trendy and collectible items, such as when Beanie Babies were first introduced. In addition to the word of mouth, the manufacturer has an excellent marketing strategy to compel the consumer to buy now. For example, the public could be told a product will only be available until a specified date after which it will not be manufactured any longer.
- Some marketers announce that a given item will only be made in a specified quantity and then discontinued. This enhances the collectability value. Another ploy is to embed a number, or issue a certificate with a number, with each individual piece of the item. This validates the authenticity of the collectible value. An example is the birth certificate that was issued with each Cabbage Patch Kid doll.
- Publicity companies can also get a product subtly placed in a scene of a movie, a television show, or stage play. There is a reason an actor in a movie or television show drinks a Coca-Cola instead of a Pepsi Cola. The reason is that Coca-Cola paid for that exposure. This is not an ad, but a subtle impression on the viewer's mind of the brand. Impression counting is measuring the strength of an advertising and/or publicity campaign.
- Some products can be demonstrated in the retail store on a periodic basis. There are also electronic demonstrations using video displayed on monitors, tablet devices, and so on.

Acquiring appropriate licenses is a method of gaining consumer recognition. For example, just about everyone is familiar with the McDonald's golden arches or Ronald McDonald; the use of recognizable images or characters such as these can be part of a license. However, licenses can be a costly and risky business. The licensor usually has control of the product's appearance, the package design, and other aspects. There are many approval steps that must be fitted into the development timeline. When making a product that is an exact replica, a license is a legal requirement. But acquiring a license needs to be weighed against the cost and extra work.

Manufacturing in a Foreign Country for Import to the United States

The decision to have an internally designed proprietary product manufactured in a foreign country depends on several factors:

- The sales volume of an item is sufficient to purchase in minimum order quantities that will afford the target cost. The minimum quantities should be measured against the anticipated rate of sales to determine the quick response time. The cost of warehousing between shipments must also be justified, as those expenses affect the bottom line profits.
- The purchased quantities for each shipment qualify for the best container rates, or shipments can be consolidated with other purchased goods.
- Direct import items are customarily purchased on a "no recourse" or no-return basis. New factory relationships require due diligence before being consummated to protect an importer from unscrupulous foreign sellers. Factories in other countries sometimes compromise on quality to offer the lowest prices. Quality control inspections before shipment, especially at the manufacturing site, can be expensive, but they are necessary to protect the importer's investment.
- Factory compliance with U.S. social and safety ordinances is required.
- There is also the risk of foreign manufacturers creating intentional overruns that they sell to customers in other countries.
- If the item is a packaged consumer product, it may be prudent to bring the product into the United States in bulk and package it domestically. The package can be printed overseas, if that reduces cost, and brought in flat in the container with the

product. If the product requires assembly, parts can be imported and assembled or completed in the United States. The use of free trade zones can be a cost-saving idea for both packaging and assembly.

- Currency exchange rates with the foreign country must be considered, to be sure all costs are less than domestic manufacturing would be.
- It is important to be sure the selected factory has the capacity and financial resources to produce the anticipated demand. It is also urgent to have a back-up source—even in another country—when planning foreign production.

The decision process for new product designs is often the most time-consuming and critical for the eventual success or failure of manufactured products companies. Whether it's fashion, flora, or fine china, the design is usually what attracts wholesalers and retailers to carry the line, and ultimately for consumers to purchase an item in a store or online.

Source: Author interviews with Bob Rosenbaum, owner, Market Sourcing, on December 11, 2013, and February 12, 2014.

Questions

1. How does a company publicly justify overseas design and production when so many American factory workers are unemployed?

2. If design is often contingent upon a current assessment of consumer's needs and wants, as well as contemporary tastes, how can outsourced designs meet market requirements?

3. How can a U.S. company monitor the "fair trade" principles an international manufacturer does or does not employ?

GLOSSARY

Numbers in brackets indicate the chapters where the terms are used.

A

ABSOLUTE QUOTAS [7]: Specific quantities of products that may enter the country during a given time period.

ACQUISITIONS [1]: Occur when one company buys another.

AD VALOREM RATE [7]: A duty percentage added to imported goods based on their value.

ADVISED LETTER OF CREDIT [9]: Issued by a bank in the seller's country, which advises the letter of credit to the beneficiary. The advising bank may eventually assume the role of confirming bank, but, until they do, it is an unconfirmed letter of credit.

ADVISING OR NEGOTIATING BANK [9]: A bank that advises or negotiates a letter of credit and receives payment on behalf of a beneficiary.

AESDIRECT [5]: U.S. Census Bureau's free, Internet-based system for filing shipment export declaration forms.

AIR WAYBILL [4, 5, 9]: A non-negotiable type of bill of lading that serves as a receipt of goods shipped by an airline; a contract of carriage between the shipper and the carrier.

AMENDMENT [9]: Any change that is made to a letter of credit.

AMOUNT [9]: The sum of credit allowed as stated in a specific currency.

ANTI-DUMPING DUTIES [6]: Taxes on imported goods priced to sell at less than in the country of origin.

APPLICANT [9]: The term used for buyer in a letter of credit.

ATA CARNET [5]: "Admission Temporaire/Temporary Admission." A Carnet or ATA Carnet (pronounced kar-nay) is an international customs temporary export-import document. It is used to clear customs in 83 ATA countries and territories without paying duties and import taxes on merchandise that will be re-exported, usually within 12 months.

AUTOMATED BROKER INTERFACE (ABI) [7]: An integrated part of the Automated Commercial System (ACS), used by U.S. Customs to track, control, and process commercial goods imported into the United States.

AUTOMATED COMMERCIAL ENVIRONMENT (ACE) [8]: An online access point connecting the Customs and Border Protection agency and the international trade community, increasing the effectiveness of trade enforcement, by preventing cargo from becoming tools of terrorism.

AUTOMATED EXPORT SYSTEM (AES) [5]: The electronic way to file the Electronic Export Information (EEI) and ocean manifest information directly to U.S. Customs.

B

BALANCE OF PAYMENTS [1]: A record of all export-import trade and other financial transactions, including investments and gold, flowing in and out of each country.

BALANCE OF TRADE [1]: The difference between a country's total imports and its exports over a set time period. Should exports exceed imports, a favorable balance of trade, or a *surplus*, occurs; if imports are greater than exports, the country experiences an unfavorable trade balance, or a *deficit*.

BANKER'S ACCEPTANCE [9]: A time draft accepted by a bank, which then may be sold at a discount for immediate payment.

BENEFICIARY [9]: The term for exporter in a letter of credit.

BILATERAL ALLIANCES [2]: Agreements between two sovereign nations.

BILL OF LADING (B/L) [4, 5, 9]: A document issued by a carrier (ship, rail, truck) to a shipper (exporter) verifying specific goods have been received for delivery to a named place, to a certain consignee.

BLOCKED PERSONS LIST [5]: See "Specially Designated Nationals and Blocked Persons List."

BRETTON WOODS CONFERENCE [2]: The name given to the United Nations Monetary and Financial Conference held at Bretton Woods, New Hampshire, July, 1944.

BUREAU OF INDUSTRY AND SECURITY (BIS) [5]: An agency of the U.S. Department of Commerce, the Bureau's mission is to protect the national, economic, cyber, and homeland security of the United States through a law enforcement program focused on sensitive exports to hostile entities or those that engage in onward proliferation; prohibited foreign boycotts; and related public safety laws.

C

CASH-IN-ADVANCE [9]: Payment prior to shipment of purchased goods.

CE MARKING [2]: A mandatory conformity mark on many products placed on the single market in the European Union (EU). It certifies that a product has met EU consumer safety, health, and environmental requirements for selling to any EU member country.

COMMERCE CONTROL LIST (CCL) [5]: The first step in determining whether an intended export item needs an export license from the U. S. Department of Commerce. The Export Control Classification Numbers (ECCN) are listed on the CCL.

COMMERCE COUNTRY CHART (CCC) [5]: Identifies reasons for U.S. export controls, by country.

COMMERCIAL INVOICE [5, 8]: A bill for goods from the seller to the buyer showing the value and description of the merchandise plus payment terms.

COMPLIANCE ASSESSMENT [8]: The systematic evaluation of importers' systems supporting their Customs and Border Patrol-related activities.

COMPONENTS [6]: Materials and parts that go into finished goods.

COMPOUND RATE [7]: A combination of ad valorem and specific duty rates.

CONFIRMATION FEE [9]: Paid by an importer or exporter to obtain a bank's confirmed letter of credit.

CONFIRMED IRREVOCABLE LETTER OF CREDIT [9]: An irrevocable letter of credit whose payment is guaranteed by a bank. It provides the highest level of protection to the seller because the L/C cannot be canceled or changed unilaterally by the buyer or any other party to the credit without the consent of all parties involved.

CONFIRMED LETTER OF CREDIT [9]: An L/C that adds the endorsement of a seller's bank (the accepting bank) to that of the buyer's bank (the issuing bank).

CONSIGNMENT [9]: The transfer of possession of a seller's goods to a buyer without any formal commitment to pay for the goods unless they are sold. A very risky payment method, especially for the exporter in international trade. .

CONSULAR INVOICE [5]: Required by certain importing countries, this describes the goods to be shipped and their value, and it designates the buyer and seller—usually in the language of the importer's country and obtained from the Consulate of that country.

CONSUMER DEMAND [4]: The amount consumers are willing to buy.

CONSUMPTION ENTRY [8]: Usually for perishable goods; the importer indicates the tariff classification and pays estimated duties and processing fees.

CONTAINER SECURITY INITIATIVE (CSI) [6, 8]: A U.S. Customs control mechanism intended to avert terrorists' use of maritime containers to deliver a weapon into the United States.

COST, INSURANCE, AND FREIGHT (CIF) [7]: Term of sale indicating the cost of the goods, insurance, and freight.

CURRENCY REVALUATION [6]: The government initiated, official changes in the value of a country's currency relative to other currencies.

CUSTOMS: See U.S. Customs and Border Protection.

CUSTOMS AUTOMATED COMMERCIAL SYSTEM (ACS) [7]: Electronically receives and processes entry documentation and provides cargo disposition information.

CUSTOMS BROKER [7]: An independent business licensed by the Treasury Department and engaged in clearing goods through U.S. Customs.

CUSTOMS DUTIES [7, 8]: Government-imposed taxes on certain goods or services brought into a country from a foreign source; also known as *duties* or *tariffs*.

CUSTOMS MODERNIZATION ACT (THE MOD ACT) [7]: Declares that it is the importer's responsibility to use reasonable care in classifying imported goods and estimated values to enable Customs to accurately assess duties and ascertain that other legal requirements have been met.

CUSTOMS-TRADE PARTNERSHIP AGAINST TERRORISM (C-TPAT) [8]: The Customs-Trade Partnership Against Terrorism (C-TPAT) is a joint effort between the United States government and businesses involved in importing goods into the United States. Membership is voluntary, and open to most businesses who import goods into the United States, including freight carriers, brokers, manufacturers, and importers.

D

DATA WAREHOUSE CONCEPT [1]: Monitoring retail sales in order to replace in-store inventory swiftly.

DATE DRAFT [9]: Specifies the date a payment for goods or services is due.

DEBARRED LIST [5]: A list of parties to whom exporting is controlled by licensing or denied by the Bureau of Industry and Security.

DECLARATION FOR FREE ENTRY OF NON-ACCOMPANIED ARTICLES [8]: A form, to be completed by the owner, importer or agent of an importer of personal and household effects for which free entry is claimed.

DENIED PERSONS LIST [5]: A list of individuals and entities that have been denied export privileges. Any dealings with a party on this list that would violate the terms of its denial order are prohibited.

DEPARTMENT OF HOMELAND SECURITY (DHS) [8]: The primary U.S. government agency responsible for preventing terrorism and enhancing security; managing our borders; administering immigration laws; securing cyberspace; and ensuring disaster resilience.

DOCK AND WAREHOUSE RECEIPTS [5]: Documents used to transfer accountability when moving goods from the exporter to the port of embarkation.

DOCUMENTARY DRAFT [9]: In international trading, a bill of exchange or commercial draft that is presented for payment with the required documents such as a clean bill of lading, certificate of insurance, certificate of origin.

DOHA DEVELOPMENT ROUND [2]: The latest round of trade negotiations among the WTO membership. Its aim is to achieve major reform of the international trading system through the introduction of lower trade barriers and revised trade rules.

DUAL-USE ITEMS [5]: Items with both commercial and military applications.

DUMPING [6]: The practice of selling products in foreign countries at less than the fair value price in the originating country in an attempt to dominate regional markets for certain targeted industries.

DUTIABLE VALUE [7]: The value of the shipment subject to import duties.

DUTIES [7]: See Customs duties.

DUTY FREE [3]: Goods that are imported free of import taxes.

E

E-COMMERCE [6]: The buying and selling of products over electronic systems such as the Internet and other computer networks.

E-TAILERS [6]: Retailers operating their own Web sites.

EAR 99 [5]: An export control classification number for items that are subject to the Export Administration Regulations (EAR), but not specifically described by an Export Control Classification Number (ECCN) on the Commerce Control List.

EARLY-PAY PROGRAM [9]: Full payment to a manufacturer before shipment and sometimes before production, usually to earn a discounted price.

ELECTRONIC EXPORT INFORMATION (EEI) [5]: Electronic Export Information (EEI), formerly known as the Shipper's Export Declaration (SED), is used for compiling official U.S. export statistics and to enforce U.S. export laws. By law, all EEI filing records must be retained for five years from the date of export.

ELECTRONIC TRANSFER OF FUNDS (ETF) [9]: Payments are transferred by computer, from one bank to another, such as a wire transfer, to pay for the international exchange of goods or services.

END USE [5]: The ultimate application for which a product has been designed.

END-USERS [6]: The final consumers of a product.

ENTITY LIST [5]: Informs the public of parties whose activities imposed a risk of diverting exported and re-exported items into programs related to weapons of mass destruction.

ENTRY [7, 8]: The presentation of all documents necessary to clear the U.S. Customs, allowing foreign goods to enter the United States.

EQUITY [1]: Ownership.

EURO [2]: The official currency of the Eurozone member countries.

EUROPEAN UNION (EU) [2, 3]: The EU is a unique economic and political partnership among 28 European countries that together cover much of the continent. It was created in the aftermath of the Second World War, to foster economic cooperation.The EU encompasses 493 million people in its member countries.

EUROZONE [2]: Countries using the euro as currency include the European states of Austria, Belgium, Finland, France, Germany, Greece, Ireland, Italy, Luxembourg, the Netherlands, Portugal, Slovenia, and Spain, plus the islands of Cyprus and Malta.

EVERYTHING INTERNATIONAL (EI) [3]: A university-sponsored collection of resource links to many aspects of international trade found on the Web.

EXPIRATION DATE [9]: The final date for the beneficiary to present documents against a letter of credit in international trade finance transactions.

EXPORT ADMINISTRATION REGULATIONS (EARS) [4]: Regulate the export and re-export of most commercial items. Usually refers to regulation of "dual use" items—those that have both commercial and military or proliferation applications—but purely commercial items without an obvious military use are also subject to the EAR.

EXPORT CONTROL CLASSIFICATION NUMBER (ECCN) [5]: The code identifying the level of export control on the Commerce Control list.

EXPORT CONTROL REFORM INITIATIVE [5]: A series of programs to simplify U. S. Export Control laws, as a means to encouraging more exports.

EXPORT ENFORCEMENT ARM (EEA) [5]: That part of the Bureau of Industry and Security (BIS) which protects national security by intercepting illegal exports and prosecutes export violations.

EXPORT-IMPORT TRADE [1]: The marketing and physical distribution of goods, services, and technologies or ideas to countries other than that of their origin.

EXPORT LICENSE [5]: A transaction-based requirement for an exporter to obtain a license from the U.S. Department of Commerce, Bureau of Industry and Security if there is no assumed grant of authority to export goods, services, or other specific "items," under No License Required or License Exception. There is no License designated as an "Exporter's License"; each transaction will be judged by BIS to determine export requirements.

EXPORT MANAGEMENT COMPANY (EMC) [4]: An independent firm that acts as the exclusive export sales department for non-competing manufacturers. An EMC functions in foreign markets in a way similar to how a sales representative or exclusive wholesaler functions for a manufacturer in the U.S. EMCs should not be confused with Export Trading Companies (ETCs), which are organizations that specialize in procurement on behalf of foreign clients. An ETC has no "loyalty" to a particular manufacturer. It is just looking for the best terms for their clients.

EXPORT PACKING LIST [5]: Itemizes the contents of each shipment.

EXPORTING [4]: The distribution of a product, service, technology, or idea beyond the originating country's borders for the purpose of re-selling it.

EXPORTS [1]: Sales of goods that flow out of the country.

EXTENDED TERMS [9]: Allowing payments for goods and services to be made later than the traditional 30 days as in domestic sales.

EZCERTORIGIN [5]: A source that provides Chamber of Commerce-certified Certificates of Origin that may be required for certain exports.

F

FAIR TRADE [INTRODUCTION]: An organized social movement and market-based approach that aims to help producers in developing countries obtain better working conditions and minimize the environmental impact of production.

FIRST PRICE [6]: The manufacturer's selling price in the factory showroom.

FOREIGN DIRECT INVESTMENT [1, 3]: Occurs when an investor, an individual, company, or even a government organization gains an equity (ownership) interest in a foreign operation.

FOREIGN INVESTMENT [1]: Financial transactions involving loans or ownership of international enterprises and institutions.

FOREIGN POLICY CONTROLS (FP) [5]: Export controls placed on some commodities or specific countries, as necessary, to further the foreign policy of the United States or to fulfill its declared international obligations.

FORMAL ENTRY [8]: Imports of commercial or non-commercial (personal) shipments that exceed $2,500 in value; usually require a surety bond to guarantee payment of government-imposed duties.

FREE TRADE [INTRODUCTION, 3]: A government trade policy that allows importers and exporters to interact without interference from government laws or protectionist policies. Under such policies, prices for international trade transactions are primarily based on market forces—supply and demand—and are not subjected to import tariffs or non-tariff barriers to trade.

FREE TRADE AGREEMENTS (FTAS) [1, 2]: Bi-lateral or multi-lateral agreements eliminating all or most tariff and non-tariff barriers to international trade.

FREE TRADE AREA [2]: A region without trade borders or restrictions; often an area fenced off at an airport or shipping port that allow storage of imports to delay customs' tariffs (taxes) on incoming goods until they leave the designated free trade area.

FREIGHT FORWARDER [5, 9]: An independent, third-party international logistics specialist offering exporters transportation, documentation, and, in some cases, financial services, for a fee. Forwarders are usually licensed by the Federal Maritime Commission if they are involved in ocean transportation, and by the International Air Transport Association (IATA) if they act as an air cargo agent.

G

GENERAL AGREEMENT ON TARIFFS AND TRADE (GATT) [2]: A multi-national agreement to encourage free trade among members by negotiating substantial reductions of tariffs and other trade barriers. Its duties were assumed by the World Trade Organization (WTO) in 1995.

GLOBAL BUSINESS [1]: All commercial transactions—private and governmental—between individuals or enterprises of more than two countries.

GLOBAL SOURCING [6]: The process of purchasing imports from markets throughout the world.

GLOBAL TRADE [1]: The exporting and importing of goods and services among the countries of the world.

GLOBALIZATION [1]: The increasing interdependency and interaction of nations, economies, and businesses all over the world.

GROSS DOMESTIC PRODUCT (GDP) [1]: The monetary value of all the finished goods and services produced within a country's borders, typically within a one-year period.

GROUP OF EIGHT (G8) [2, 3]: An international forum for promoting trade liberalization and economic cooperation. Current members are: Canada, France, Germany, Italy, Japan, the United Kingdom, the United States, and Russia.

GROUP OF TWENTY (G20) [2]: A group of finance ministers and central bank governors from 19 of the world's largest economies and the European Union; formed in 1999 to broaden the dialogue on key economic and financial policy issues and to promote global cooperation.

GUANXI [1]: Connections, usually referring to government contacts and influence (Chinese term).

H

HALAL CERTIFICATE [5]: An official recognition that certain products are permissible under Islamic law. These products are then edible, drinkable, or usable by Muslims.

HAMILTON TARIFF ACT [8]: In 1789, the second statute of the U.S. government authorized the collection of duties on imported goods.

HARMONIZED TARIFF SCHEDULE OF THE UNITED STATES (HTSUS) [7]: A classification system to determine the amount of duties, or tariffs, U.S. Customs will assess on certain imports into the United States, as prescribed by law. The importer must determine the classification number of the merchandise being imported, as a prerequisite to the entry process, but Customs makes the final determination of the correct rate of duty.

I

IMMIGRATION AND CUSTOMS ENFORCEMENT (ICE) [8]: The principal investigative arm of the U.S. Department of Homeland Security, ICE was created in 2003 through a merger of the investigative and interior enforcement elements of the U.S. Customs Service and the Immigration and Naturalization Service

IMPORT LICENSE [5]: Documentation required for certain foreign goods.

IMPORT QUOTA [7]: A quantity or volume limit on certain imported merchandise from a specific country for a stated period of time.

IMPORT TRADERS [6]: Business people who import goods for resale.

IMPORTER SELF-ASSESSMENT (ISA) [8]: A voluntary, self-governance program that encourage compliance with Customs and Border Protection import guidelines, in exchange for less government oversight.

IMPORTS [1]: Purchases of foreign goods or services that enter a country in various forms, including raw materials, component parts, and finished goods. Imports into the United States are generally controlled by the U.S. Customs and Border Protection agency of Homeland Security.

IN-BOND ENTRY [8]: Arrangements made by exporter permitting duties to be paid upon arrival of the goods at the final port.

INBOUND FDI [1]: Direct Investment flowing into the United States.

INFORMAL ENTRY [8]: A process covering personal, commercial, and mail shipments that enter the United States to be consumed; in most cases the value is under $2,500.

INFRASTRUCTURE [8]: A nation's bridges, highways, communications, and transportation systems.

INSPECTION CERTIFICATE [5]: Required by some purchasers and countries in order to guarantee the goods shipped are the same as ordered.

INSURANCE CERTIFICATE [5]: Used to assure the buyer that insurance will cover the loss of or damage to the cargo in transit.

INTELLECTUAL PROPERTY [2]: Patents, trademarks, and copyrights.

INTELLECTUAL PROPERTY RIGHTS (IPR) [2, 8]: The rights to creative works that may be protected by patents, trademarks, or copyrights.

INTERNATIONAL MONETARY FUND (IMF) [2, 8]: An organization of 185 countries, working to foster global monetary cooperation, secure financial stability, and facilitate trade by providing temporary financial aid to countries with balance-of-payment problems.

INTERNATIONAL TRADE [1]: Trade between businesses or governments in two or more countries.

IRREVOCABLE LETTER OF CREDIT [9]: A legally binding document that can't be changed by any parties to an L/C, unless all parties agree.

ISOLATIONISM [6]: Limiting international trade and political relations.

ISSUING BANK [9]: The bank that issues the letter of credit and assumes the obligation to make the payment.

J

JOINT VENTURE [1]: A direct investment in which two or more partners share specific percentages of ownership.

L

LANDED COST [6]: The cost of goods at the final port-of-entry; includes shipping and entry costs, and duty charges to the foreign port of entry.

LEAD TIME [6]: The amount of time between ordering goods and receiving shipments.

LEAST-DEVELOPED COUNTRIES [2]: The least developed countries (LDCs) are a group of countries that have been classified by the UN as "least developed" in terms of their low gross national income (GNI), their weak human assets and their high degree of economic vulnerability.

LETTERS OF CREDIT (L/Cs) [10]: A bank's commitment to pay, on behalf of the buyer (importer), a specific sum of money, in a stated currency, within a fixed time period, to the seller (manufacturer/exporter), provided that the seller meets the terms as stated in the L/C and presents all required documents. L/Cs are common in international trade as they reduce the risk levels for both the seller and the buyer, since established banks are negotiating the documents and facilitating payments.

LICENSE EXCEPTION [5]: An export item that normally would require a license, but is exempted due to special circumstances. Do not require written export control approval.

LICENSING AGREEMENT [1]: An arrangement between a company with a well-known name and a manufacturer who pays a royalty to create goods using that name.

LIQUIDATION [8]: The final step of the customs entry process, liquidation signifies the settlement of accounts between importer and the Government, and the importer's taking possession of the goods.

M

MANAGEMENT INFORMATION SYSTEMS (MIS) [1]: A combination of customized computer technologies and processes that provide information for management decision-making.

MANUFACTURER'S SUGGESTED RETAIL PRICE (MSRP) [8]: The amount of money for which the company that produces a product recommends that it be sold in stores.

MARKET [6]: (a) A concept or place where producers of goods or services can offer their wares to buyers willing to pay the negotiated prices for those goods or services. International trade markets now include electronic venues such as eBay, Amazon, and Yahoo, as well as a number of social networks like Facebook and Twitter; (b) a business or consumer demand for a specific product.

MARKET RESEARCH [4]: Primary or secondary data collection and analysis to determine the needs or wants of a target market participant, including manufacturers, distributors, retailers or consumers.

MERGERS AND ACQUISITIONS (M & AS) [1]: A merger occurs when two or more firms join together for a specific purpose, with each participant retaining a portion of ownership or control over the new entity; an acquisition takes place when one firm buys another.

MIXED VENTURE [1]: A commercial operation in which ownership is shared by a government and a business.

MULTINATIONAL AGREEMENTS [2]: Agreement among more than two independent countries.

N

NO LICENSE REQUIRED (NLR) [5]: Most U. S. exports do not require a license and can be exported under the designation NLR. There is an assumed grant of authority, provided it meets the transaction guidelines of: what the item is, where it is going, who will receive it and what will it be used for.

NATIONAL EXPORT INITIATIVE [3]: The National Export Initiative (NEI) is the Obama administration's initiative to improve conditions that directly affect the private sector's ability to export. The goal, announced in 2010, was to create jobs in the U. S. by doubling exports over a 5-year span—by removing trade barriers abroad, by helping firms—especially small businesses—overcome the hurdles to entering new export markets; by assisting with financing, and promoting a Government-wide approach to export advocacy abroad.

NATIONAL SECURITY CONTROLS (NS) [5]: Controls placed on exports of certain strategic commodities or technology that would make a significant contribution to the military potential of any other country or combination of countries that would prove detrimental to the national security of the United States.

NON-TARIFF BARRIERS TO TRADE (NTBS) [7]: All international trade barriers that do not involve the assessment of duties, or taxes, in order to manage trade. Examples include quotas, standards, and special certifications, such as Underwriters Laboratory certifications and French language labeling requirements for exports to Canada's Quebec Province.

NORMAL TRADE RELATIONS [7]: Relationships with the countries with whom the United States trades and regularly maintains the lowest duty rates; formally referred to as "most favored nations."

NORTH AMERICAN FREE TRADE AGREEMENT (NAFTA) [2]: An agreement among Canada, Mexico, and the United States, establishing the world's largest free trade area (in terms of GDP). NAFTA was launched 20 years ago to reduce trading costs, increase business investment, and help North America be more competitive in the global marketplace.

O

OCEAN BILL OF LADING [9]: Required for transport of goods by sea; it serves as both the carrier's receipt to the shipper and as a collection document. The document specifies the details of the goods being transported, such as quantity, type and destination.

OFF-SHORE PRODUCTION [6]: Goods produced in another country.

OFFSHORING [3]: Manufacturing outside of the country where the producer is located.

OFFICE OF FOREIGN ASSETS CONTROL (OFAC) [5]: An office of the U.S. Treasury Department that administers and enforces economic and trade sanctions based on U.S. foreign policy and security goals.

OPEN ACCOUNT [9]: Goods are shipped first and paid for within a predetermined specified time, typically 30 days.

OUTSOURCING [1]: (a) Shifting factory production, or services, such as call centers, to less developed, cheaper labor countries; (b) domestic retailers purchasing imports.

P

PACKING LISTS [7]: Documents that include information needed for transport such as the number and kinds of items in the shipment.

PIGGYBACKING [4]: Seeking out and tying in with other non-competing, complementary product line exporters to achieve overseas distribution.

PORTFOLIO INVESTMENT [1]: A non-controlling interest in a venture made in the form of either debt or equity.

PRINCIPAL PARTIES IN INTEREST [5]: The persons in the United States who receive the primary benefit monetary or otherwise of the export transaction.

PRIMARY DATA [4]: Original data collected for a specific research project.

PRODUCTS [4]: Designed items for exchange that have physical properties, such as clothing, food, or electronics; items for exchange that are not services.

PRO FORMA INVOICE [4]: An exporting form describing the merchandise, its specifications, packaging, per unit price, and payment terms. Used in advance of a shipment, but not for payments which are based upon commercial invoices.

PROTECTIONISM [6]: Government motivated trade barriers, such as tariffs and non-tariff barriers used to protect home markets and domestic manufacturers from foreign competition.

PROTECTIONIST POLICIES [3]: Government-imposed barriers to imports into a country, usually in the form of tariffs.

PROTEST [8]: An objection; within 90 days after the date of liquidation of an import shipment, an importer or consignee can protest the Customs valuation and duty assessment and receive an administrative review. Any person whose protest has been denied may contest the ruling by filing a civil action in the U.S. Court of International trade.

Q

QUICK RESPONSE [6]: The computerized replenishment system of popular items while still in demand.

QUOTAS [1]: Limits on the amount or volume of imports of certain categories of goods from specific countries over a set period of time, usually one year.

R

RED FLAGS [5]: Any abnormal circumstances in a transaction that indicate that the export may be destined for an inappropriate end-use, end-user, or destination. Exporters have a duty to inquire about red flags before exporting to firms exhibiting them.

REVOCABLE LETTER OF CREDIT [9]: A letter of credit that can be withdrawn or modified at any time without notice to the seller; not a legal contract.

RULES OF ORIGIN/KYOTO CONVENTION [2]: The rules that determine the country where an imported product was originally manufactured, as determined at an international meeting on trade held in Kyoto, Japan.

S

SECONDARY DATA [4]: Research data previously compiled by various sources inside or outside an organization.

SHIPMENT MANIFEST [8]: Official papers filed and sworn to as being accurate accompanying shipments.

SHIPPER'S EXPORT DECLARATION (SED) [5]: Replaced by the Electronic Export Information (EEI) filing, which is generally required by the U.S. Census Bureau for U.S. exports that contain a single commodity's value exceeding US$2,500.

SHORT SUPPLY CONTROLS (SS) [5]: Are used where necessary to protect the domestic economy from the excessive drain of scarce materials and to reduce the serious inflationary impact of foreign demand.

SIGHT DRAFT [9]: Payment method for international trade. It is on demand or on presentation of the negotiation documents to the paying bank or the importer. In practice, the bank may pay within three (3) working days (not instantly) after the receipt and review of the negotiation documents and if they are in order, that is, the documents comply exactly with the letter of credit (L/C) stipulations. Enables the exporter to retain title to a shipment until it reaches its destination and payment is made.

SIMPLIFIED NETWORK APPLICATION PROCESS REDESIGN (SNAP-R) [5]: Allows users to submit export license applications, commodity classification requests, encryption registration, re-export license applications, and license exception notifications via the Internet.

SMALL BUSINESS NETWORK OF THE AMERICAS (SBNA) [3]: A network of counterpart small business centers in the Western Hemisphere linked to centers throughout the United States.

SPECIALLY DESIGNATED NATIONALS AND BLOCKED PERSONS LIST [5]: A list maintained by the U. S. Department of Treasury's Office of Foreign Assets Control (OFAC) comprising individuals and organizations deemed to represent restricted countries or known to be involved in terrorism and narcotics trafficking.

SPECIFIC RATE [7]: Duties set at a measurable rate such as per piece, liter, or kilo.

SPECIFICATION BUYING [6]: A domestic retailer designs the product and has it produced overseas according to the buyer's directions.

STOCKING DISTRIBUTOR [4]: Overseas intermediary who purchases products in quantity and maintains staff and facilities for international marketing.

STOPFAKES.COM [8]: StopFakes.com aims to educate consumers about counterfeit products and the web sites that sell them. StopFakes.com also directs consumers to industry-approved retailers.

SURETY BOND [8]: Required for all formal entries as a guarantee of payment duties posted with Customs.

SWOT ANALYSIS [6]: An assessment of an organization's strengths, weaknesses, opportunities, and threats.

SYSTEM FOR TRACKING EXPORT LICENSE APPLICATIONS (STELA) [5]: An automated voice response system that will provide the up-to-the-minute status on any pending license application or commodity classification.

T

TARIFF PREFERENCE LEVELS (TPL) [7]: Under NAFTA, administered like tariff-rate quotas.

TARIFF RATE QUOTAS [7]: Provide for the entry of a specified quantity of quota products during a given time period. Most "quotas" have been eliminated.

TARIFFS [1]: Tariffs are taxes imposed by governments on imports that may compete unfairly with domestically produced goods, usually due to cheap labor, as a way of controlling the number of foreign products that can enter a domestic market. Also known as *duties*.

TERMS [9]: The requirements in a purchase agreement that must be met for the collection of the credit.

TEXTILE PRODUCTION VERIFICATION TEAMS (TPVTS) [8]: Enforcers of U.S. customs laws with respect to imports of textile or apparel articles, particularly as they relate to enforcement of the North American Free Trade Agreement (NAFTA), the Dominican Republic-Central America-United States Free Trade Agreement (CAFTA-DR), and other free trade agreements and trade preference programs to prevent trans-shipments and origin fraud.

TEXTILE VISA [7]: An endorsement in the form of a stamp on an invoice or export control license, which is executed by a foreign government. It is used to control the exportation of textiles and textile products to the United States and to prohibit the unauthorized entry of the merchandise into this country.

TIME DRAFT [9]: When the exporter extends credit to the buyer, the draft states when the payment is due (e.g., 30 days after acceptance).

TRADE DEFICIT [1, 3]: When a country's imports are higher than its exports.

TRADE DIVERSION [2]: The process of shifting purchasing patterns from one producer to another. In an international trade, when a business that is able to offer a lower cost product for importation into a certain country tends to create a trade diversion away from another importer or local producers whose prices are higher for a similar product.

TRADE SHOWS [4]: Periodic wholesale markets for buyers and sellers in related fields, e.g., the MAGIC Apparel show in Las Vegas.

TRADE SURPLUS [1, 3]: When a country's exports are higher than its imports.

TRANSACTION VALUE [7]: The price actually paid or payable by the buyer to the seller for goods sold for export to the U.S.

TRANS-PACIFIC PARTNERSHIP (TPP) [2]: The Trans-Pacific Partnership Agreement (TPP) is a free trade agreement currently being negotiated by nine countries: The United States, Australia, Brunei Darussalam, Chile, Malaysia, New Zealand, Peru, Singapore, and Vietnam.

TRANSATLANTIC TRADE AND INVESTMENT PARTNERSHIP (TTIP) [2]: A trade agreement that is presently being negotiated between the European Union and the United States. It aims at removing trade barriers in a wide range of economic sectors to make it easier to buy and sell goods and services between the EU and the United States.

U

UNVERIFIED LIST [5]: Composed of firms for which BIS was unable to complete an end-use check. Firms on this list present a "red flag" that exporters have a duty to inquire about before exporting to them.

U.S.-COLOMBIA TRADE PROMOTION AGREEMENT [3]: Over 80 percent of U.S. exports of consumer and industrial products to Colombia became duty free with implementation, with remaining tariffs to be phased out over 10 years. The U.S.–Colombia Trade Promotion Agreement (TPA) supports more American jobs, increases U.S. exports, and enhances U.S. competitiveness.

U.S. COURT OF INTERNATIONAL TRADE [8]: Established under Article III of the Constitution, this Court has nationwide jurisdiction over civil actions arising out of the customs and international trade laws of the United States.

U.S. CUSTOMS AND BORDER PROTECTION (CBP) [7, 8]: The government agency responsible for the legal movement of goods into the U.S.; a name given the U.S. Customs Service as a result of the merger of Customs with other government agencies.

U.S. CUSTOMS AND BORDER PROTECTION DECLARATION FORM [8]: A full and accurate description of imported merchandise that must be attached to the outside of each shipment.

U.S-KOREAN FREE TRADE AGREEMENT [3]: Offers new opportunities for U.S. exporters to sell more Made-in-America goods, services, and agricultural products to South Korean customers—and to support more good jobs in the U.S.A. Entered into force on March 15, 2012.

U.S.-PANAMA TRADE PROMOTION AGREEMENT [3]: The United States and Panama signed a trade promotion agreement, sometimes called a Free Trade Agreement (FTA), on June 28, 2007. Panama approved the TPA on July 11, 2007. The TPA was signed into law in the United States on October 21, 2011.

V

VOLUNTARY SELF-DISCLOSURES (VSD) [5]: When individuals and companies admit to violating Export Administration Regulations or other export laws.

W

WAREHOUSE RECEIPTS [5]: See dock and warehouse receipts.

WIRE TRANSFER [9]: See electronic transfer of funds (ETF).

WORLD BANK [2]: A specialized agency of the U.N. consisting of 184 countries whose goals are to give long-term financial assistance to middle-income nations and to poorer countries to alleviate poverty and encourage economic development.

WORLD CUSTOMS ORGANIZATION (WCO) [7]: A global organization of some 171 Customs administrations that in total processes 98 percent of the world's trade.

WORLD TRADE ORGANIZATION (WTO) [2]: The only global organization providing a forum for governments to negotiate trade agreements and a place for them to settle trade disputes.

CREDITS

CHAPTER 1
1.1 © Dave Yoder/Polaris
1.2 Courtesy of U. S. Customs and Border Protection/Charles Csavossy
1.3 © ACDI/VOCA
1.4 Don/WWD/ © Conde Nast
1.5 Recreated by Alisha Neumaier
1.6 © Johnny Jones/Alamy
1.7 © Mario Tama/Getty Images
1.8 AP Photo/Katsumi Kasahara
1.9 © david pearson/Alamy
1.10 © Dimitrios Kambouris/Getty Images
1.11 © Bloomberg/Getty Images
1.12 © Jeff Greenberg/Alamy2.2

CHAPTER 2
2.1 Aquino/WWD/ © Conde Nast
2.2 Courtesy of the International Monetary Fund
2.3 © IMF Photo/Stephen Jaffe
2.4 © IMF Photo/Michael Spilotro
2.5 © World Bank
2.6 Courtesy of the Royal Society
2.7 iStockPhoto
2.8 © imagestock/istock
2.9 © Jim West/Alamy

CHAPTER 3
3.1 © Keith Beaty/Getty Images
3.2 © Ric Frantz/ LR International Inc.
3.3 Courtesy of the U.S. Census Bureau
3.4 Courtesy of the U.S. Census Bureau
3.5 Courtesy of the U.S. Census Bureau
3.6 U.S. Department of Commerce
3.7 © EPA/Rungroj Yongrit/Alamy
3.8 Courtesy of the Ambassador Bridge
3.9 © aerialarchives.com /Alamy
3.10 Courtesy of Department of Commerce/Office of Textiles and Apparel
3.11 © SCPhotos/Alamy
3.12 © Aflo Co. Ltd /Alamy
3.13 © Kevin Foy/Alamy
3.14 © JIM WATSON/AFP/Getty Images

3.15 © Joerg Boethling/Alamy
3.16 © Robert Harding Picture Library Ltd/Alamy

CHAPTER 4
4.1   Weng lei - Imaginechina/AP Image
4.2   WWD/© Conde Nast
4.3   Centeno/WW D/© Conde Nast
4.4   Courtesy of the CIA
4.5   WWD/© Conde Nast

CHAPTER 5
5.1   Bureau of Industry and Security, U.S. Department of Commerce
5.2   U.S. Department of Commerce
5.3   U.S. Department of Commerce
5.4   U.S. Department of Commerce
5.5   U.S. Department of Commerce
5.6   U.S. Department of Commerce

CHAPTER 6
6.1   © Michael Matthews/Alamy
6.2   WWD/© Conde Nast
6.3   Courtesy of U.S. Customs and Border Protection
6.4   Courtesy of U.S. Customs and Border Protection
6.5   Courtesy of U.S. Customs and Border Protection
6.6   Recreated by Alisha Neumaier
6.7   Copyright 2008 Columbia Books, Inc. www.associationexecs.com; www.columbiabooks
      .com
6.8   Courtesy of Metropolitan Pier and Exposition Authority
6.9   © Aurora Photos/Alamy

CHAPTER 7
7.1   Courtesy of U.S. Customs and Border Protection/James Tourtellotte
7.2   Courtesy of U.S. Customs and Border Protection/James Tourtellotte
7.3   Courtesy of U.S. Customs and Border Protection/James Tourtellotte
7.4   Courtesy of Department of Commerce
7.5a Giannoni/WWD/© Conde Nast
7.5b Giannoni/WWD/© Conde Nast
7.5c Giannoni/WWD/© Conde Nast
7.5d Giannoni/WWD/© Conde Nast
7.6   CBP Officers-Cargo and Seaport Image Library/James R. Tourtellotte
7.7   Federal Trade Commission

CHAPTER 8
8.1   National Archives photo 532892
8.2   Courtesy of U.S. Customs and Border Protection, Office of International Trade, U.S.
      Department of Homeland Security
8.3   Courtesy of U.S. Customs and Border Protection, Office of International Trade, U.S.
      Department of Homeland Security

8.4   Courtesy of U.S. Customs and Border Protection/James Tourtellotte
8.5   Courtesy of U.S. Customs and Border Protection/James Tourtellotte
8.6   © nick baylis/Alamy
8.7   Courtesy of U.S. Customs and Border Protection
8.8   Courtesy of U.S. Customs and Border Protection
8.9   Courtesy of U.S. Customs and Border Protection

CHAPTER 9

9.1   © Rob Wilkinson/Alamy
9.2   iStockPhoto
9.3   Courtesy of Department of Commerce/International Trade Administration
9.4   Courtesy of Department of Commerce/International Trade Administration
9.6   Recreated by Erin Fitzsimmons
9.7   iStockPhoto
9.8   Yuri/istock
9.9   starfotograf/istock

CHAPTER 10

10.1   © PhotoAlto sas/Alamy
10.2   © Gerry Sky/Le Fleur Imports, Ltd
10.3   © Ric Frantz/LR International Inc.
10.4   © blickwinkel/Alamy

INDEX